# Tracking Rural Change:

## Community, Policy and Technology in Australia, New Zealand and Europe

# Tracking Rural Change:
## Community, Policy and Technology in Australia, New Zealand and Europe

EDITED BY FRANCESCA MERLAN
AND DAVID RAFTERY

Published by ANU E Press
The Australian National University
Canberra ACT 0200, Australia
Email: anuepress@anu.edu.au
This title is also available online at: http://epress.anu.edu.au/tracking_citation.html

National Library of Australia
Cataloguing-in-Publication entry

Title: Tracking rural change : community, policy and technology in Australia, New Zealand and Europe / editors, Francesca Merlan, David Raftery.

ISBN: 9781921536526 (pbk.) 9781921536533 (pdf.)

Subjects: Sociology, Rural.
Rural development.
Social policy.
Rural conditions.

Other Authors/Contributors:
Merlan, Francesca.
Raftery, David.

Dewey Number: 307.72



Cover design by ANU E Press

Cover image: The editors thank Dörte Süberkrueb for the cover photo, and to Sepp Frankl for the spelt.

# Table of Contents

# Introduction

## The rural future in Australia and New Zealand: mapping the terrain of rural change

**Francesca Merlan and David Raftery**

On 16 October 2006, Australian Prime Minister, John Howard, announced funding of $350 million to assist Australian farmers struggling with drought, whose circumstances had been declared 'exceptional'. This announcement has many precedents: since 2001, $1.2 billion worth of such payments has been disbursed to Australian farming families (Peatling 2006). What was distinctive about the announcement of the drought payments of 2006 was the assertion of national agricultural values that accompanied such routine implementation of policy. The Prime Minister, in announcing these disbursements, stressed that farming was central to Australia's psyche and that family farms should not be allowed to die:

> It is part of the psyche of this country, it is part of the essence of Australia to have a rural community...Not only would we lose massively from an economic point of view [but] we would lose something of our character. We would lose something of our identification as Australians if we ever allowed the number of farms in our nation to fall below a critical mass. (Peatling 2006)

In January 2007, the Australian Federal Government unveiled its $10 billion National Water Plan, a scheme that purported to reform systems of irrigation management. This plan sought federal control of the Murray-Darling Basin river system, formerly managed by the states of Queensland, New South Wales, Victoria and South Australia. The plan conceded the need for 'structural adjustment' and made provisions for relevant structural assistance, including the buy-out of water resources previously allocated to irrigators. The Prime Minister, in this case, was explicit about the need, and the political will, to 'buy out' particular agricultural interests: 'Enhancing the overall viability of irrigation districts will require structural adjustment...The Government stands ready to provide structural assistance and, if necessary, to purchase water allocations in the market' (Howard 2007). We see here a moment in which a familiar rhetoric of support for free enterprise and opposition to state intervention is submerged in an appeal to national and associated 'rural' values.

As well as underscoring the need to better control irrigation allocations, the plan devoted considerable attention to the restoration of environmental flows: water that was not allocated to commercial agricultural purposes, but was dedicated to the ecological health of the river system and its associated biodiversity (<http://www.environment.gov.au/water/action/npws.html>).

A third major policy announcement relating to rural Australia came on 25 September 2007. At this time, the Federal Government announced further drought assistance measures, valued at $714 million. What was especially significant about this announcement was the juxtaposition of the established drought relief payments with the 'Exceptional Circumstances Exit Package'. This package provided a means by which farmers could receive some financial compensation for selling their farms and assistance in adapting to new business or employment. Such assistance, however, was conditional on those farmers leaving their farms and not returning to farming in an owning or operating capacity. This government-sponsored departure from farms was clearly at odds with earlier assertions of the inviolability of the rural–agricultural nexus.

The political motivations that lie behind such contradictory policy positions have been interpreted elsewhere (Cockfield and Botterill 2006; Botterill 2003; Halpin and Martin 1996). What is of most interest to us, however, are the ways in which this chain of policy events clearly reveal three things: 1) that the Australian family farm has become increasingly difficult to sustain; 2) that this is acknowledged at the level of government and bureaucracy; and 3) that the rural future is one in which the diverse and often competing social and political interests that are physically and economically vested in ruralism compete keenly at the level of political, scientific and cultural discourse.

## The developed world and its rural future

These issues are not new ones. From many parts of the developed world comes sobering evidence of rapid rural change. Many rural spaces have been emptied. In Australia, Cribb (1994) asserted some years ago that the rural population had 'tipped' due to the exit from rural land to the point where rural populations were unable to replace themselves. In the United States, entire areas where there were formerly small towns and working farms have been vacated, or are only sparsely occupied, while other areas are undergoing forms of 'regional suburbanisation', reversing the twentieth-century pattern of rural exodus (Salomon 2003). There is evidence in such parts of the 'post-agrarian' rural Midwest of aggressive marketing of small-town life with different 'growth machine' trajectories. The emergent landscape is a spatial structure with economic and social differentiation among what were formerly more self-sufficient small communities.

In relation to these and other trends, there is some measure of agreement that the entire developed world is participating in yet another, perhaps intensifying, phase of what Lobao and Meyer (2001:103) have called, with reference to the United States, the 'great agricultural transition'. They describe this bluntly as the 'national abandonment of farming as a livelihood strategy' (Lobao and Meyer 2001), evidenced by the exit of many farmers and the increasing concentration and industrialisation of agricultural production. These changes are heralded in different ways. There is a dramatic and persistent discourse of rural decline, while at the same time, resistant, somewhat nostalgic urgings to return to former agrarian practices and values can be found (Montmarquet 1989). Other commentators, in describing rural scenarios, look more to the future (Bonnano and Constance 2001; DeLind 1993) and highlight the position of rural communities and spaces within densely integrated chains of mass-produced and marketed food and fibre (Wilkinson 2002; Schusky 1989). The point found consistently through these analyses is that rural areas and rural-dwelling people can be an increasingly negligible concern in the production of food and fibre (Wilkinson 2002). Set against this depiction of an industrialised and de-socialised rural landscape is the description of 'new' agricultural practices and values (DeLind 1993; McMichael 1999; Barham 2003) that stress the *necessity* of a sustainable relationship among rural people, places and products.

In all of this, it is important to recognise the ambiguity and variability of the term 'rural': take note of comments of the form, 'national distinctions between rural and urban are arbitrary and varied' (IFAD 2001:17). There is nevertheless agreement that what are referred to as 'rural' spaces are undergoing rapid and continuing change, including a continuing decline in the proportions of populations resident rurally and engaged in agricultural production, a rise in occupations that are non-agricultural in origin (though sometimes with links to agriculture) and increasing vulnerability to extra-local forces (Ray 1998).

There is no doubt about the reality of some of these trends. To adopt a 'calamity' view of rural change, however, would be to abdicate the effort to critically engage with these diverse and novel intersections of social, economic and cultural phenomena. It is in rural spaces, among rural populations, that these intersections can be tracked, charted and critically analysed. One of the intended contributions of this volume is to develop a critical understanding of the institutional vehicles by which change is being driven. Beyond the pronouncements of politicians lies a densely networked array of governmental bodies and processes, commercial interests and social institutions through which agrarian, financial and environmental imperatives are channelled. The authors of this volume are concerned to map the terrain on which these contests for the rural future are being staged.

Specifying the challenges to the reproduction of the present into a rural future requires a depth of empirically and experientially based understanding. The way that governance both enables and impinges on rural livelihoods, the challenges that demographic trends pose for succession within farming families and the commoditisation of land, labour and resources all form part of the analyses contained within this book's case studies.

The contributors to this volume came together in an attempt to stimulate collective insight into trends of rural change. We have especially attempted to build on insights that we accept as fairly well established and that also are indicative sources of unpredictability and instability in rural transition: first, that rural areas and people have been brought with greater intensity into complex and global chains of food and fibre production; second, that globalisation and neo-liberalism produce new vulnerabilities and uneven effects for rural people (Gray and Lawrence 2001); third, that almost everywhere in the 'developed' world, there are big questions about how rural spaces are to be managed and governed, and how rural populations can participate in their own governance and that of the wider societies they inhabit. There was a concentration of contributors with Australian perspectives, but New Zealand and Europe were also represented.

Most of us accept that there has been rapid agrarian change, but for that very reason we agree that it is important to transcend the customary identification of 'rural' with 'agrarian' activity, or orientation to farming and related primary production, for these developed-world countries in particular. A significant literature of the past few years proposed the phrase 'post-productivism' in order to describe the contemporary condition of rural spaces (Wilson 2001). This term denotes the declining relative importance of agriculture and signals the importance of understanding contemporary rural practices, and their regulation, in new ways. This label, however, yields to the 'post' phenomenon, in that it suggests a framework in which agrarian rurality still dominates one's thinking. Recently, Australian geographer John Holmes (2006) has used the phrase 'multifunctional transition' to refer to continuing change and diversification in rural spaces, whereby varying mixes of production, consumption and protection values underscore differing modes of rural occupancy. This phrase perhaps better captured the spirit of exploration and possible plurality of rural futures, which motivated the small conference in July 2007 at The Australian National University at which most of the following chapters were first presented.

The literature on rural transformation is vast, but remains fragmented and is often consigned to specialist publications and professional fractions (Lobao and Meyer 2001). Why should this be so? The changes that such literature attempts to chart affect us all and the spectrum of issues involved is great, so any attempt at insight must continue to be multidisciplinary. And though coming from different disciplines—policy and political science, anthropology, sociology and geography—contributors to this volume also agreed on some of the questions that needed to be asked and answered in new ways.

1. What can we mean by 'rural'? A vast amount of literature has probed the meanings of this word, attempting to identify 'rurality' as a spatial and social category. It appears, however, that the implications of the changing character and porosity of contemporary ruralism still need clearer recognition. People might live and work in what are conventionally defined as 'rural' spaces, but highly variable combinations of cultural and social experiences, access to information, training and engagement with policy processes converge in new ways to define the attitudes, expectations and aspirations of those who occupy rural spaces. We can assume no simple or even 'ideal type' of contrast between country and city, farmer and urbanite, but must understand some of the recent trends in order to appreciate increasing diversification in the formation of rural experience, and changing implications attaching to uses of 'rural' as a descriptive category.
2. What are some of the trends transforming and taking shape in rural areas, and how might these condition possible futures? These include, and the following chapters explore, changes in: a) demography; b) combinations of rural activities; and c) implications of greater connectedness and technologisation of rural areas.
    a. Daniela Stehlik's chapter and, in a different way, Lesley Hunt's, analyse the challenge of demographic transition, a well-recognised phenomenon of developed-world societies. Farmers in the developed world are ever older as a group, not simply because those who continue to farm are ageing, but because fewer young people are entering farming.
    b. What else is going on in relation to this trajectory of an ageing farm population? No longer can we rest content with 'pluri-activity' as an adequate label to describe the increasingly 'other' engagements of those who farm and those who decide not to. For example, it is insufficient to view participation in other forms of income earning—so-called 'non-farm income'—as if this were simply supplementary to farming. There is evidence of more profound transitions. The very expectations of many entering farming, even at advancing age, as in Hunt's paper, and those choosing not to enter it, have changed. Those who farm engage in new mixes of activities and are less accepting of isolated farm life. In some cases, this drives the development of niche and boutique production nearer to population centres, new blends of farming with other activities and the creation of new occupational portfolios that could eventually reshape quite substantially the demands on those who farm as one of their activities. These sorts of transitions bring about challenges to the reproduction

of rural life. If occupations and activities other than agriculture are increasingly important factors within rural communities, how do these new roles constrain or enable those striving to ensure their rural futures?

c. What role does technology play in these transformations? Connectedness of rural areas generally continues to develop, with more roads and other infrastructure. There have been many studies that have stressed the critical importance of telecommunications in enhancing the economic competitiveness of rural-based industries (Commonwealth of Australia 2008). But what of the changes in rural communities that technological innovations such as broadband can facilitate? Rather than simply a case of technology boosting or enhancing existing economic structures, technology does have the ability to collapse distance, create markets and provide the hardware for new rural dynamics. Aitkin (2007) points the way to some of these possibilities. From the perspective of representative politics, do these changes mean new constituencies? Is the role of local government ever more critical, given that the rural is more diffuse in its political and cultural involvements?

3. What is the evidence of change and persistence in values relating to rurality? To answer this question there needs to be a consideration of the influence of long-term structural tendencies in developed-world countries. The structure and persistence of certain values could be the clearest areas of difference between 'developing' and 'developed' world rurality and its regulation. Several of the chapters in this volume (Botterill, Morris) refer to the character and persistence of developed-world 'agrarianism' and its political and cultural influence—the explicit celebration of values and social forms associated with agricultural activity, in complex but generally inverse relationship to real small-scale ownership and occupancy of rural land. Others (Peace) take as their chief focus related preservationist and restorative efforts to sustain ruralism as it is thought to have been or as it should be. Most interestingly, there is suggestion of shifts in terms of who is able to claim legitimacy in their assertion of rural values, with agrarian values encountering competition from other sources (Morris). Over a long period, farmers and farming have tended to occupy a moral 'high ground' of positive national and ethical values, even if this has been an idealised image. In the context of agrarian transformation, in which many farmers leave the land and the positions of those who remain change, this high ground is being at least claimed, if not usurped, by environmentalists advocating abstention from, or variation of, productivist land use.

4. What are the political and policy structures that have shaped rurality and the relationship between country and metropole in particular ways? Several

chapters address the question of the extent of influence of policy, its long-term effects and the power differentials between policymakers and 'policy-takers' (those subjected to policy). John Gray discusses the 'policy effect' of defining rural spaces, while Ian Gray discusses a long-term policy and practice of administrative centrism in Australia. Peace and Morris explore the contest for the legitimacy of different uses for rural spaces in Australia and New Zealand, respectively. Some of these chapters look at the lasting impacts of policy, and others at the disjuncture between policy (especially of the recently influential 'neo-liberal' kind) and practice. From anthropological contributors, we also receive accounts of the implementation and consequences of policy from below—from the perspectives of farmers and other rural dwellers who critically focus their relevant experience and knowledge on policy and its likely impacts. The diverse regulatory and governmental settings from which these accounts are drawn bring together points (1–4) in real ethnographic detail. These ethnographic accounts are drawn from situations that feature dynamic interactions among governmental bodies, people, values and policy.

5. For developed-world contexts in which technological change has been at the heart of agrarian and social change, when do we pay attention to 'science' and technology in relation to rural issues, and when do we not? What happens when rural spaces are in effect laboratories of the latest scientific technologies, but the expertise, technology and motivations for farming are being transformed at a remove from any identifiable rural population? Lyons and Scrinis detail the emerging regulatory networks that could pertain to future nanotechnological developments in Australia. The convergence of nanotechnology with already entrenched biotechnological agricultural applications has produced speculation of an impending 'bio-serfdom' (Rural Advancement Foundation International 1997), whereby farming livelihoods are dependent on the use of agricultural inputs that are in effect privatised genetic resources. Such scenarios are indeed future oriented, and the contribution of Lyons and Scrinis is a concrete analysis of the regulatory systems applying to nanotechnology and its potential rural impacts.

In order, the chapters, with identified central themes, are as follows.

## Diversification and reorganisation of ruralism

John Gray distinguishes different attempts to define 'rurality', as a concrete social space definable in terms of quantifiable measures and as an imagined category or representation. He also presents a picture of the interrelationship at the level of the European Union between continuing transformations in rural areas and in policy, and underlines the significance of a 'feedback' relationship between these two. Gray argues that while agrarian (and especially agricultural) activity was formerly seen as central, rurality has become increasingly decoupled from agriculture, and this has been at least partly reflected in changing positions of the European Union's Common Agricultural Policy (CAP). Having arrived at recognition of the heterogeneity of rural spaces and types of activities, and the relative decline of agriculture among these, Gray foreshadows future research and consideration of new forms of rurality from the vantage point of his long-term field site in the Scottish Borders.

## Policy and its long-term effects

Ian Gray explores the legacy of Australia's long-practiced administrative centrism. Under the label of 'administrative geography' of Australian rural development, this chapter examines grain handling, irrigation and railways as examples of administrative relations between rural areas and centres. He argues that centrism has contributed to a culture of 'rural dependency' that continues to leave rural people and areas averse to the idea and practice of governmental devolution, and implies that such aversion is a current liability for devolved governance options.

## Values: persistent and changing

Linda Botterill asks for Australia in particular—but with implications for other developed-world contexts—why there is little critical public analysis of rural policy. She argues that all developed countries display forms of 'agrarianism'—that is, belief in agrarian activities as worthwhile and inherently wholesome, in greater measure than other forms of occupation. That agrarianism persists, Botterill argues, is one of the reasons for the absence of rural policy critique despite great change in the rural sector. Also, so deeply ingrained is agrarianism that it can remain inexplicit as a ground of thinking and action. Drought policy receives particular attention in her account of the influence of agrarian values on the conceptualisation of legitimate rural activity.

Adrian Peace considers the implications of, and local community objections to, the reintroduction of a vanished wallaby species to a national park in South Australia adjacent to agricultural landholders. The tammar wallaby was considered to properly belong in this area by national park managers and other environmental and heritage bodies, but was experienced as a pest by farmers and other locals. Peace argues that such institutions are ineffective in taking local perspectives into account, and suggests the 'ritual' nature of much community consultation. He thus highlights the issue of asymmetry of power between state environmental and heritage institutions on the one hand and local communities on the other, but also the pressures that have given rise to such institutions and the imperatives that they must be seen to consult and to elicit local participation. This chapter thus has implications for many other cases of similar interaction and for questions of rural management of competing land uses.

## Diversification and reorganisation of ruralism

Carolyn Morris illuminates the historical conditions under which high country farmers of New Zealand's South Island have been able to occupy the position of 'stewards' of the country they preside over as lessees, and an iconic position as the 'real' New Zealanders in the national imaginary. Neo-liberalism emerged in the 1980s as the principal ideological vehicle for the regulation of rural activities and spaces in Australia and in New Zealand (and less consistently, but nevertheless also elsewhere, in the developed world; see Pritchard 2001; Pritchard and McManus 2000). This change brought with it overt disjunctions between neo-liberal ('free market') rhetoric and practice, compared with earlier conditions. Contradictions inherent in these new relations constantly surface against the background of the global political–economic context in relation to which rural policy is constructed. And, as illustrated above by the Australian Government's buy-out of irrigation interests in the Murray-Darling system, practices under what is proclaimed to be neo-liberal policy can depart significantly from the template the theory of neo-liberalism provides.

In New Zealand, these recent dramatic shifts to neo-liberal rural policy (from 1989) were shortly followed by 'tenure review' in the South Island high country. This brought with it the possibility of privatisation of some areas—with massive rates of profit for farmers in some cases resulting from the sale of portions of privatised land, and assignment of some former pastoral areas to national conservancy. These changes have altered the position of high country farmers and farming in many ways—socioeconomically and ideologically. Morris argues that high country farmers' moral position has become more tenuous and that the positive morality of stewardship that they formerly enjoyed could be shifting to 'greenies' not engaged in commodity production on the land. This chapter illustrates and amplifies some of the kinds of openness, and instability, that neo-liberal rural policy can bring with it.

Lesley Hunt describes as a vehicle of change the increased tendency of ageing 'baby boomer' farmers to take up kiwifruit farming as an activity bridging the transition between greater activity and retirement. She considers its implications with respect to farmer subjectivities, person–land relationships and rural occupation.

Daniela Stehlik in her chapter reconfigures some of the classic considerations of 'rural sociology'. Stehlik asks what we can make of the ageing of developed-world (and global) rural populations, and of farmers in particular, from her perspective of concern with natural resource management systems in south-western Western Australia. Concerned with the question of the relationship between intergenerational transition and sustainability, she adapts a framework for consideration of the kinds of goods that can be intergenerationally transmissible, placing emphasis on knowledge and social capital rather than on more conventional 'material' goods.

Stehlik's contribution importantly highlights two issues that relate to changing directions and plurality of rural futures: a) transmission of knowledge in an environment in which it is ever clearer that people seek 'options' and new ways in which they can engage in rural occupation; and b) the creation of governing structures that take the 'environment' as their concern, rather than necessarily being delimited by other, pre-existing political boundaries.

## New technology

Lyons and Scrinis take as their point of departure the widespread observations that a nanotechnology revolution in the agri-food sector is well under way, but remains largely beneath 'policy and regulatory radars'. What are the potential impacts and risks of this technological change with particular reference to the agri-food sector? Why has nanotechnology elicited so little regulatory attention? The convergence of biotechnology, nanotechnology and technical applications such as precision farming collate unprecedented levels of site-specific information relating to land, soils, water and organic life. The ownership of such technical information, however, is largely privatised. This would seem to promote a further dependence of rural communities on so-called 'off-farm services and support'. The convergence outlined above has been heralded by some as a greater revolution than that of farm mechanisation (ETC Group 2004). The chapter explores these issues and argues that a regulatory framework is urgently required. The environmental, health and ethical controversies surrounding the cultivation of genetically modified crops and the sale of genetically modified foods have attracted widespread attention (UNESCO 2006; Lin 2007). Nanotechnology—the technical manipulation of molecular material of one-billionth of a metre—poses, however, a regulatory challenge to which no government has yet developed an adequate response (ETC Group 2004).

Given the high level of technical expertise and political cooperation demanded by the advent of genetically modified crops in Australia—even during trial stages—it would be likely that one or more regulatory bodies would be created to manage nanotechnological developments. The power invested in such bodies would flow from many areas and interest groups—business, consumers, scientific communities—all of whom have established procedures for engaging in the resolution or management of highly technical problems and challenges. Where, however, do rural people and rural lands find a place in such dialogues? Lyons and Scrinis's chapter opens up this wider anthropological and sociological question of the relationship between scientific innovation and the public. What can be an effective modality in the management and oversight of rural technological activities?

## Bibliography


Aitkin, D. 2007, *'Building Australia'. Under construction: nation-building in Australia, past, present and future*, Canberra.

Barham, Elizabeth, 2003, 'Translating terroir: the global challenge of French AOC labeling', *Journal of Rural Studies*, vol. 19, pp. 127–38.

Bonnano, A. and Constance, D. H. 2001, 'Globalization, Fordism, and post-Fordism in agriculture and food: a critical review of the literature', *Culture and Agriculture*, vol. 23, no. 2, pp. 1–18.

Botterill, L. 2003, 'Uncertain climate: the recent history of drought policy in Australia', *Australian Journal of Politics and History*, vol. 49, no. 1, pp. 61–74.

Cockfield, G. and Botterill, L. 2006, 'Rural adjustment schemes: juggling politics, welfare and markets', *Australian Journal of Public Administration*, vol. 65, no. 2, pp. 70–82.

Commonwealth of Australia 2008, *Regional Telecommunications Review Report: Framework for the future*.

Cribb, J. 1994, 'Farewell to the heartland', *Australian Magazine*, 12–13 February, pp. 11–16.

DeLind, L. 1993, 'Market niches, "cul de sacs", and social context: alternative systems of food production', *Culture and Agriculture*, vol. 47, pp. 7–12.

ETC Group 2004, *Down on the Farm: The impact of nano-scale technologies of food and agriculture*, ETC Group, Ottawa.

Faludi, A. 2000, 'The European spatial development perspective—what next?', *European Planning Studies*, vol. 8, no. 2, pp. 237–50.

Gray, I. and Lawrence, G. 2001, *A Future for Regional Australia: Escaping global misfortune*, Cambridge University Press, Melbourne.

Halpin, D. and Martin, P. 1996, 'Agrarianism and farmer representation: ideology in Australian agriculture', in G. Lawrence, K. Lyons and S. Momtaz (eds), *Social Change in Rural Australia*, Central Queensland University, Rockhampton.

Holmes, J. 2006, 'Impulses towards a multifunctional transition in rural Australia: gaps in the research agenda', *Journal of Rural Studies*, vol. 22, pp. 142–60.

Howard, John 2007, 10 billion dollar 10 point plan, National Press Club Address, (viewed 25 January), <www.abc.net.au.rural/vic/content/2006/s18333636.htm>

International Fund for Agricultural Development (IFAD) 2001, *Rural Poverty Report 2001: The challenge of ending rural poverty*, Oxford University Press for IFAD, Oxford.

Lin, Patrick 2007, 'Nanotechnology bound: evaluating the case for more regulation', *Nanoethics: Ethics of the Nano Scale*, vol. 2, pp. 105–22.

Lobao, L. and Meyer, K. 2001, 'The great agricultural transition: crisis, change, and social consequences of twentieth century US farming', *Annual Review of Sociology*, vol. 27, pp. 103–24.

McMichael, P. 1999, 'The power of food', *Agriculture and Human Values*, vol. 17, pp. 21–33.

Montmarquet, J. A. 1989, *The Idea of Agrarianism: From hunter-gatherer to agrarian radical in Western culture*, University of Idaho Press, Moscow, Idaho.

Peatling, Stephanie 2006, '"I'll never shut failing farms," Howard vows', *Sydney Morning Herald*, 17 October 2006, <smh.com.au>

Pritchard, B. 2001, 'On Australia's pursuit of agricultural free trade', *The Drawing Board: An Australian Review of Public Affairs*, 28 September.

Pritchard, B. and McManus, P. 2000, *Land of Discontent: The dynamics of change in rural and regional Australia*, UNSW Press, Kensington.

Ray, C. 1998, 'Culture, intellectual property and territorial rural development', *Sociologia Ruralis*, vol. 38, pp. 3–20.

Richardson, T. 2000, 'Discourses of rurality in EU spatial policy: the European spatial development perspective', *Sociologia Ruralis*, vol. 40, no. 1, pp. 53–71.

Rural Advancement Foundation International 1997, *Bioserfdom: Technology, intellectual property and the erosion of farmers' rights in the industrialised world*.

Salomon, S. 2003, *Newcomers to Old Towns: Suburbanization of the heartland*, University of Chicago Press, Chicago.

Schusky, E. L. 1989, *Culture and Agriculture: An ecological introduction to traditional and modern farming systems*, Bergin and Garvey Publishers, New York.

Shucksmith, M., Thomson, K. J. and Roberts, D. 2005, *The CAP and the Regions: The territorial impact of the Common Agricultural Policy*, CABI Publishing, Wallingford, Oxford.

United Nations Educational, Scientific and Cultural Organisation (UNESCO) 2006, *The Ethics and Politics of Nanotechnology*, UNESCO, Paris.

Wilkinson, J. 2002, 'The final foods industry and the changing face of the global agro-food system', *Sociologia Ruralis*, vol. 42, pp. 329–46.

Wilson, G. 2001, 'From productivism to post-productivism—and back again? Exploring the (un)changed natural and mental landscapes of European agriculture', *Transactions of the Institute of British Geographers*, vol. 26, no. 1, pp. 77–102.

# 1

# Rurality and rural space: the 'policy effect' of the Common Agricultural Policy in the Borders of Scotland

John Gray


## Abstract

A central aim of the European Union's Common Agricultural Policy (CAP) since its inception in the 1970s has been to sustain rural society, the landscape and the environment, particularly those areas with less favourable production conditions—that is, land with poor productivity, low production and declining populations. Since 2003, the European Union's CAP has undergone two major reforms, the aim of which is to ensure the vitality and sustainability of rural communities. The first focuses on market-related support and direct aid to farmers for agriculture, including the Less Favoured Area Support Scheme. The second focuses on broader rural development including diversification of economic activities and stewardship for the environment. The aim of this chapter is to trace changes in rural land use and landscapes on hill sheep farms that result from the policy effect of the CAP: the dialectic evolution of the concept of rurality embedded in the European Union's CAP and the rural landscapes shaped and used by hill sheep farmers in the Scottish borderlands.


## Introduction

This chapter is a case study of the relationship between agricultural policy and human activity as it is manifest in rural landscapes and concepts of rurality. The particular case I analyse is the European Union's Common Agricultural Policy (CAP) and the activities and experiences of hill sheep farmers in the Scottish borderlands. My aim is not just an analysis of the production of rural space in this particular locality but a more general understanding of rural space/landscapes (in Australia, Europe and North America) as materialisations of policy-motivated formulations of rurality by governments (whether local, national or supranational) and practically generated activities of those living in the locations deemed to be rural by the policy. One of the characteristics of this dialectic of government policy and local practice is what Bourdieu calls 'the theory effect':

> Due to the existence of a social science, and of social practices that claim kinship with this science, such as...the conduct of politicians or governmental officials...there are, within the social world itself, more and more agents who engage in scholarly, if not scientific, knowledge in their practices and more importantly in their work of production of representations of the social world and of manipulating these representations. So that science increasingly runs the risk of inadvertently recording the outcome of practices that claim to derive from science. (Bourdieu 1992:249–50)

In the case presented here, I am illustrating an analogous 'policy effect': the representations of and policies for rural spaces devised by the European Community in its CAP set the conditions for hill sheep farmers to produce in their practices a concrete rural locality as a version of the rurality represented in the CAP. The CAP records these mediated effects on agriculture and rural landscapes of its policy in its analysis of the nature of rural spaces within the European Community for which it has to devise further representations and concomitant policies. In addition, not just a mutually entailed emergence of policy and practice, the production of rural space/landscapes in the European Union is also a dialectic of rurality as locality and rurality as representation.

## Rural image/rural locality

In a survey of academic definitions of the 'rural', Halfacree (1993:32) posits a distinction between rural as locality and rural as social representation. As locality, rurality is a specific type of space that has a concrete geographical location where its character is objectified in the physical and social attributes of that location. In this mode, rural locations can be observed, analysed and mapped in various terms: topographical attributes, the social composition of the people living and/or working there, forms of activity, the nature of social relations and relations with other spaces of similar or different type in other geographical locations. In the mode of social representation, rurality is a de-spatialised cultural concept that has a 'disembodied and virtual character' because it is not linked to a concrete geographical location and thus it 'lacks empirical clarity' (Halfacree 1993:32). Instead, it is a discourse about a type of space that is usually morally charged and about the kind of social life that occurs in it. Often it includes landscape images, either visual or verbal, placing the rural at a distance and thereby presenting idealised pictures of society that are implied by but can never be attained in everyday life (see Hirsch 1995:9, 23). In this mode, the rural is something expressed rather than observed, interpreted rather than explained. It is related culturally (by meaningful contrast and similarity of image) to other representations of other types of spaces, particularly those of urban space (see Williams 1975; Creed and Ching 1997).

Since its inception in 1958 and throughout its ensuing development in the next five decades, the CAP has conflated these two modes of conceiving rurality, alternately adopting them first in producing agricultural policy on the basis of an image of rurality and then in analysing the concrete rural localities that are its effects. A third form of rurality mediates this dialectic of image and locality: rurality as place. Here, I am referring to the way in which rurality is experienced and practised by rural people in their everyday activities. I illustrate this mode of rurality in the activities of hill sheep farmers as they respond strategically to agricultural policy to maintain the economic and intergenerational viability of their farms.

I trace the development of the CAP from its inception as part of the Treaty of Rome establishing the European Community to the recent changes of the Agenda 2000 and Fischler II Reforms (2003). The development of the CAP is also a 'history' of the concept of rurality as it moves through its various forms—locality, representation, particular experience of place—in the progressive dialect of policymaking and agricultural practice through which rural space is produced.

My analytical location is a function of the timing of my ethnographic research among hill sheep farmers in Teviotdale, a locality of 15 farms that straddles an 18-kilometre stretch of the River Teviot from its source to the mill town of Hawick (see Figure 1.1). It is a landscape of a river valley surrounded by steep hills reaching 600 metres high at the watershed and gradually decreasing in height and density as one moves in a north-westerly direction towards Hawick. The farms range in size from 160 to more than 2000 hectares, carrying 400 to 4000 breeding ewes. Hill sheep farmers differentiated the physical terrain in terms of two categories of farmland. 'Out-bye'—rough grazing or hill land—is predominant in the locality. It is characterised by steep gradients, altitudes in excess of 300 metres, harsh weather, boggy soil and nutrient-poor vegetation. 'In-bye'—or park—are areas of lower-altitude flat fields that become increasingly prevalent nearer to Hawick. All farms in the valley have some of both types of land. The nine larger farms (more than 500ha) on the higher ground nearer the watershed have a greater proportion of hill land (more than 75 per cent) and the six smaller farms on generally lower ground have a smaller proportion of hill land (less than 50 per cent). I did fieldwork in Teviotdale from 1981 to 2001. It was during this period that I was able to describe how hill sheep farmers strategically implemented the contemporary policies of the CAP with which they were confronted. These policies reflected the CAP's representation of rurality during the 1960s and 1970s and the effects this had on rural landscapes before my fieldwork. Assuming the actions of hill sheep farmers that I have observed are indicative of how other farmers have responded to the CAP during the 1980s and 1990s, I describe how their activities and their effects on rural space/landscape have been recorded and objectified in the understanding of rurality on which the Agenda 2000 and Fischler II reforms of the CAP are based.

## Rurality as agricultural

Creating a unified European Community in the late 1950s and early 1960s from a context of national boundaries, wars and political fragmentation required a communal space and common meanings. Because of its importance for food supply, consumer costs and political importance, agriculture was the primary vehicle for the construction of European communal space and the integration of the member states (see Bowler 1985:10–12).[1] Its three guiding principles were: 1) a single market, with no internal tariff protection imposed by member states, which allowed labour, capital and agricultural products to circulate freely throughout the community at comparable costs; 2) a community preference for agricultural goods backed by an external tariff on products imported into the community; and 3) a sharing of the financial burdens and benefits of the CAP by the community as a distinct entity, rather than by distributional procedures to and from member states.

**Figure 1.1 Teviotdale**

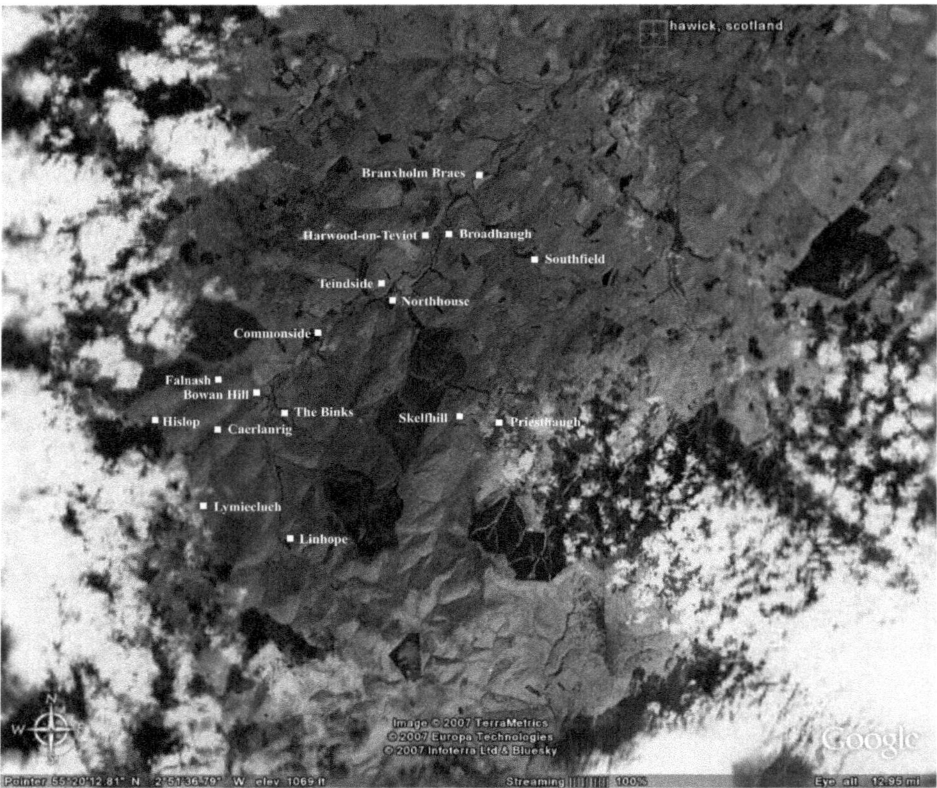

While these principles were overtly economic in character, they also identified the types of practices that would produce the internal nature and geographical limits of a distinct European space. The unified market, free internal movement of agricultural products and common prices and common financial responsibility de-emphasised the national partitioning of the European Community epitomised by pre-existing import levies of member states to protect their agricultural industry and by separate financial responsibility for their national agricultural sectors. Simultaneously, the uniform external tariff and the sharing of the financial burden of the CAP was the boundary that marked the limits of the European Community.

Within this European space, a major difficulty in formulating agricultural policy was the diversity of farming in member states in terms of resource endowment, the range and average size of farms, the density of population, the level of food self-sufficiency and the importance of agriculture in national politics. There were, however, two similarities on which a commonness could be 'codified' (see Bourdieu 1990:80) in formulating a European agricultural policy. First, all prospective member states had established tariff mechanisms to protect their farmers' incomes and their agricultural sectors from cheaper imported agricultural products and, remembering the privations during and after World War II, to maintain strategic self-sufficiency in food supplies. Second, in all member states there was an image of rural society portraying people and their agricultural way of life in the countryside that had cultural value and political significance. The five objectives of European Community's agricultural policy[2] that emerged from these two points of convergence addressed issues of economic efficiency of the agricultural sector and stability of prices, political issues of national self-sufficiency of food supplies and reasonable prices for consumers, and social issues of the equitable distribution of income to farmers. The two most important objectives for understanding the effect of the CAP on rural landscapes and concepts of rurality relate to the incompatible aims of achieving social equity for individual farmers and promoting economic efficiency in the agricultural sector. With respect to the former, the Treaty of Rome set as an explicit objective for the CAP 'to ensure a fair standard of living for the agricultural population, particularly by increasing the individual earnings of persons engaged in agriculture' (Article 39[1b]). With respect to the economic efficiency of farming, the Treaty of Rome set the objective of increasing 'agricultural productivity by promoting technical progress and by ensuring the national development of agricultural production and the optimum utilisation of all factors of production, particularly labour' (Article 39[1a]).[3]

The social equity objective of maintaining farmers' standard of living was vital to an abiding goal of CAP—to preserve the image of rurality and the family farm as the major feature of agriculture that in turn was the condition for rural society—even if this inhibited the process of increasing economic efficiency in the agricultural sector. At the Stresa Conference in 1958, where the European Community's original objectives for agricultural policy were defined, it was explicitly stated that 'the structures of European agriculture were to be reformed and become more competitive, without any threat to family farms' (CEC [1958], quoted by Folmer et al. 1995:12; see also Pearce 1981:7). This implied causal link between family farming and the preservation of rural society continued to be central to the European image of rurality throughout the 1980s. The 1987 Green Paper, Perspective for the Common Agricultural Policy, states that its aim is 'to maintain the social tissue in the rural regions' by ensuring continued employment opportunities in agriculture. Moreover, the paper presents the community's image of rural space: 'An agriculture on the model of the USA, with vast spaces of land and few farmers, is neither possible nor desirable in European conditions, in which the basic concept remains the family farm' (European Commission 1985:II). The same aim and image of rural space were reaffirmed a year later in the European Commission's paper 'The future of rural society': 'This communication...reflects the Commission's concern to avoid serious economic and social disruption [caused by structural measures] and to preserve a European rural development model based on the promotion of family farms' (CEC 1988:67).[4]

In these statements, EC policy represented a rurality in which agriculture was the encompassing activity defining the nature and values pervading the whole of rural space.[5] Rural space is a function of and is constituted by farming, family-based production units and a specific form of social life. While there is little specification of the attributes of farm, family and social life, family-based agriculture and rural society are portrayed as mutually constitutive: farming carried out by family production units is the condition for the kind of landscapes and social life characteristic of rural space (Marsh 1991:16) and rural space is the condition for and outcome of family farming.

This representation of ruralism as agricultural and vice versa is a version of 'rural fundamentalism', an urban-based and edifying image of agrarian society pervasive in the member states of the European Community at the time: 'farm people...were thought to make a special contribution to political, economic and social stability, economic growth and social justice' and the ownership of small parcels of land characteristic of the family-sized farm was considered to be 'the basis of a vigorous democracy' (Bowler 1985:16).[6] In this image, agriculture, rural space and society are relatively homogeneous—it is where agriculture is carried out predominantly on small-sized farms managed by families. In addition, there is a causal relation between a specific form of agricultural production and exemplary society. Family farming creates the kind of space where rural society can flourish and where the ideals of wider society are nurtured and preserved. Family farming sustains not just rural society, but society as a whole, characterised by the ideals of stability, justice and equality. Thus despite the claimed academic marginality of such romantic representations of peripheral rural farming communities (Macdonald 1993:10–11), it was this morally charged image of rurality that was codified in the CAP. The link between material (agricultural) production and moral reproduction that is characteristic of this image of rural space continues through the progressive development of the CAP.

## Intensification and diversification of agricultural space/landscape

In the 1970s and 1980s, the effect of the CAP's original market and price-support mechanisms on agriculture began to be analytically identified as two interrelated predicaments that threatened the viability of farming and rural society central to the image of rural fundamentalism. They derived from the CAP's conflicting aims of social equity and economic efficiency; paradoxically, the programs aimed at ameliorating them instead intensified them. The predicaments were known as 'the farm [income] problem' (Bowler 1985:46–8; Garzon 2006:28, 42) and 'the rural problem' (Kearney 1991:126).

The farm problem refers to the effects of general economic processes on the agricultural sector, in particular the accelerating inverse relation between increasing agricultural production by farmers and slackening demand for food by consumers. On the one hand, as national economies in Europe develop in a context of slow population growth, consumers spend less of their increasing income on food. Thus growth of demand for agricultural products is less than growth in income. On the other hand, as farmers use more and more technology to increase agricultural production, the supply of food expands faster than consumer demand. This process suppresses the prices of agricultural commodities and the income of farmers. Low farm income, which threatens the viability of rural society, is one of the two central issues of the farm problem specifically addressed by the CAP. Since one of its goals is to ensure a fair standard of living for farmers by maintaining income equity with other sectors of the economy, market intervention mechanisms have been developed to prop up the prices farmers receive for their products.[7] Because support prices were above those of the world market, however, there was a need to protect them by erecting a clear boundary around the European agricultural market with import duties. Thus a European space was created where family farms and rural society could flourish, even if 'artificially' in economic terms.

Since EC analysts defined the essence of the farm problem as overproduction, the second and more fundamental solution to the farm problem and the increasing financial burden of price-support mechanisms was to decrease the size of the agricultural sector. This was the central point of the review of the CAP carried out by Sicco Mansholt in 1968. He suggested decreasing the amount of land in production and decreasing the numbers of people engaged in farming. Such 'structural' changes would force small, economically inefficient farms (that is, family farms) to go out of business and allow their consolidation into larger productions units. As a result, there would be larger farms with fewer farmers producing a greater share of food required in the European Community, thus increasing their incomes. This type of 'resource adjustment' (Bowler 1985:47) requires people leaving the agricultural sector to look for employment in other sectors. Spatially, this has meant that people leave the place where agricultural production is carried out to look for work where industrial production occurs. As I have argued above, in the early years of the European Community, agricultural production was the essence and defining feature of rural space while industrial production served the same signifying function for urban space. The point, then, is that resource adjustment has a severe impact on the small, inefficient family farms and society that the CAP was designed to preserve. Structural adjustments caused depopulation of rural areas and jeopardised the financial health of small family farms; they led to the establishment of large, mechanised farms with absent owners and local managers—the 'vast spaces of land with few farmers' that the European Community found undesirable. The 'rural problem' (Kearney 1991:126) refers to these threats to the mutual dependence between small family farming and rural society brought about by structural adjustments in the agricultural sector.

## Producing rural localities

In order to address the incompatible aims of preserving rural society and farmers' incomes on the one hand, and increase the economic efficiency of the agricultural sector on the other, the CAP in the 1970s and 1980s introduced three instruments: regional diversification, price-support mechanisms and structural measures. Regional diversification and price-support mechanisms exemplified the way in which the design of CAP instruments was based on the image of rurality as a mutually constitutive relation between agriculture and rural society and on the consequent analysis of agriculture in marginal agricultural areas, such as hill sheep farming in the Scottish Borders. The analysis runs as follows: because of the poor quality of the land there is inherent low productivity and poor financial returns; in turn, these characteristics of hill sheep farming mean fewer employment opportunities and less incentive to take it up as an occupation; further, while consumer demand for lamb is relatively constant, hill sheep farming is seasonal so that farmers sell their lambs when supply is high; this depresses demand, the prices farmers receive and the level of income they can expect. Together, these were the ways hill sheep farms manifested the 'farm problem', and they threatened the viability of rural society by causing depopulation in locations such as the Scottish Borders.

The implementation of all three measures required that real rural localities be identified and this necessitated engaging in theoretical practices (Bourdieu 1992:250) to define rurality 'objectively' in terms of measurable attributes of landscape, topography and spatial relations and in social attributes of farm size, family personnel and interpersonal relations. A principle means of doing this was the Nomenclature unités territorial statistiques (NUTS) developed in 1980 by the European Union to statistically compare regional units from the level of nation-state (level zero) to smaller regions (level three) (see Figure 1.2). On this basis, rural localities could be made real through mapping and analytical comparisons of demographic, economic and agricultural data. At first, rural regions were defined solely by population density (more than 100 people/square mile). This was later refined through the use of the Organisation for Economic Cooperation and Development (OECD) typology in which rural was differentiated from urban solely on the basis of population density (more than 150 people/square mile); within the rural areas, degrees of rurality were distinguished in terms of the percentage of the population living in rural communities, from less than 15 per cent to more than 50 per cent.

Through the farming practices of hill sheep farmers in the Scottish Borders, all three measures had the effect of transforming agricultural landscapes through regional diversification of agricultural space within the community, intensification of production and diversification of agricultural land.

## Less favoured area: regional diversification of rural space

While the CAP defined a common space for the agricultural sector by de-emphasising internal national partitioning, the policy instruments created a different kind of internal partitioning. The community was divided into 166 NUTS 3 regions (CEC 1987) as a way conceptualising and ameliorating the effects of structural transformations on rural society. This NUTS 3 regional spatialisation was not based on the political differentiation of nations but on diversity in topography, resources and potential for development in rural areas. This marked an era of regional policymaking (Shucksmith et al. 2005; Bowler 1985:57) that was lacking in the original formulation of the CAP. For the Borders of Scotland, the most important of these regionalising polices was Directive 75/268, establishing Less Favoured Areas within the European Community (see Figure 1.3). The stated objective of the directive was, again, social rather than economic: to ensure the continuation of farming in areas characterised by poor natural resources for agricultural production and to maintain the density of the rural population in these areas. Less Favoured Areas were mountainous and hilly regions with marginal agricultural potential because of the topography and soil quality, low and declining population and/or poor infrastructure. They were also the localities where family farms were concentrated.

## Figure 1.2 NUTS regions of Scotland

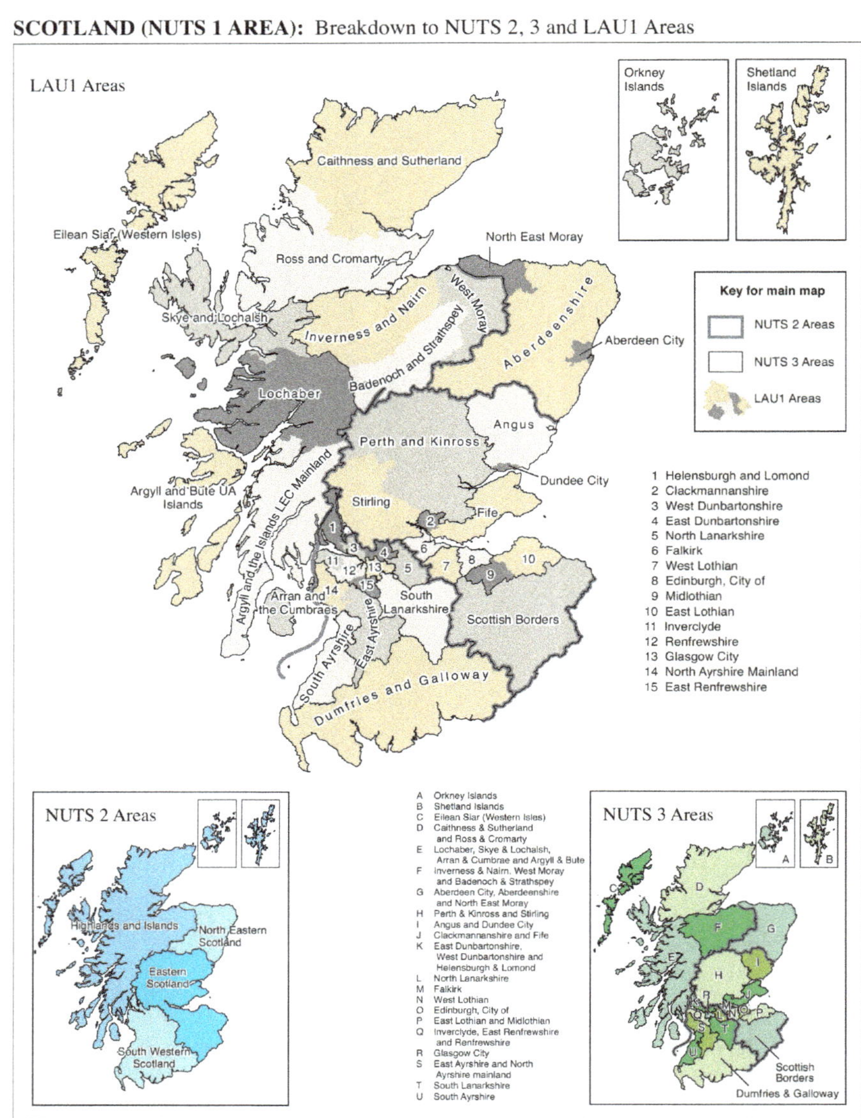
SCOTLAND (NUTS 1 AREA): Breakdown to NUTS 2, 3 and LAU1 Areas
LAU1 Areas
Orkney Islands
Shetland Islands
Caithness and Sutherland
Eilean Siar (Western Isles)
Ross and Cromarty
North East Moray
Skye and Lochalsh
Inverness and Nairn
West Moray
Aberdeenshire
Aberdeen City
Badenoch and Strathspey
Lochaber
Angus
Perth and Kinross
Dundee City
Argyll and Bute UA Islands
Argyll and the Islands LEC Mainland
Stirling
Fife
Arran and the Cumbraes
South Lanarkshire
Scottish Borders
South Ayrshire
East Ayrshire
Dumfries and Galloway
Key for main map
NUTS 2 Areas
NUTS 3 Areas
LAU1 Areas
1 Helensburgh and Lomond
2 Clackmannanshire
3 West Dunbartonshire
4 East Dunbartonshire
5 North Lanarkshire
6 Falkirk
7 West Lothian
8 Edinburgh, City of
9 Midlothian
10 East Lothian
11 Inverclyde
12 Renfrewshire
13 Glasgow City
14 North Ayrshire Mainland
15 East Renfrewshire
NUTS 2 Areas
Highlands and Islands
North Eastern Scotland
Eastern Scotland
South Western Scotland
A Orkney Islands
B Shetland Islands
C Eilean Siar (Western Isles)
D Caithness & Sutherland and Ross & Cromarty
E Lochaber, Skye & Lochalsh, Arran & Cumbrae and Argyll & Bute
F Inverness & Nairn, West Moray and Badenoch & Strathspey
G Aberdeen City, Aberdeenshire and North East Moray
H Perth & Kinross and Stirling
I Angus and Dundee City
J Clackmannanshire and Fife
K East Dunbartonshire, West Dunbartonshire and Helensburgh & Lomond
L North Lanarkshire
M Falkirk
N West Lothian
O Edinburgh, City of
P East Lothian and Midlothian
Q Inverclyde, East Renfrewshire and Renfrewshire
R Glasgow City
S East Ayrshire and North Ayrshire mainland
T South Lanarkshire
U South Ayrshire
NUTS 3 Areas
Scottish Borders
Dumfries & Galloway

## Figure 1.3 Less Favoured Areas, 1997, showing NUTS 3 regions

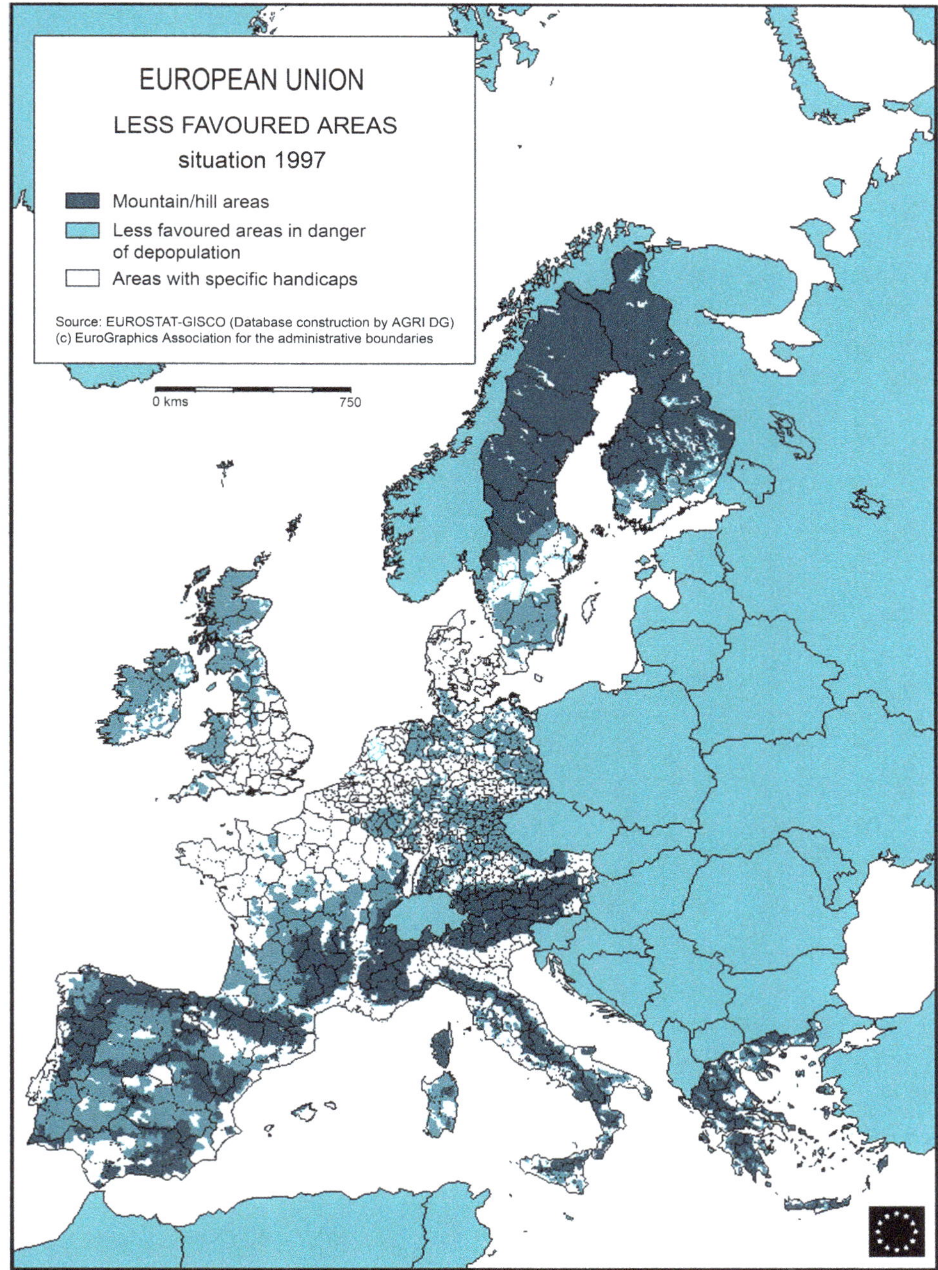

As a result of this directive, the hill sheep farming area of the Borders took on a specific spatial quality. As a Less Favoured Area, it was a productively marginal but still rural space for moral reproduction within the European Community that needed special assistance. It was necessary to differentiate this type of rural space because price-support mechanisms and structural measures by themselves were insufficient 'to sustain the traditional pattern of small-scale family farming in the Community and to encourage the continued population of some remote rural areas' (Marsh 1991:16). Thus farms in Less Favoured Areas were eligible for direct payments to compensate for the impediments to production imposed by the environment or caused by CAP instruments that were beyond the control of farmers. In the 1980s and 1990s, these payments, known as Hill Livestock Compensatory Allowance (HLCA), were targeted to directly increase farmers' incomes by being based on input (livestock numbers grazing on hill land) rather than on output, as were the price-support mechanisms.[8] As a result, farmers were motivated to increase the numbers of stock on their land to increase the HLCA payment.

## Price-support mechanism: intensification of production

The second type of measures adopted by the CAP to address the farm income problem and the concomitant rural problem and to preserve the localities where farming and rural society could flourish were market-intervention schemes. These worked by supporting the minimum prices individual farmers received for their products. The most important of these schemes for hill sheep farmers was the Sheep Meat Regime introduced in 1980. The Sheep Meat Regime was a 'variable premium' paid to farmers on their 'finished' or fat lambs.[9] The variable premium supplemented the market price a farmer received up to a CAP-determined seasonally adjusted, weekly market price (the 'variable' component of the premium) that represented what farmers should receive for their lambs to realise a fair income level. In addition, the regime included a 'ewe premium' paid to farmers for every breeding ewe maintained on their farms. This headage payment was meant to fill the gap between the UK guide price and the EC-wide basic price for fat lambs. In Less Favoured Areas, the rate for ewes on severely disadvantaged hill land was twice the rate for ewes on better quality low-lying fields. Hill sheep farmers were unanimous in saying that without these two price supports, which represented at least 25 per cent of their turnover, hill sheep farming would not be viable.

The general effect of these price-support schemes on the agricultural sector was to (over)-stimulate farm production: the more products sold on the market, the more a farmer received in price subsidies and the greater the income; the more ewes on a farm, the greater the total ewe premium received. They represented nearly 90 per cent of the CAP budget. This reflects the importance to the

European Community of rural space and the link between material production in agriculture and moral reproduction in social life.

## Structural measures: diversification of agriculture

In order to achieve economic efficiency in agriculture, the CAP adopted structural measures or resource adjustments. These were aimed at controlling the productive capacity of the agricultural sector so that the supply of agricultural products matched the demand for food in the European Community. Structural measures involve decreasing the amount of land in agricultural production, increasing the size and technology input of farms in order to take advantage of economies of scale and transferring labour and capital from farming to other sectors of the economy. The two structural adjustment schemes that were used by almost every Borders hill sheep farmer during the 1980s were the Agricultural Development Scheme (European Community) and the Agricultural Improvement Scheme (United Kingdom). These grant schemes provided financial support for modifying the natural qualities of agricultural land, particularly the marginal land in Less Favoured Areas, as a means of increasing the efficiency of labour and the product efficiency of the farm. This is explicitly conveyed in an explanatory leaflet:

> The aim of an improvement plan is to bring about a lasting and substantial improvement in the economic situation of your farms. The plan must therefore show that, within a period of not more than 6 years, the investments you propose to make will increase the earned income of each labour unit needed to run the business. (Department of Agriculture and Fisheries for Scotland 1986:1)

Grants, which in the Less Favoured Areas can cover up to 60 per cent of the costs, are given to assist in a wide variety of expensive and technologically based improvements to hill pasture: planting shelter belts; building and repairing stone dykes and fencing for controlled grazing and lambing; spraying bracken to improve the pasturage on hills; building roads for improved access to hill grazing areas for delivery of supplementary feeding; building sheds to house ewes during lambing; and, most important of all for hill sheep farmers, installing land drainage, reseeding and regeneration of grassland for permanent high-quality pasturage. These schemes were designed to improve the economic viability of farms by increasing labour productivity, maximising profit and maintaining rural society.

The way hill sheep farmers used these programs led to a diversification of agricultural practice and rural landscape within and between their hill sheep farms. Those farms with a high proportion of rugged hill land that could not be converted into improved pasture were unable to switch production from purebred hill lambs to crossbred field lambs. Since hill lambs are often too small to meet fat-lamb certification standards, they were sold on the store market where they were not eligible for the variable premium. While these farms used grants to convert as much land as possible to increased lamb production on improved pasture and used supplementary feeding to fatten more of their hill lambs, they largely remained 'breeding' farms in the sense that the majority of their production was purebred hill lambs sold on the store market. Those farms that had a greater proportion of low-lying hill land and flat fields converted the former to improved pasture where they could raise less hardy but more prolific field sheep and where the larger lambs could be fattened to the certification standards of the Sheep Meat Regime. These farms sought to increase the production of crossbred fat lambs that were eligible for the variable premium. They were labelled 'commercial' farms because there was less emphasis on breeding programs for purebred hill sheep and more emphasis on feeding programs for crossbred field sheep.

The CAP's representation and analyses of and policies for rural spaces within the European Community that I have described thus far were thoroughly agricultural and focused on issues of production (see also Ward and McNicholas 1998:28). Regions in the European Community were defined in terms of their economic dependence on agriculture, policy issues within these regions were seen to emerge from the 'farm problem' and the 'rural problem', and the mechanisms devised to deal with these issues—price supports and structural measures—were targeted at agricultural production. Further, the Less Favoured Area directive was aimed at propping up with direct income support farming in areas of marginal potential for agricultural production where small inefficient family farms tended to predominate. These policies are consistent with a representation of rurality in which rural space and society are a function of, constitute and are encompassed by agriculture, particularly family farms. In the next phases of the process, there is a significant change in the representation such that rurality becomes autonomous from and encompasses agriculture. This leads to a shift from agricultural policy to rural development policy in which rural space becomes a location for consumption rather than primarily for agricultural production.

## Diversification of rural space

In the late 1980s and throughout the 1990s, the European Community began to revise the representation of ruralism and the revisions appeared to appropriate the changes the CAP had wrought on rural locations: regional diversification of rural space, intensified production and agricultural diversification. I begin my analysis of this newly formulated representation of ruralism with the 1988 European Community Commission report, 'The future of rural society'. This report is a reflective portrayal of rural space that describes the effects of the CAP on farming (brought about by the actions of farmers in appropriating policy measures into their farming practices), the current problems facing rural society and strategies for addressing these problems.

The report begins with the following description of rurality, which I quote at length not only because it highlights the emerging autonomy of ruralism from agriculture and the different types of spaces that now exist within it, but because it still recognises: 1) the need to support farming in rural areas to offset the effects of structural change on rural society; and 2) the mutually constitutive relation between human activities in rural space and forms of social life—a more general version of rural fundamentalism.

> The concepts of the countryside or of rural society are by no means merely geographic in scope, since economic and social life outside our towns and cities is of great complexity, embracing a wide range of activities... (CEC 1988:5)
>
> Rural society [as locality], as it is generally understood in Europe, extends over regions and areas presenting a variety of activities and landscapes comprising natural countryside, farmland, villages, small towns, regional centres and industrialised rural areas. It accounts for about half of the population and a little over 80% of the territory of the Community.
>
> But the concept of rural society [as representation] implies more than geographical limits. It refers to a complex economic and social fabric made up of a wide range of activities: farming, small trades and businesses, small and medium-sized industries, commerce and services. Furthermore, it acts as a buffer and provides a regenerative environment which is essential for ecological balance. Finally, it is assuming an increasingly important role as a place of relaxation and leisure.
>
> [After the expansions of the European Community in 1973 and 1987,] the Community has acquired a distinctly higher proportion of areas the structures of which militate against proper economic—and social—development. Most of these areas are rural in the extreme, sometimes with 20–30% of the population still employed in farming. (p. 15)

Notable in this description is the change in the relation between agriculture and rurality. Agriculture exists within and is encompassed by rural space and society rather than the other way around, as it was in the earlier representation. This change foreshadows a major theme of the report: the decrease in the importance of agriculture in rural regions. It proposes an urban-centric spatial model that identifies three types of rural regions. Each of these regions is defined by its relation to large conurbations; each is described as experiencing a different problem brought about by the overall decrease in the importance of agriculture within the European Community; and together these are referred to in the report as the 'three standard problems' (CEC 1988:28–9). First, there are areas close to cities experiencing 'the pressure of modern life' due to an influx of population and competition for the use of land where agriculture is least important and where there is a diversification of land uses between agriculture, industry and leisure. Second, there are 'outlying regions' experiencing 'rural decline' due to out-migration where agriculture remains relatively important but with decreasing employment opportunities because of technological improvements in production. Third, there are the 'very marginal areas' experiencing more marked rural decline and depopulation where agriculture remains the most important sector of the local economy and where there is little potential for economic diversification because of the difficulty of providing services and infrastructure. The second and third standard problems portray rural areas experiencing what Kearney earlier called the 'rural problem' (1991:126). In this sense, the report appropriates into its revised representation of rural space the effects of the structural adjustments brought about by the implementation of the CAP.

The last paragraph of the quote is also significant to the revised representation of ruralism. It describes a reconfiguration of the relation between agriculture based on family production units and rurality. Now in relation to the large, technologically advanced agribusiness farms, leisure areas and environmental buffer zones, the spaces 'furthest from the mainstream of Community life' (CEC 1988:7)—where small family farming of the rural fundamentalist image continues—are 'rural in the extreme': remote, depopulated and economically marginal because of their heavy dependence on agriculture. The word 'extreme' is important in the paragraph because it is a narrative form of distanciation as well as authenticity. Its use makes poorer agricultural regions, the Less Favoured Areas like those of the hill sheep farming area of the Scottish Borders, into a kind of distanced and marginal landscape—a museum-like place portraying the original image of rural space where family farming and a valued form of society continue to exist.

Overall, then, 'The future of rural society' records the marginalisation of agriculture—especially small family-based farming—into the European Community's revised representation of rurality. Unlike the original 'agrarian' (Bonanno 1991) configuration, rurality is now portrayed as incorporating heterogeneous activities and types of spaces. The nature of rural space is not defined only by agriculture, even a diversified agriculture. Instead, the rural is also a place for small industry and leisure activities in those areas where structural adjustment mechanisms of the CAP have lead to a rural decline; and it is also a place for environmental preservation in those areas where the price-support mechanisms have led to farmers adopting intensive but ecologically damaging methods of agricultural production as a means of maximising income from subsidies. This representation of rural areas for leisure and environmental preservation continued the moral-reproductive function of the earlier rural fundamentalist image that the CAP originally envisioned for farming in rural society. In the former case, there is rural space for relaxation and recreation necessary for regenerating the human spirit for people throughout the entire European Community; and, in the latter case, there is rural space for regenerating the environment essential to the ecological balance of the entire community. Rural locations should be preserved not just for the farmers living there but for the benefit of society as a whole.

Another implication of representing the rural as constituted by a diversity of activities and spaces is that it also has a diversity of endogenous resources—not just land for agriculture—that can be developed to expand and reinvigorate the economy and society of rural areas. Instead of local farmers relying on CAP price-support mechanisms to produce agricultural commodities for people outside their rural locality, rural localities are now places that people from outside come into to consume the diversity of things that now constitute rural localities: the environment, heritage, beautiful natural landscapes, local customs and artefacts.

## Agenda 2000 and beyond

I am now moving into a period of CAP policy development and the changes in the measures designed to achieve the aims of the reformed CAP that occurred after my last period of fieldwork among hill sheep farmers in 2001, just before the outbreak of foot-and-mouth disease. Four farms in the fieldwork area had to destroy all their sheep and the others were quarantined throughout the outbreak. What follows, then, is suggestive of how these policy documents construct the nature of rurality and an image of rural landscapes. It also sets a framework for future research into the way in which hill sheep farmers have practically adopted these policy measures together with the effects of the 2001 outbreak of foot-and-mouth disease.

To achieve the development of rural regions, the European Commission produced a number of documents that transposed the image of diversified rurality into tangible localities exhibiting characteristics of the pressure of modern life, rural decline and very marginal areas and exemplifying the mediated effects of previous agricultural policies. All of them envisioned a phasing out of price-support schemes and placed a revised CAP within the broader agenda of integrated rural development. This is a shift from a sectoral approach of assisting agriculture throughout the European Community to a more territorial approach supporting agricultural, infrastructural, educational, social and economic development in specific localities. The principal analyses and policy statements are: the MacSharry Reforms (1992), the Community Initiative for Rural Development (LEADER), the Cork Declaration (1996), the Buckwell Report (1997), culminating in Agenda 2000 (July 1997).

Agenda 2000 identified four aims for the CAP. First, 'ensuring continued agricultural land use and thereby contributing to the maintenance of a viable rural community; note here the continuing importance of agriculture to the viability of rural communities'. Second, 'preserving the countryside'. Third, 'maintaining and promoting sustainable farming systems'. Fourth, 'assuring environmental requirements'. Agenda 2000 also re-conceptualised the CAP as based on two 'pillars'. Pillar one includes market and price mechanisms to support agricultural production. Pillar two consolidates various programs and mechanisms that contribute to rural development, including economic diversification, infrastructural improvement, rural heritage, protection of the environment, maintenance of the countryside, restoration of landscapes, extensification, and set-aside. Less Favoured Areas continue in the CAP, now explicitly as a component of Rural Development (pillar two), not only because of the impact of the poor land on agricultural production and the decline in farming and rural populations, but because of the environmental 'high nature value' of Less Favoured Area landscapes. As a result, rural areas are now like areas of European nature conservation interest—in fact, the two types of areas have large expanses of overlap (see Figure 1.4).

A common theme in these policy statements and reports culminating in the Agenda 2000 reforms is a reiteration of the effects that previous measures, particularly price-support schemes such as the Sheep Meat Regime and support through the Less Favoured Areas policy, have had on rural localities: overproduction, polarisation of incomes between small family farms and large technologically based farms, environmental degradation and continued rural decline. Based on this analysis, Agenda 2000 stated the objectives for a reformulated CAP for 2000–06. They incorporated the original aims identified in the Treaty of Rome of achieving social equity for farmers and promoting economic efficiency with new aims of environmental management and multidimensional rural development to maintain the viability of rural society:

> ensuring a fair standard of living for the agricultural community and contributing to the stability of farm incomes; increased competitiveness internally and externally in order to ensure that EU producers take full advantage of positive world market developments; food safety and food quality which are both a fundamental obligation towards consumers; integration of environmental goals into the Common Agricultural Policy; and creation of alternative job and income opportunities for farmers and their families. (European Commission 1997b)[10]

## Figure 1.4 Less Favoured Areas (LFAs) and areas of European nature conservation interest (EECONET) in the European Union

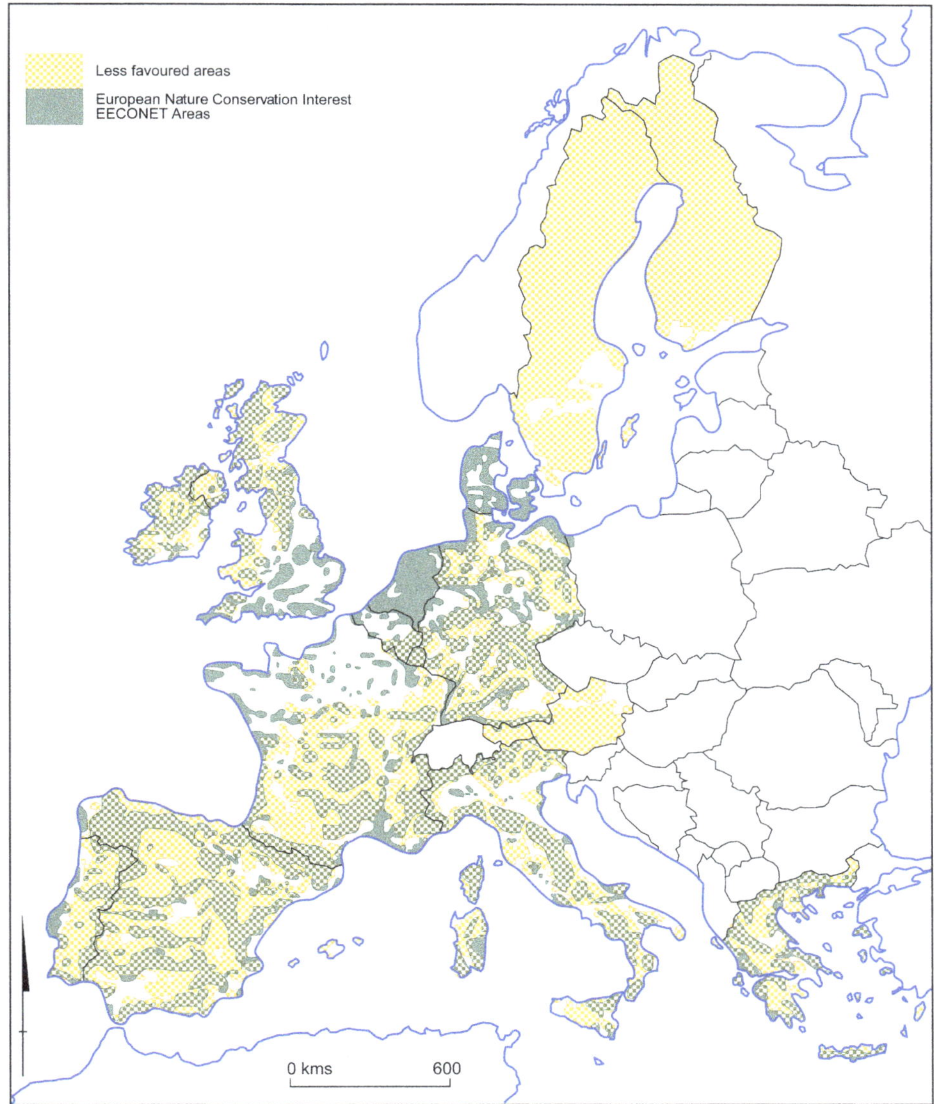


Source: EECONET.

## Figure 1.5 Objective one and objective two areas of the European Union

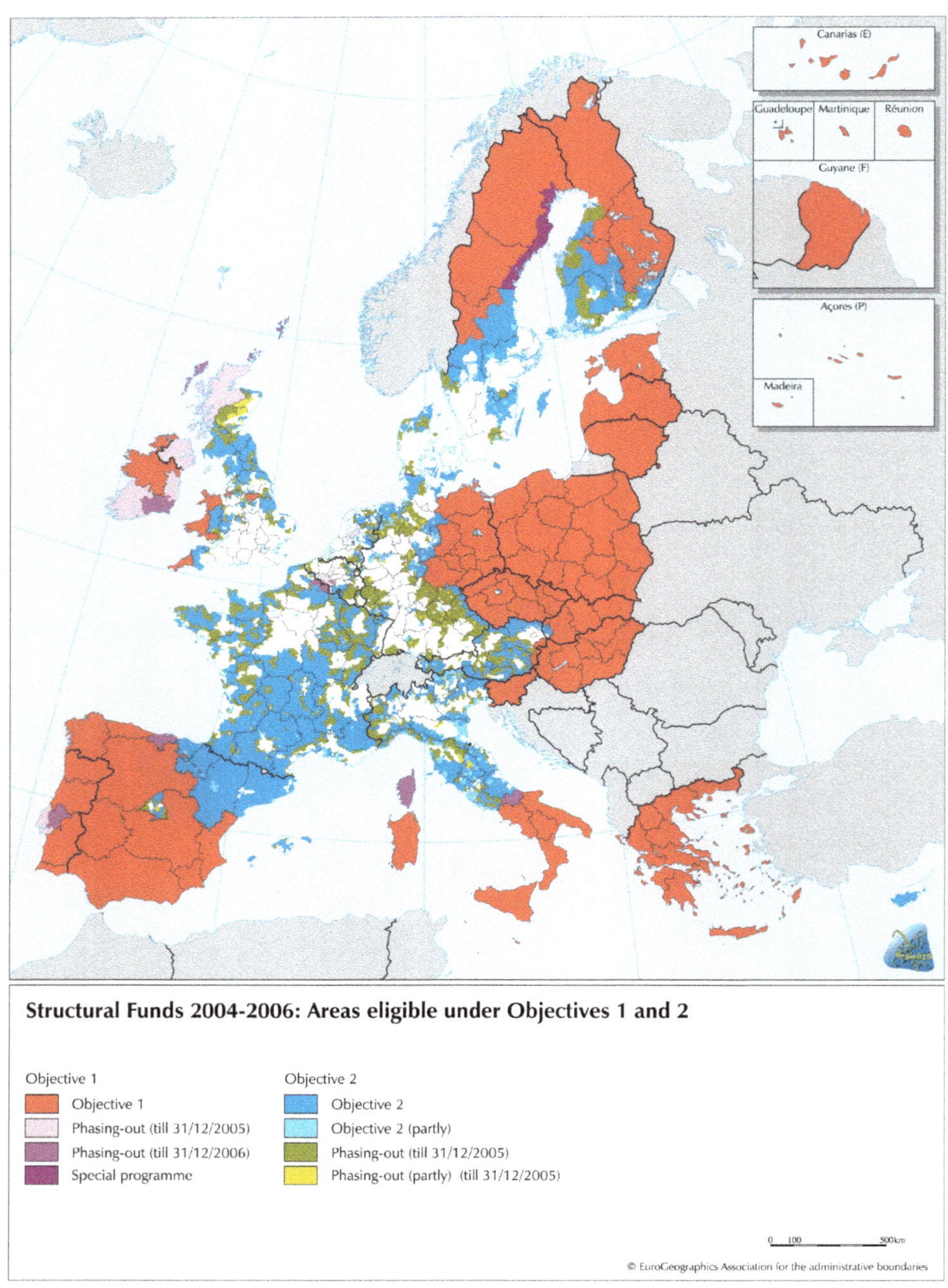

In the Explanatory Memorandum accompanying Agenda 2000 (European Commission 1997b), the 'European model of agriculture' is explicitly described as competitive, using environmentally friendly production methods and including a diversity of agriculture 'rich in tradition...[and seeking] to maintain the visual amenity of our countrysides [sic] as well as vibrant and active rural communities' (European Commission 1997b, Explanatory Memorandum:5). Again, as in the 1987 Green Paper, there is an explicit juxtaposition of European agriculture with Europe's major competitors (that is, the United States), particularly the part it plays 'in society and in preserving the landscape, whence the need to maintain farming throughout Europe and to safeguard farmers' incomes' (European Commission 1997b, Explanatory Memorandum:6).

All payments to farmers under the CAP were dependent on their compliance with ('cross-compliance') requirements to maintain their land in good agricultural and environmental condition including appropriate stocking densities on the land, and to ensure plant and animal health, environmental protection and animal welfare. Recognising the consequences of price supports on inputs (that is, headage payment on stock) for intensification and overproduction, financial support under the Single Farm Payment Scheme for achieving these aims was now to be made on a land-area basis. In recognition of the detrimental environmental effects of intensive production, area-based direct support payments were linked to requirements for farmers to use the land less intensively in order to preserve the high nature value of landscapes in the Less Favoured Areas (European Commission 1997a:20).

In order to achieve these policy aims in the 2000–06 period, European space was re-spatialised to reflect the three priority objectives for the use of structural funds under Agenda 2000. Two of them address the development problems in remote areas (objective one) and rural areas facing a decline in traditional activities (objective two)—that is, agricultural activities in the Scottish Borders, by providing financial assistance for the creation of the heterogeneous activities and spaces now represented as constitutive of rurality. As a result, rural regions are now defined in 'objective' terms. The pun—referring to the objectives for the structural funds and to the mode of defining and identifying real locations of such ruralities in terms of objective measures such as population density—is here intended. In the first sense of objective, rural localities are theoretically characterised using a combination of the OECD measure of population density at local and regional levels and the Eurostat approach of measuring the degree of urbanisation by population density. On this basis, the European Community is divided into 'predominantly rural regions' (about 10 per cent of the population covering about 47 per cent of the European Community's territory), 'significantly rural regions' (about 30 per cent of the population and 37.4 per cent of the community's territory) and 'predominantly urbanised regions' (about 60 per cent of the population and 15.6 per cent of the community's territory). The geographical reality of these regions is attested to by the maps included in the report, which objectify the characteristics of rural localities and spatialise the community into tangible geographical spaces according to population density, degree of urbanisation and rural and urban regions. In the second sense of objective, these rural spaces are then assessed in terms of criteria relevant to each of the three objectives for the use of structural funds. On this basis, maps are produced that spatialise the European Community into tangible geographical regions that objectify these problems; it is these regions that qualify for structural funds to support rural development (see Figure 1.5).

## Conclusion: future research

My description has chronicled revised representation of rurality as incorporating heterogeneous types of spaces and activities, and has summarised policies and mechanisms for implementation that objectify resulting images as concrete rural localities. Only one of these activities, now in decline, is agriculture. I have now reached the limits of my analysis. The next step is to conduct further ethnographic research in Teviotdale. As I mentioned previously, Teviotdale was also part of the area infected with foot-and-mouth disease in 2001. These two events provide a complex context within which hill sheep farmers have adapted their farming practices. My aim for my next period of fieldwork in Teviotdale is to find out what has happened to its rural landscape and society as a result of the way hill sheep farmers have appropriated the reformed policies and mechanisms into their farming practices, and the effects on their sense of what it means to live on family farms in a rural place.

## Bibliography

Bonanno, A. 1991, 'From an agrarian to an environmental, food, and natural resource base for agricultural policy: some reflection on the case of the EC', Rural Sociology, vol. 56, no. 4, pp. 549–64.

Bourdieu, P. 1990, In Other Words: Essays towards a reflexive sociology, Stanford University Press, Stanford.

Bourdieu, P. 1992, 'The practice of reflexive sociology (the Paris workshop)', in P. Bourdieu and L. J. D. Wacquant, An Invitation to Reflexive Sociology, University of Chicago Press, Chicago.

Bowler, I. 1985, Agriculture Under the Common Agricultural Policy: A geography, Manchester University Press, Manchester.

Creed, G. W. and Ching, B. 1997, 'Recognizing rusticity: identity and the power of place', in G. Ching and G. W. Creed (eds), Knowing Your Place: Rural identity and cultural hierarchy, Routledge, London.

Department of Agriculture and Fisheries for Scotland 1986, Agricultural improvement scheme, improvement plans, Explanatory Leaflet, Leaflet AIS (EC) 1, 1986.

Dumont, L. 1980, Homo Hierarchicus: The caste system and its implications, University of Chicago Press, Chicago.

European Commission 1985, Perspectives for the CAP, COM (85) 50 Final, 30 January.

European Commission 1997a, CAP 2000, Directorate General VI, viewed 15 January 1999, <http://europa.eu.int/comm/dg/new/cap2000/index_en.htm>

European Commission 1997b, Commission Orientations: Agenda 2000—Agriculture, Directorate General VI, viewed 15 January 1999, <http://europa.eu.int/comm/dg06/ag2000/sum/sum_en.htm>

European Community—Commission (CEC) 1987, The Regions of the Enlarged Community: Third periodic report on the social and economic situation and development of the regions of the community, Office for the Official Publications of the European Communities, Luxembourg.

European Community—Commission (CEC) 1988, 'The future of rural society', Bulletin of the European Communities, Supplement 4/88, Office for the Official Publications of the European Communities, Luxembourg.

European Community—Commission (CEC) 1997, Towards a Common Agricultural and Rural Policy for Europe: Report of an expert group, <http://europa.eu.int/en/comm/dgo6/new/buck_en>

European Spatial Planning Observation Network 2005, ESPON Project 2.1.3: The territorial impact of CAP and rural development policy, <http://www.espon.eu/mmp/online/website/content/projects/243/277/index_EN.html>

Folmer, C. et al. 1995, The Common Agricultural Policy Beyond the MacSharry Reform, Elsevier Science, New York.

Garzon, I. 2006, Reforming the Common Agricultural Policy, Palgrave Macmillan, New York.

Halfacree, K. H. 1993, 'Locality and social representation: space, discourse and alternative definitions of the rural', Journal of Rural Studies, vol. 9, no. 1, pp. 23–37.

Hirsch, E. 1995, 'Landscape: between place and space', in E. Hirsch and M. O'Hanlon (eds), The Anthropology of Landscape: Perspectives and place and space, Clarendon Press, Oxford.

Kearney, B. 1991, 'Rural society—disparities in incomes and alternative policies', in J. Marsh, The Changing Role of the Common Agricultural Policy: The future of farming in Europe, Belhaven Press, London.

Macdonald, S. 1993, 'Identity complexes in Western Europe: social anthropological perspectives', in S. Macdonald (ed.), Inside European Identities: Ethnography in western Europe, Berg, Oxford.

Marsh, J. 1991, 'Initial assumptions', The Changing Role of the Common Agricultural Policy: The future of farming in Europe, Belhaven Press, London.

Newby, H. 1979, Green and Pleasant Land: Social change in rural England, Penguin Books, Harmondsworth.

Pearce, J. 1981, The Common Agricultural Policy: Prospects for change, Routledge and Kegan Paul, London.

Shucksmith, M., Thomson, K. J. and Roberts, D. 2005, The CAP and the Regions: The territorial impact of the Common Agricultural Policy, CABI Publishing, Wallingford, Oxford.

Taylor, C. 1979, 'Interpretation and the sciences of man', in P. Rabinow and W. M. Sullivan (eds), Interpretative Social Science: A reader, University of California Press, Berkeley.

Ward, N. and McNicholas, K. 1998, 'Reconfiguring rural development in the United Kingdom: Objective 5b and the new rural governance', Journal of Rural Studies, vol. 14, no. 1, pp. 27–39.

Williams, R. 1975, The Country and the City, Paladin, Frogmore, St Albans, Herts.

## Endnotes

[1] I use the term 'common' in the sense that Charles Taylor does in drawing a distinction between common and shared meanings: 'Common meanings are the basis of community. Intersubjective meaning gives people a common language to talk about social reality...what it meant here is something more than convergence. Convergence is what happens when our values are shared...But we could also say that common meanings are quite other than consensus, for they can subsist with a high degree of cleavage; this is what happens when common meaning comes to be lived and understood differently by different groups' (Taylor 1979:51, italics added).

[2] The five objectives were: increasing agricultural productivity, ensuring a fair standard of living for farmers, stabilising markets, guaranteeing food security and ensuring reasonable prices for consumers.

[3] These are only two of the five objectives of agricultural policy identified in the Treaty of Rome. They foreshadow larger policy initiatives, termed Pillar 1 and Pillar 2 in the Agenda 2000 reforms.

[4] 'The future of rural society' paper, however, puts this image in a new configuration of agriculture and ruralism.

[5] The use of the term 'encompassing' follows Dumont (1980:239–45).

[6] There is some support for Bowler's assertion of the persuasiveness of this image in Europe at the time when the CAP was being developed. His description of rural fundamentalism is reminiscent of William's (1975) historical analysis of the changing representation of the 'country' in English literature and of Newby's (1979:14, 18) notion of rural Romanticism as British society's living 'museum' of its cherished

values. In addition, Creed and Ching (1997:19) point to the notion of the 'romantic trope of the countryside as idyllic retreat' in America. Unlike Bowler, however, these analysts also identify the negative images and realities of living in rural society.

[7] As we will see below, there was an explicit social policy to preserve rural society by ensuring that farmers as the pivots of rural society were maintained.

[8] In the early 1990s, the Beef Special Premium was introduced. This was a headage payment for beef cattle. Since most hill sheep farms also carry some cattle, this was another important source of income. I do no more than mention this scheme because sheep are the most financially and socially important livestock for a hill sheep farm.

[9] Fat lambs are ready for slaughter at the time of sale.

[10] These objectives are presented in a different order in Agenda 2000. I have changed the order so that it accords with the order in which I list the aims of the reformulated CAP.

# 2

# Has Australia's administrative heritage maintained a culture of agrarian dependency?

Ian Gray

## Abstract

The Australian Federation brought together colonies that had developed centralised administrative systems over an equally centralised pattern of settlement. Rural society was developed under agrarian ideals that differentiated country from city in social and political as well as cultural terms. While similar ideals were held in Europe and North America, the colonial administration of such important instruments of rural development as railways and local government left Australian rural areas in a condition of dependency that the regionalist traditions and stronger local governments of Europe and North America might not have permitted. The expression of 'country-mindedness' and the establishment of the almost unique National (formerly Country) Party alongside administrative tradition have helped to preserve a climate in which appeals to administrative apparatuses firmly based in state capitals have been the principal recognised means of solving local problems. Rural culture as well as the structural conditions of dependency could have blinkered community perception of possible means of local advancement by way of self-governance, other than where business opportunities are presented in familiar industries. Much has been said and written about rural communities being blinkered to economic opportunity, but despite some penetrating analysis, conflation of economic and political dimensions remains a problem. Criticism of rural communities for being blinkered and passive is paradoxical in a cultural context in which self-reliance at the individual level is held as an important ideal and farmer organisations have been very active. After examining some literature, this chapter illustrates these points with brief references to the history of grain handling, irrigation, natural resource management and railways in New South Wales, from their establishment through to the restructuring that occurred during and since the 1990s. In concluding, this chapter suggests appropriate dimensions for cultural research and analysis.

## Introduction

Any comparison between Australia and Europe—most obviously, the United Kingdom—could not escape the fundamental point that Australia was colonised while industrialising Europe was colonising. Colonial settlement grew relatively rapidly during the late eighteenth century and, although much growth occurred inland, each colony was administered from a capital city located on the coast with very little delegation to local communities. The colonial relationship is still apparent in each state's administrative hierarchy and the federal system, making reasonable overseas comparisons in governance enduringly difficult, even though neo-liberalism and parallel new models of localising and regionalising governance have been very influential in Australia and Europe.

This chapter focuses on a cultural element that is associated with this centralised administrative system. The structure of the metropolitan–regional system in Australia has been analysed extensively, and likewise rural cultures, but the connection with governance is not made so often. There has long been a broad interpretation of the rural Australian world view, or 'community self-concept' (Curry 2000:694, drawing on Clifford Geertz), available alongside the political economy of regional development and disadvantage (see Gray and Lawrence 2001). Much has been written about farm cultures and their significance for farm practice and environments (such as Vanclay et al. 1998). The rural community studies literature has explored town culture in relation to ruralism (see, for example, Gray 1991). The history of the National Party, 'country-mindedness' (Aitkin 1985) and new state movements have shown a radical, sometimes almost revolutionary, element in rural culture. Though waning at times, this element has been significant historically, but in the research literature it has generally not been tied to current problems of economic and social restructuring. There is a case for making this connection and reinterpreting metropolitan–regional relations accordingly. The case is made below with an eye to administrative structures and the prospects for regionalisation.

## The administrative geography of Australian rural development

Unlike the comparable countries of North America, and other than the national capital created after federation, inland cities that could rival the capitals did not arise in Australia. Inland Australia has possessed relatively little secondary industry or commercial administration. No inland city has been able to rival the administrative and commercial strengths of the coastal state capitals. A by-product of this early dominance was the capacity of each colony to ignore the others, except to attempt to ensure that neighbouring colonies did not siphon trade. This rivalry substantially affected the pattern of settlement and administrative relations among the state capitals.

It is, however, possible to identify sub-state regions in terms of economic, demographic and environmental characteristics to which the state boundaries have little or no relevance. The states are sometimes said to be unnecessary historical anomalies, hindering rational planning and development (see, for example, Soorley 2004). Nevertheless, the states and particularly their capitals dominate Australia's political and economic geography. Despite a significant drift of population to dispersed coastal towns where tourism and service industries are growing, the state capitals remain demographically dominant and are likely to remain so. For example, Sydney is projected to show about 70 per cent of the population growth of New South Wales in 2031. Coastal areas are expected to grow the most rapidly in percentage terms, while inland areas are expected to continue to lose population (Transport and Population Data Centre 2004).

This relationship between country and city has a political element. It has provided the basis of an important dimension of Australian politics with the development of a continuing national political party, which has attempted to represent the views of rural residents (see Costar and Woodward 1985). It was founded on the ideology of country-mindedness: belief in the distinctiveness, value and legitimacy of rural interests founded on agrarian values and counterpoised with city interests. The city–country relationship is also expressed in state–local government relations. Rural local government is a product of colonial governments' attempts to force local people to take responsibility for some of the costs of development. From the outset, rural communities had to seek favours from colonial governments for development to occur, and leaders emerged around the need to promote local interests (Chapman and Wood 1984). From the 1850s, the colonies permitted incorporation of local councils having taxation (rating) capability. Many local government areas have relatively small populations and hence have very limited revenue-raising capacity. The governments of New South Wales and Tasmania found it necessary to enforce incorporation in many areas. Chapman and Wood (1984:39) mention that in the mid 1980s, just more than half of all local authorities had populations smaller than 5000 people, despite some recent amalgamations of small rural councils. Local councils have generally been reluctant to extend their responsibilities by increasing their taxation revenue, and have been reluctant to combine with other councils to form larger organisations. Local government continues to exist only under the authority of state government legislation and administration. With the likely exception of the one very large council, that of Brisbane City, Australian local government is not capable of accepting sufficient effective responsibility to become a likely vehicle for regionalisation, decentralisation and certainly not devolution.

The Australian tradition of local government is one of small and subservient institutions. State governments remain entrenched in the overwhelmingly populous and economically strong state capitals. Although appearing to attempt decentralisation from time to time by transferring departments or parts of them to regional cities, and sometimes later transferring them back again, the hierarchy of state administration extends outwards and downwards, with some variation among the states, from the capitals, as it has always done. Debate about the size and strength of Australian local government has focused on economic efficiency arguments rather than power and devolution (Dollery and Crase 2006). Where devolution has occurred it has tended to be functions and responsibilities that are devolved rather than power—a situation leading Dollery and Crase to support the view that Australian local government is financially unsustainable.

## Dependency, governance and rural restructuring

The culture of rural local government, and rural communities more broadly, has been one in which subservience to the state government is understood—in the sense that it is taken for granted as well as in the sense of familiarity. Debates about rural restructuring among researchers and practitioners, including small-town 'revivalists' (Gray 2005a) who seek to reverse the detrimental economic and social effects of change, illuminate this culture. The researchers do so as they implicitly propose that exerting influence over state governments either amounts to expression of autonomy or at least indicates something other than an absolute power relationship as rural interests are 'translated' (see Herbert-Cheshire 2003) rather than exerted independently. The practitioners are similar as they identify the culture to be changed as one of dependency identifiable among individuals and expressed as the absence of entrepreneurialism. Both groups—the researchers and the activists—are at least partly correct in what they see and what they conclude. The problem is that they tend to be a little myopic. Moreover, they conflate political powerlessness and economic passivity.

Those who perceive a power structure see it in terms of struggle against central government, while those who take an apolitical view see business failure amid opportunity. Among those who acknowledge local–central power relations, Herbert-Cheshire (2003:255) identifies previous research that shows 'local people to negotiate, challenge and ultimately transform rural policy' but not create policy for themselves as a truly autonomous organisation might be expected to do. In her own research, Herbert-Cheshire uses actor network theory to circumvent conceptualisation of power in terms of either passivity or resistance and admits the possibility that those in power might be displaced by the translation of interests towards something more consistent with those of the formerly powerless. Herbert-Cheshire presents a scenario in which local people are able to persuade a state government to modify and reverse its decisions to terminate a train service and close a courthouse. She presents another scenario through which local people persuade a Commonwealth Government department to change an industry-support funding formula.

While these cases certainly illustrate 'translation' and validate the rejection of absolute conceptualisations of power, it is notable that in neither instance did a community act without reference to a central government. They apparently did not, for example, attempt to recreate the courthouse for themselves, start their own freight service or establish their own sources for industry support. In some parallel analysis, Herbert-Cheshire and Higgins (2004) contrast small rural communities in terms of the response to decline as occurring in a single dimension: one community heeding the neo-liberal dictum of the revivalists and redefining itself as entrepreneurial while the other remains reactive to government. They contrast entrepreneurialism with continuing political weakness rather than, as they might, distilling two dimensions: economic passivity–activity and political subservience–autonomy. An economically active, entrepreneurial community can remain dependent, while it is conceivable, though admittedly unlikely given the structure and culture of local government, that an economically passive community could have some autonomy.

In Herbert-Cheshire's comparison, the apparently economically successful community ceased or reduced its level of protest to government while the unsuccessful case chose to continue traditional anti-government protest, contributing further to its own illegitimacy in the neo-liberal ideological framework. The latter also did what we might predict given the tradition of political/administrative subservience. What, however, of the former entrepreneurial and apparently successful community? Herbert-Cheshire and Higgins attributed the success to the enrolment of outside expertise, which, under neo-liberal logic, was able to change the attitude of local people away from dependency towards entrepreneurialism. They use success in obtaining central government grant funding as an indicator of reform and renewal, as well as some business development. As Herbert-Cheshire and Higgins note, however, this success has not gone so far as reversing population decline and the problems of agricultural industries. It has more to do with the ability of neo-liberal rhetoric to define success and, I would add, its capacity to distract attention from the political subservience–autonomy dimension.

In political terms, the successful community acted neither independently nor in concert with other communities. It might have changed its economic world view, but only at the prompting of central government and apparently only in terms of its perception of local business. This observation prompts, at very least, some critical questioning of whether or not this 'success', which Herbert-Cheshire and Higgins show to be at least questionable, will prove to be in the community's long-term interests. It also prompts questioning of this world view in which community action is seen only as entrepreneurialism to the denigration of political action, or the viewing of it as such becomes legitimate. From the perspective of the history of Australian administrative tradition, this looks like the untranslated (Herbert-Cheshire 2004) exercise of metropolitan power. For present purposes, the important point is that although an entrepreneurial culture seems to have emerged or an old one has been strengthened, the relationship with government has not changed.

Is there any evidence of the relationship changing? Local government has been changed by amalgamation of small councils into large ones, most dramatically in Victoria. O'Toole and Burdess (2004) portrayed this as the emergence of a new mode of governance because a variety of community organisations grew in Victoria in response to local government amalgamations and the consequent loss by some local communities of their own council. Changes to local government have been and are being considered and implemented in other states, almost always involving amalgamation. There is no evidence that amalgamations create politically stronger institutions in their relations with central government. O'Toole and Burdess (2004) discuss change in terms of the creation of community organisations that react to enlarged local government in the familiar way—just as local government is reactive to state government.

Of course it is easy to make accusations of passivity from a distance in time and space, with no knowledge of the circumstances other than the communities being small and suffering from restructuring. It is also absurd to expect a small community to establish its own legal system or development funding independently of central government. It is, however, reasonable to surmise, for purposes of further investigation, that the traditional world view of the community members would not have prompted them to consider non-government (as Herbert-Cheshire and Higgins suggest) or locally governed alternatives. It is hard to see success in obtaining central government funding as a sure step towards autonomy. Very many small rural communities have organised themselves to retain or develop local industries (Cocklin and Dibden 2005). Perhaps the best type, or certainly best-known example, of a non-government alternative is that promoted by the Bendigo Bank. The Bendigo Bank works in partnership with local people to re-establish branches in small towns after the metropolitan banks have withdrawn. While only partially localised, the rise of Bendigo Bank branches in small towns does illustrate local participation in development without central government involvement. It hints at what might be done with greater cooperation and resource pooling among rural communities.

This view has a point of consistency with those who advocate community self-help and entrepreneurship: 'revivalists', as apparent in Kenyon and Black (2001) and Stoeckel (1998). From this perspective, the correct response to neo-liberalism and restructuring is the development of local business and industry of the kind that Herbert-Cheshire and Higgins identify in their successful case.

This does not contradict the power relationship models, but it does ignore the history of development through which rural localities have been created as political dependencies of the metropolitan cities. It is frequently and reasonably criticised for promoting or at least risking victim blaming. Nevertheless, it is worth noting for the way it points towards a culture in which local self-governance does not come to mind as a response to economic and social decline. The existence of work such as Kenyon and Black's and exhortations like that of Stoeckel's implies a cultural problem, though not necessarily one that can be solved at the individual level, and not without reference to the development of rural local cultures in a political relationship with metropolitan Australia.

## Radical rural governance

Locally governed alternatives are even more difficult to imagine given the status of local government. What, then, of the National Party? Has it operated in the political dimension that the revivalists ignore? The answer must be yes, but it operates in the same governance framework as it has sought to change relations within the political dimension rather than change the institutions of it. There is, however, a streak of radicalism in Australia's rural history. The proponents of new states apparently have had no difficulty in imagining drastic institutional change towards more regionalised governance.

The creation of new states has been a popular idea in many regional areas. It effectively means secession from existing states, but it is specifically allowed under the Australian Constitution if certain requirements are met. The new-state movement has roots in the creation of existing states, but has progressed no further despite the idea still retaining considerable support in Queensland and New South Wales at least. The idea that regional government should replace the states is also relatively popular, and not just in the rural areas that have been the wellsprings of new-state movements (Brown et al. 2006). While country-mindedness has promoted a rural-based political party, provided foundations for new-state movements in rural areas and generally been consistent with agrarian ideals of self-reliance, it has not helped to strengthen the only form of government residing in rural areas: local government. Nor has it successfully prompted effective agitation for reform of the federal system towards regionalisation.

Australia faces a governance dilemma: there is popular support for regionalisation at the same time as the states are losing influence to the Commonwealth, but local government does not currently provide a platform for devolution. The significance of the problem grows a little when trends towards 'new local governance' elsewhere, particularly in the United Kingdom, are considered. Here we see promotion of the idea of devolution alongside improvements in local governance (Stoker 2004). This comes amid the ever-present evidence that bottom-up, local initiative provides the best platform for promoting or ameliorating change and its effects and that central control can be unnecessary and undesirable (for a British environmental example, see Hinshelwood 2001). The significance of any change for the better in local governance has, however, been vigorously questioned (Bonney 2004). Some change to rural local governance, towards more participatory models, has been noted in Australia, but some of the old structures are persistent (Pini 2006). Moreover, it is hard to imagine 'new localism' taking hold in Australia: no Australian local council, with the possible exception of Brisbane City, has anything like the capacity to improve its environment as some of the big British cities have done. The debate in Australia remains focused on amalgamations of very small councils into slightly larger ones.

Research on rural local government has shown that the legitimacy of rural elected councillors rests on their ability to defend the interests of the locality, frequently against what are seen to be threats from central government, and initiatives that could conceivably bring rate increases are resisted (Gray 1991). The amalgamation of councils and the application of new management techniques, such as competitive tendering, have partially redefined local government, but nothing appears to have changed the traditional criteria for popular legitimacy (Welch 2002, using New Zealand and Australian illustrations). If there is a cultural problem, as suggested above, there doesn't seem to be any change happening in local government to solve it. There could be something happening through central government attempts at 'whole-of-government' programming and participatory planning, but none of this indicates the rise of local institutions that could be expected to take initiatives in a climate of relative autonomy. In New Zealand, engagement and partnership have recently illuminated the continuing problems of local government legitimacy and implicitly support arguments for stronger regional governance (Scott and McNeill 2006). There is no institutional basis for such change in Australia. Just as the revivalists seek cultural change towards entrepreneurialism and have apparently found a platform for it in some towns, so we might consider the existence of a platform for more political cultural change towards the legitimisation of regionalism.

## A culture of political subservience?

Given the enthusiasm with which the new entrepreneurialism of the revivalists has been accepted in some communities, what has become of country-mindedness? Looking at the National Party, one might think it has faded at least a bit. The National Party, however, is still a country party and it retains its country-mindedness, with indications of agrarianism (as with its recent support for the 'single-desk' wheat exporter). The National Farmers Federation (NFF) continues to represent rural industry, though it is an industry organisation with only weak connections to rural communities and cannot be said to have been driven by agrarianism (Connors 1996) to the extent that the National Party has. Nevertheless, both organisations represent the rural interest, to the extent that there is a singular rural interest, though particularly the NFF is industry rather than community focused. Their level of political activity and activism contrasts with the passivity of the communities discussed above.

This could reflect the view that what is good for industry is good for the community. Giving priority to farmer interests has been noted in regional local politics (Gray 1991). When we consider the strength of activism, however, and the high level of political organisation among farmers, it is surprising that there has been so little activity at the local community level for the sake of local community interests. The reason for this paradox might lie in the rigidity of the state administrative apparatus and the low status of local government. In some circumstances, rural organisations seem very keen and able to take over government activities. In other circumstances, there seems to be no recognition of the possibilities. Some examples will illustrate this problem by way of contrasting the processes of privatisation in which opportunities have arisen for rural industries and communities.

## Grain handling

The privatisation of grain handling in New South Wales was taken on by a farmer organisation as a great entrepreneurial opportunity and the capture of a government function to which farmers had been subservient. The Grain Handling Authority, previously known as the Grain Elevators Board, was sold in its corporatised form, the NSW Grain Corporation, by the Prime Wheat Association in 1992. In 2000, it merged with its Victorian counterpart. It merged with Queensland-based Grainco in 2003. In a letter to the Leader of the NSW Opposition, the Prime Wheat Association states:

> We appreciate the support of your Party in our objective to acquire NSW Grain Corporation Ltd on behalf of the growers of NSW. It is essential that the privatisation of GrainCorp results in ownership by the users of the system as a natural and logical extension of their production process.

The letter goes on to state that the association has 8000 grower members and has been in existence since 1958. It concludes by saying: 'Your policy of growers acquiring ownership of GrainCorp as expressed by Mr Jack Hallam, Shadow Minister for Agriculture, Rural Affairs and Forests receives our strong endorsement' (Parliament of New South Wales 1992).

Elias (2005) reports that only 22 per cent of Graincorp shares are in the hands of farmers, but this does not alter the apparent enthusiasm and competence of a farmer organisation through acquiring not just a business, but a government function, which had been managed from Sydney since 1917. Farmers, at least for a time, placed themselves much further towards the entrepreneurial autonomous ends of the economic and political dimensions of their relationship with metropolitan Australia.

## Irrigation

The recent history of irrigation is more complex, and differs among the states and within states. Unlike Victoria, New South Wales privatised its water distribution agency at the community level during the 1990s. The farmers were, according to parliamentary statements, keen to take over the provision of irrigation water at the local or regional level. 'The irrigators are eager to be handed the task of privatisation' (Member for Murray, in Parliament of New South Wales 1993). An interesting example of community involvement in the process is that of Coleambally Irrigation Co-Operative Limited (CICL), which took over from what was once the NSW Water Conservation and Irrigation Commission (from 1976, the Water Resources Commission) in 2000. All 373 of the cooperative's customers are also members (Meyer 2005:116). In the same year that the cooperative was corporatised (1997), the future membership was facing uncertainties of water supply and pricing as the state government discussed capping the quantities of water that could be diverted, issues that had been on the political agenda for several years (Parliament of New South Wales 1997). Water conservation measures were required of the privatised entities and were funded by the NSW Government (with respect to Murray Irrigation Limited, see Meyer 2005:105). In drought conditions, however, on top of environmental concerns and infrastructure problems, the management of water provision has been difficult.

This is especially so for locally or regionally based organisations that are required to manage state policy. It is reasonable to ask about the extent to which local people, including cooperative members, are able to interpret and act on their own interests. Just what privatisation and localisation/regionalisation have meant to farmers and other local people should be questioned. An anecdote of potential interest has been provided by an anthropologist working among irrigation farmers in an area managed by a cooperative (A. Brown, personal communication). In conversations about water and its management during some research on the values and interests of irrigation farmers, a privatised irrigation organisation was consistently referred to as 'the commission', being a reference to the Water Resources Commission, which had ceased to exist in 1986. 'The commission' was seen to have been an authoritarian, almost foreign, organisation. It did, as the privatised entities must still do, police the use of water. This raises the possibility that after the irrigation provider has been transferred to local ownership, though not entirely local control, it is seen to remain unchanged. It is reasonable to propose that the idea of local control is foreign to the irrigation farmer's world view. While grain handling indicates the legitimacy of the regionalisation of industry functions and the ease with which the ideas of privatisation and farmer control fit into the rural world view, government functions might not be so easily reconceptualised in regionalist terms.

## Natural resource management

Among the rural functions of government, natural resource management (NRM) has become the most regionalised. Before discussing the process, it is worth differentiating regionalisation from regionalism. The latter refers to the idea, held among regional people, that regional-level administration is preferable to central administration. In the rural context, it is consistent with country-mindedness, though it has no necessary agrarian element. Regionalisation refers to the actions of central governments when they devolve responsibility, with or without significant authority, to sub-state organisations. The Commonwealth Government, with the cooperation of the states, has been responsible for regionalising NRM since the national Landcare program was established on a localised basis from 1988, but more significantly since the National Action Plan for Salinity and the Natural Heritage Trust provided substantial funding to organisations established on a regional basis (Moore and Rockloff 2006). It is hard, however, to see much regionalism in these changes. They have been instituted and delivered by central, state and the Commonwealth governments in terms laid down by those governments.

Regional NRM organisations, typically known as catchment management authorities (CMAs), have considerable power and resources. Although their constitutions vary among the states, they are not, however, particularly democratic. The CMA boards are often appointed rather than elected and central government is seen to maintain control. In Moore and Rockloff's (2006:268) research, the idea that a local government's elected representatives might participate was rejected by NRM group members interviewed on the grounds that local government was too parochial, despite local government being more democratic and accountable to its constituents.

These organisations have a very shaky status on the political dimension of regional–metropolitan, local–central relations. Despite having resources, they do not have regionalist origins and are very much creatures of state governments, although Moore and Rockloff see some opportunities for the exertion of regional agency. They conclude that the challenge of democratised NRM is that of transforming local government to suit effective regional delivery and democratic accountability, something that is apparently absent from at least some regional participants in CMAs.

## Railways[1]

The examples above indicate the limitations of regional autonomy after some of the major changes of the past 20 years in the context of neo-liberalisation of rural, industrial and environmental policies. They show that although an entrepreneurial spirit has existed among farmers and others as members of industry organisations, and can be stimulated by central government activity at the local level, and although the interests of rural and metropolitan people and institutions have been and continue to be counterpoised in the tradition of country-mindedness, there seems to be limited readiness to become involved in ways that, in the context of 'new localism' and potentially 'new regionalism', could drive substantial change.

While it is problematic to explain the absence of a phenomenon, particularly when it is basically ideological, I propose that the problem could be due to the embedded nature of the rural world view in a tradition of administrative dependency and a reluctance to break away from that tradition. We have seen that reluctance, possibly in terms of the failure of Graincorp to maintain farmer ownership, but more evidently in the hint of a culture of subservience to the old irrigation provider and the rejection of local government as a vehicle for regionalisation.

A historical explanation for this non-phenomenon is offered by the history of the railways. More than any other institution, the railways, with some variation among the states, present the history of administrative dependency. This is partly because they were a very significant institution in rural development economically and culturally. Blainey (1968) sees the steam locomotive as so significant to the history of rural Australia and particularly the National Party that he suggests that a steam locomotive rather than a sheaf of wheat should be the centrepiece of its coat of arms, were it to have one. The railways established the pattern of rural settlement. While doing so, they focused the economy of each state, to slightly varying degrees, on the capitals. The railways were planned and administered from the colonial capitals in ways that ensured that metropolitan interests were furthered and alternative ports did not develop sufficiently to compete, or develop at all. Among transport historians, Lee (2003) makes this point about centralisation, though he does note variation among the colonies, later the states.

New South Wales and Victoria developed railway systems that focused the exportation of primary products on the colonial capitals and a few other ports, such as Newcastle in New South Wales and Geelong in Victoria. The more decentralised Queensland pattern is a consequence of the great distance between Brisbane, the capital, and the important northern port of Townsville, rather than any decentralising design by the colonial government. The other states' railway systems were centralised to varying degrees, with Western Australia being the most like Queensland due to its possession of a long coastline and a small number of widely separated ports. The idea of creating more ports in the centralised states was floated. For example, in 1911, a Royal Commission recommended to the NSW Government that a port be developed north of Newcastle and another south of Sydney, with systems of railway lines to serve them, in order to effect decentralisation (Gunn 1989). No such development occurred, though inland extensions of the system connecting Sydney continued into the 1930s. The Commonwealth Government has worked with the states on the interstate railway system, but has left the regional lines entirely to the states.

The railways enabled the creation of a rural society consistent with the image valued by an urban mercantile class rather than that valued by the rural aristocracy. Railway development was part of a deliberate program of social change, by way of the creation of a yeoman farmer class, conducted amid conflict between the 'squatters' and urban dwellers dominated by commercial interests. Change was fuelled by an ideology of civilisation. The railway would bring law and order and the institutions of religion and education to the inland. The railway was seen as one of 'the rudiments of bourgeois civilisation': a means to 'tether the mighty bush to the world' (Clark 1978:96). After noting how appreciative local populations were to the railway service, Gammage (1986:217) puts it bluntly: 'But the railways were built to serve men in Sydney who equated progress with the economic advancement of the metropolis.'

Gammage (1986:219) illustrates the subservience of a small town to the Sydney railway authorities: 'railway people, including railway workers, were convinced that some Narrandera street trees had been accidentally poisoned from a railway drain, but in 1983 the men in Sydney decided that this was not the case, and the [local government] council was obliged to let the matter drop'. Even local construction works were contracted to Sydney builders (Sharp 1998). Rural people have been well aware of their place in the relationship between rural interests and railway administrations.

Corresponding with the rise of road transport since the 1950s, the railway systems have come to be defined politically as problems more than as assets. Regional railways have been seen as problems almost from their opening. In New South Wales during the 1960s, the railways' finances rather than their capacity to provide transportation became a serious political problem, despite the railways still being able to cover operating expenses into the 1970s and freight services doing so into the 1990s (Industry Commission 1991). Nevertheless, the solution adopted by all governments except that of Queensland has been to privatise freight services and, in some instances, passenger services as well. In each case, buyers willing to continue regional services, for at least some period, were found.

While this change has been going on, the practice of 'cost shifting' has worsened. Cost shifting occurs when a regional railway is abandoned without any compensation to local government for the increased damage to be suffered consequently by local roads. The additional road maintenance costs can be substantial, which when accompanied by local concerns about road safety, gives local government an interest in rail transport. Such is the weakness of the still highly dispersed local government system that it has been unable to counter the problem. Many councils have protested to state governments about the deterioration of services and appealed for them to be improved, or in some cases restored, after cessation. At least one council has considered taking over a railway (Bourke Shire in 1989; see Industry Commission 1991). It was not successful. There has been no organisational platform and not much indication of enthusiasm among rural people for running their own railway system—certainly nothing comparable with the levels of enthusiasm and organisation shown by farmers through the privatisation of grain handling and irrigation. This differs substantially from the experience in North America, where there are now many locally and regionally operated railways, which are products of local initiative (Beingessner 2003). It should not be attributed to a lack of enthusiasm on the part of rural people or to a lack of entrepreneurialism or to the absence of the idea (see Lander and Smith 2004). Rather, sense can be made of it in terms of the centralised administrative tradition maintained by government and the contradictory nature of the relationship between railways and local communities.

## Conclusion: some research directions

In concluding her discussion about potential applications of anthropology to regional development, Eversole (2005) points to the potential that the 'insider's perspective' has to illuminate and explain some of the problems faced by people seeking to develop Australia's non-metropolitan regions. She advocates application of ethnographic methods to interpret the 'ways of doing things' of regional people. In this chapter, I have explored some recent literature on local–central, or regional–metropolitan, relations in the context of the processes of neo-liberalisation and restructuring. I have attempted to refine current conceptualisation of economic dependency and political subservience. Consideration of these two elements as separate dimensions, alongside the problems of restructuring, provides a more penetrating analysis of the condition of rural communities, particularly potentially those not doing well: those most likely to be subject to the exhortations of the revivalists.

Having separated the economic from the political, for present analytical purposes at least, attention is turned to the political dimension. For present purposes and in the context of Australian history, this means state government administration and its relationship with local institutions, particularly local government. We find that centralism at the state level has been a profound element in this continuing relationship. When looking at some examples of privatisation into rural hands, we see faltering change towards devolution. Most importantly, we see a hint of evidence that rural cultural tradition does not easily accept devolution and probably lacks the resources to manage it to advantage. When we look at what might be or become significant devolution in the NRM context, we see no evidence of regionalism of a kind that seeks genuine devolution. This does not indicate an absence of regionalism but rather an application of a kind of regionalisation from the state that does not facilitate devolution. When we look at the history of the railways, we see an administrative institution that has cemented centralisation, in New South Wales at least, and very little evidence of regionalist thinking about transport problems.

Where to for anthropology? There are obviously some propositions here that ethnography could help to test. Even if the propositions are ultimately seen to fall over, exploration and interpretation of relations between rural people and the institutions of the state hold some promise for those, such as Herbert-Cheshire and Moore and Rockloff, who are concerned with regional sustainability and good governance. It is probably no coincidence that it is the traditionally well-organised farmers who have responded to regionalisation, even if they have neither seized nor maintained control. What of the other members of rural communities? What of their relations with farmers? What of relations between local government, its constituents and the states? All three of these questions have been tackled in the past. It might now be time to tackle them ethnographically again to build a platform for equitable and sustainable models of regional governance.

## Acknowledgment

The gathering of material for this chapter was assisted by 'Towards Sustainable Regional Institutions', Discovery Project DP0556168, funded by the Australian Research Council.

## Bibliography

Aitkin, D. 1985, 'Countrymindedness: the spread of an idea', *Australian Cultural History*, vol. 4, pp. 34–41.

Beingessner, P. 2003, 'Saskatchewan short line rails', in H. P. Diaz, J. Jaffe and R. Stirling, *Farm Communities at the Crossroads*, Canadian Plains Research Center, University of Regina, Regina, pp. 191–203.

Blainey, G. 1968, *The Tyranny of Distance: How distance shaped Australia's history*, Macmillan, London.

Bonney, N. 2004, 'Local democracy renewed?', *Political Quarterly*, vol. 75, no. 1, pp. 43–51.

Brown, A. J., Gray, I. and Giorgas, D. 2006, 'Towards a more regional federalism: rural and urban attitudes to institutions, governance and reform in Australia', *Rural Society*, vol. 18, no. 2, pp. 283–301.

Chapman, R. J. K. and Wood, M. 1984, *Australian Local Government: The federal dimension*, George Allen and Unwin, Sydney.

Clark, C. M. H. 1978, *A History of Australia. Volume IV: The earth abideth forever, 1851–1888*, Melbourne University Press, Melbourne.

Cocklin, C. and Dibden, J. (eds) 2005, *Sustainability and Change in Rural Australia*, UNSW Press, Sydney.

Connors, T. 1996, *To Speak With One Voice: The quest by Australian farmers for federal unity*, National Farmers Federation, Canberra.

Costar, B. and Woodward, D. 1985, 'Conclusion', in B. Costar and D. Woodward, *Country to National: Australian rural politics and beyond*, George Allen and Unwin, Sydney, pp. 135–8.

Curry, J. M. 2000, 'Community worldview and rural systems: a study of five communities in Iowa', *Annals of the Association of American Geographers*, vol. 90, no. 4, pp. 693–712.

Dollery, B. and Crase, L. 2006, 'Optimal approaches to structural reform in regional and rural local governance: the Australian experience', *Local Government Studies*, vol. 32, no. 4, pp. 447–64.

Elias, D. 2005, 'Victoria unshackled: the good and bad', *Age*, 13 August 2005.

Eversole, R. 2005, 'The insider's perspective on regional development: using the anthropological perspective', in R. Eversole and J. Martin (eds), *Participation and Governance in Regional Development*, Ashgate, Aldershot, pp. 1–53.

Gammage, B. 1986, *Narrandera Shire*, Narrandera Shire Council, Narrandera.

Gray, I. 1991, *Politics in Place, Social Power Relations in an Australian Country Town*, Cambridge University Press, Cambridge.

Gray, I. 2005a, What can railway organisations learn from railway cultural traditions?, Paper presented at the National Railway Heritage Conference, Tamworth, 28–30 September 2005.

Gray, I. 2005b, 'Challenges to individual and collective action', in C. Cocklin and J. Dibden (eds), *Sustainability and Change in Rural Australia*, UNSW Press, Sydney, pp. 230–46.

Gray, I. 2006a, The centralisation of regional land transport in Australia and some of its consequences, Paper presented at the annual conference of the International Society for the Study of Transport, Traffic and Mobility, Paris, September.

Gray, I. 2006b, Transport and regionalism, Paper presented to the Australian Political Studies Association Conference, Newcastle, September.

Gray, I. and Lawrence, G. 2001, *A Future for Regional Australia: Escaping global misfortune*, Cambridge University Press, Cambridge.

Gunn, J. 1989, *Along Parallel Lines*, Melbourne University Press, Melbourne.

Herbert-Cheshire, L. 2003, 'Translating policy: power and action in Australia's country towns', *Sociologia Ruralis*, vol. 43, no. 4, pp. 454–73.

Herbert-Cheshire, L. and Higgins, V. 2004, 'From risky to responsible: expert knowledge and the governing of community-led rural development', *Journal of Rural Studies*, vol. 20, no. 3, pp. 289–302.

Hinshelwood, E. 2001, 'Power to the people: community-led wind energy—obstacles and opportunities in a South Wales valley', *Community Development Journal*, vol. 36, no. 2, pp. 95–110.

Industry Commission 1991, *Rail Transport. Volume I: Report*, Australian Government Publishing Service, Canberra.

Kenyon, P. and Black, A. (eds) 2001, *Small Town Renewal: Overview and case studies*, Rural Industries Research and Development Corporation, Canberra.

Lander, F. and Smith, G. 2004, 'NSW branch lines: has the time come for the Australian short line revolution?', *Railway Digest*, vol. 42, no. 1, pp. 26–8.

Lee, R. 2003, 'The railway age, 1874–1920', *Linking A Nation: Australia's transport and communications, 1788–1970*, Australian Heritage Commission, Canberra, viewed 30 November 2006, <http://www.ahc.gov.au/publications/national-stories/transport/>

Meyer, W. 2005, *The irrigation industry in the Murray and Murrumbidgee Basins*, Technical Report No. 03/05, Cooperative Research Centre for Irrigation Futures.

Moore, S. and Rockloff, S. F. 2006, 'Organizing regionally for natural resource management in Australia: reflections on agency and government', *Journal of Environmental Policy and Planning*, vol. 8, no. 3, pp. 259–77.

Murray Irrigation Limited 2006, *MIL Infrastructure*, <http://www.murrayirrigation.com.au/content.aspx?p=20051>

O'Toole, K. and Burdess, N. 2004, 'New community governance in small rural towns: the Australian experience', *Journal of Rural Studies*, vol. 20, no. 4, pp. 433–43.

Parliament of New South Wales 1992, 'NSW Grain Corporation Holdings Limited Bill', *Hansard*, 6 May 1992, viewed 25 May 2007, <http://www.parliament.nsw.gov.au/prod/parlment/HansArt.nsf/V3Key/LA19920506023>

Parliament of New South Wales 1993, 'Irrigation Scheme Privatisation', *Hansard*, 20 May 1993, viewed 25 May 2007,

<http://www.parliament.nsw.gov.au/prod/PARLMENT/hansArt.nsf/V3Key/LA19930520041>

Parliament of New South Wales 1997, 'Minister for Land and Water Conservation', *Hansard*, 8 April 1997, viewed 25 May 2007, <http://www.parliament.nsw.gov.au/prod/parlment/hansart.nsf/V3Key/LA19970408048>

Pini, B. 2006, 'A critique of "new" rural local governance: the case of gender in a rural Australian setting', *Journal of Rural Studies*, vol. 22, no. 4, pp. 396–408.

Scott, C. and McNeill, J. 2006, Community strategic planning and the pursuit of whole of government outcomes, Paper presented at Governments and Communities in Partnership: From theory to practice, University of Melbourne, 25–27 September 2006.

Sharp, S. A. 1998, Destined to fail: management of the New South Wales railways 1877–1995, Unpublished PhD thesis, University of Sydney.

Soorley, J. 2004, 'Do we need a federal system? The case for abolishing state governments', in W. Hudson and A. J. Brown (eds), *Restructuring Australia: Regionalism, republicanism and reform of the nation-state*, Federation Press, Sydney, pp. 38–46.

Stoeckel, A. 1998, 'Farmers can solve their problems by themselves', *Australian Farm Journal*, vol. 8, no. 9, pp. 16–17.

Stoker, G. 2004, 'New localism, progressive politics and democracy', *Political Quarterly*, vol. 75, no. s1, pp. 117–29.

Transport and Population Data Centre 2004, *New South Wales State and Regional Population Projection, 2001–2051*, 2004 Release, Department of Infrastructure, Planning and Natural Resources, Sydney.

Vanclay, F., Mesiti, L. and Howden, P. 1998, 'Styles of farming and farming subcultures: appropriate concepts for Australian rural sociology?', *Rural Society*, vol. 8, no. 2, pp. 85–107.

Welch, R. 2002, 'Legitimacy of rural local government in the new governance environment', *Journal of Rural Studies*, vol. 18, no. 4, pp. 443–59.

## Endnotes

[1] Parts of this section draw on material in Gray (2006a, 2006b).

# 3

# The role of agrarian sentiment in Australian rural policy

Linda Botterill

## Abstract

Politics has famously been described as the 'authoritative allocation of values' and the political science literature has discussed the mechanisms through which different values are represented in the policy process. Much of this research has focused on explicitly stated values that can be identified as competing interests in the community. This chapter discusses the existence of an apparently pervasive value in Australian agricultural policy development, which is rarely articulated and is not represented by an identifiable interest group or 'watchdog'. The value is agrarianism. Agrarian imagery and appeals to national identity are frequently used to explain rural policy decisions. This is ironic, given that in recent years rural policy in Australia has been dominated by neo-liberal economics with an emphasis on structural adjustment, productivity improvement and deregulation—goals that are apparently at odds with agrarian values. This chapter will explore the influence of agrarianism in Australia, including its limiting impact on the level of policy debate and its role in sustaining the National Party as a force in Australian politics.

## Introduction

Politics has been described as the 'authoritative allocation of values' (Easton 1953:129) and the public policy literature discusses how values are incorporated in policy development processes and how decision makers balance the conflicting values that inevitably arise. Almost every policy decision involves a compromise between differing objectives, many of which are anchored in particular values: the trade off between inflation and unemployment is a clear example in economic policy, as is the balance between wages and profits. With a few exceptions, the discussion of values in the policy process has focused on identifiable values promoted by particular advocates within the policy community. Using agrarianism in Australia as an example, this chapter will argue that this interpretation of the role of values is superficial—that there exist deeper, fundamental values in a polity that do not need advocates, as their influence is pervasive. These values might not even be recognised or named but their impact can be seen.

This examination of agrarianism in Australia arises from a simple question: why is there so little public critical analysis of rural policy in Australia? Rural policies are rarely subject to the general scrutiny that applies, for example, when welfare, education or health policies are considered. When public interest in rural issues is aroused, it tends to be in response to events such as drought, which evoke general sympathy and support for government efforts to provide subsidies or other forms of government intervention. Why is such unquestioning support not forthcoming for other groups in the community, such as the unemployed, the disabled or single mothers? This chapter argues that this sympathetic response is the result of a residual agrarianism in Australian culture, which is shared by many developed countries, which dates back centuries, and which attributes to farmers certain virtues and idealised characteristics that generally place them beyond reproach. What makes this agrarianism interesting in Australia is that this country is one of the most urbanised in the world and, with a highly efficient agricultural sector, has one of the lowest levels of government support for farmers. In multilateral trade negotiations, Australia has criticised the United States and, more particularly, the European Union for farm policies that are seen as trade distorting and economically inefficient. Ironically, the motivation for these policies is much the same agrarian sentiment that motivates sympathy in Australia for farmers in difficulty and which provides the basis for the image cultivated by the National Party in differentiating itself from its opponents and from its coalition partners.

The chapter is set out as follows. The first section describes the characteristics of agrarianism, its history and its Australian manifestation, 'country-mindedness'. The second section draws on the political science literature in examining the role of values in the policy process, and finally the chapter examines agrarianism and politics, specifically their role in sustaining the National Party and insulating rural policy from critical analysis.

## Agrarianism and country-mindedness

In his fascinating history of agrarianism, Montmarquet (1989) tracks the idea and its many interpretations from the early classical thinkers, through the French physiocrats and Thomas Jefferson, to Wendell Berry in the twentieth century. His book illustrates the point made by rural sociologists that the agrarian concept is both nebulous and malleable, and that it can be used rhetorically for apparently contradictory purposes (Beus and Dunlap 1994; see, for example, Halpin and Martin 1996:21). The seminal definition of agrarianism is provided by Flinn and Johnson, who identify the following five 'tenets of agrarianism':

- *'farming is the basic occupation on which all other economic pursuits depend for raw materials and food'*
- *'agricultural life is the natural life for man; therefore, being natural, it is good, while city life is artificial and evil'*
- farming delivers the *'complete economic independence of the farmer'*
- *'the farmer should work hard to demonstrate his virtue, which is made possible only though [sic] an orderly society'*
- *'family farms have become indissolubly connected with American democracy'* (Flinn and Johnson 1974:189–94; italics in original).

This description encapsulates two important features of agrarianism. First, agrarianism rests on the belief that agricultural pursuits are inherently worthwhile and wholesome. Montmarquet (1989:viii) summarises this as 'the idea that agriculture and those whose occupation involves agriculture are especially important and valuable elements of society'. Farming pursuits are regarded as conducive to the development of moral behaviour and thinkers such as J. S. Mill and Thomas Jefferson advocated small-scale agriculture for social rather than economic reasons. Mill argued of small-scale peasant agriculture as practised in Europe that 'no other existing state of agricultural economy has so beneficial effect on the industry, the intelligence, the frugality, and prudence of the population...no existing state, therefore is on the whole so favourable both to their moral and physical welfare' (Mill 1893:374).

Griswold (1946:667) explains that, for Jefferson, 'agriculture was not primarily a source of wealth, but of human virtues and traits most congenial to popular self-government. It had a sociological rather than an economic value. This is the dominant note in all his writings on the subject.'

More recently, Wendell Berry (1977:11) linked the demise of small-scale agriculture to the rise of undesirable characteristics of exploitation, waste and fraud, suggesting that modern life had caused a 'disastrous breach...between our bodies and our souls'. His contrast between the exploitative mind and nurturing is consistent with earlier interpretations of agriculture's worth, which extends beyond the economic to the moral. As well as promoting virtue, agricultural activity is seen as valuable because it is regarded as the starting point of civilisation—without settlement, art, culture and other pursuits that depend on large groups of people could not have evolved. Settlement allowed for specialisation. Agriculture, as opposed to hunting and gathering, provided the basis for settlement.

The second important characteristic of agrarianism is that it is half of a dichotomy, the other half of which is non-farm life and which on all counts fails to measure up to the morally superior, if economically inferior, status of farming. Flinn and Johnson (1974:194) refer to the agrarian perception that 'city life is artificial and evil' and they go on to argue that '[w]ithin agrarian belief there is pride, a certain nobility, in what man accomplishes by the sweat of his brow. There is suspicion about a man who makes a living by using his head and not his hands.'

This dualism was evident in Jefferson's thought. Initially, he hoped that the United States would remain an agrarian society, allowing Europe to house manufacturing activity and cities and their associated social problems. He argued that:

> The loss by the transportation of commodities across the Atlantic will be made up in happiness and permanence of government. The mobs of great cities add just so much to the support of pure government, as sores do to the strength of the human body. It is the manners and spirit of a people which preserve a republic in vigor. (Cited in Griswold 1946:668)

In the Australian context, Don Aitkin has summed up agrarianism as country-mindedness. The term is of uncertain origin but is traceable to the beginnings of the Country Party in the 1920s. Aitkin's formulation of the characteristics of Australian agrarianism reflects many of the points just discussed: the wholesome nature of agricultural activity and the contrast between the virtues of farming and the unpleasantness of urban life:

> (i) Australia depends on its primary producers for its high standards of living, for only those who produce a physical good add to a country's wealth.
>
> (ii) Therefore all Australians, from city and country alike, should in their own interest support policies aimed at improving the position of primary industries.
>
> (iii) Farming and grazing, and rural pursuits generally, are virtuous, ennobling and cooperative; they bring out the best in people.
>
> (iv) In contrast, city life is competitive and nasty, as well as parasitical.
>
> (v) The characteristic Australian is a countryman, and the core elements of the national character come from the struggles of country people to tame their environment and make it productive. City people are much the same the world over.
>
> (vi) For all these reasons, and others like defence, people should be encouraged to settle in the country, not in the city.
>
> ...
>
> (viii) But power resides in the city, where politics is trapped in a sterile debate about classes. There has to be a separate political party for country people to articulate the true voice of the nation. (Aitkin 1985:35)

Point five is of particular note given the highly urbanised nature of Australian society and it is also important in the context of the influence of agrarian ideology on Australian culture. Stehlik et al. (1996) describe the notion that Australians are

> essentially rural creatures transplanted against our will in urban metropolises around the eastern seaboard of the continent. To many of us 'the bush' evokes a natural, pristine essentially good place which may be less than the city we live in, but somehow it is still morally our national conscience. We respond emotionally to the ideology of the pioneering spirit, the challenge against the unknown, the concept of 'the rural'.

Popular culture in Australia draws on this type of rural imagery with television programs such as A Country Practice, McLeod's Daughters and Blue Heelers drawing on the rural myth with their portrayals of rugged individuals with hearts of gold facing hardship with stoicism and good humour. Many of these shows include cynical city types won over by the simplicity and basic goodness of rural living. Australian athletes have been dressed in Driza-Bones and Akubras for Olympic opening ceremonies and the Sydney 2000 Olympics drew on rural iconography in its welcome to the world. As Finkelstein and Bourke (2001:46) point out, advertising also draws on the rural–urban contrast, reinforcing this image as 'an enduring and successful element in the formation of Australian culture and identity'.

The rural myth is further strengthened by its links to the other great source of Australian identity: the ANZAC legend. Although it is debatable how accurate the sentiment is, there is a perception that Australia's diggers in World War I came disproportionately from the 'bush' (Botterill 2006:25–6). Farm groups occasionally exploit this link between the bush and the ANZAC legend—the most recent example of which is in a media release by the National Farmers Federation (NFF). Drought-affected farmers in Australia were offered free holidays in New Zealand by the Federated Farmers of New Zealand and the airline Jetstar donated 100 free air tickets to facilitate farmers taking up the offer. When it appeared that farmers might lose their drought-related welfare payments while on their free holiday, the NFF lobbied the government to change the rules. The government complied and the NFF put out a media release announcing the change, including the following statement: 'When times are tough farm communities stick together, and we appreciate our NZ counterparts' understanding and outstanding generosity very much. It is one of the best examples of the ANZAC tradition...digging in and giving each other a hand when it's needed most' (National Farmers Federation 2007).

## The role of values in Australian rural policy

As with all policy areas, agricultural policy is developed against a backdrop of conflicting values, such as the differences between environmental and production values and between importers and exporters (for example, over the stringency of quarantine requirements). In his seminal work on incrementalism, Lindblom (1959) argued that one of the advantages of incremental policy development was the capacity for policy to address values that had been overlooked in earlier iterations. He described the policy process as serial and remedial and he argued that this was an effective way for policy to be developed. He also argued that for this process to work successfully, each value should have a watchdog that focused on particular aspects of the policy to ensure that it was represented. More recently, Thacher and Rein have made a similar argument about strategies for balancing values in policy development. They suggest several approaches that can be adopted to address value conflict. The first of these, 'policy cycling', is similar to Lindblom's serial and remedial incrementalism, suggesting that policymakers 'focus on each value sequentially, emphasizing one value until the destructive consequences for others become too severe to ignore' (Thacher and Rein 2004:463). The second strategy they identify is the construction of 'firewalls' that divide responsibility for different values among institutions 'ensuring that each value has a vigorous champion' (Thacher and Rein 2004); the similarities with Lindblom's watchdogs are clear.

The interesting aspect of these approaches is that the analysis focuses on identifiable values—values that have clear advocates and that can be easily identified in the issues being debated in a particular policy area as different perspectives on complex social problems. Rokeach (1979:55) goes as far as arguing that 'there are no terminal or instrumental values that will be "left over", that are not the focus of specialization by at least one social institution'. An alternative perspective is that some values operate at a deeper cultural level and are not articulated in policy debate. Feldman (1988:418) argues that widely shared core values and beliefs 'may be so pervasive that their presence in everyday politics often goes unnoticed'. Sabatier refers to 'deep core' values that are exogenous variables in policy advocacy and 'are very resistant to change—essentially akin to religious conversion'. They consist of 'fundamental normative and ontological axioms' (Sabatier 1988:144). Williams is one of the few writers who points to explicit values and those that are not:

> some values are, indeed, highly explicit, and appear to the social actor as phenomenal entities: the person can state the value, illustrate its application in making judgments, identify its boundaries, and the like. Other standards of desirability are not explicit; and social actors may even resist making them explicit. (Williams 1979:17)

Different mixes of values will deliver different policy outcomes. In Europe, agrarian values are clearly influential in the policy settings of the Common Agricultural Policy (CAP). Ockenden and Franklin (1995:1) argue that 'the CAP provides evidence that agriculture carries a cultural and social significance far in excess of its economic importance. The policy is neither an afterthought nor an expensive irrelevance, but the manifestation of the unique place of agriculture in the psyche of industrial societies.'

In Australia, production values have dominated in recent years with policy emphasis on productivity improvement and competitiveness. The mix changes over time as different values gain ascendancy in policy debate (Botterill 2004). Rural policy communities are archetypal 'closed' networks (see, for example, Grant and MacNamara 1995; Smith 1992), which have a shared approach to policy and which exclude competing views from the process. The peak Australian farmers' representative body, the NFF, was established in 1979 and from the outset was at the forefront of neo-liberal debate. It has consistently advocated free trade, domestic deregulation and labour market reform and it has extended these policy prescriptions to its own sector. In its 1981 paper Farm focus: the '80s, the organisation stated that the 'NFF does not believe that any industry—rural, mining, manufacturing, or tertiary—whether highly protected or not—should be permanently shielded from the forces of economic change. The overall interests of the economy demand that all industries must participate in the inevitable adjustment process' (National Farmers Federation 1981:48).

As Lawrence (1987:79) wrote, in the 1980s, the NFF became 'one of the most vocal proponents of a deregulated economy and a free enterprise agriculture'. It was therefore at home in the agricultural policy community with the Australian Bureau of Agricultural and Resource Economics (ABARE) and the Commonwealth agriculture department, currently the Department of Agriculture, Fisheries and Forestry (DAFF). After several decades of highly interventionist agricultural policies in Australia, agricultural economists in the 1960s began to question policies of government intervention in agriculture (see, for example, Lloyd 1970; Makeham and Bird 1969; McKay 1967) and, by the 1980s, neo-liberal approaches to rural policy were firmly entrenched. While agrarian values were clearly articulated in the first half of the twentieth century (see, for example, Chifley 1946), they seemed to disappear from policy settings from the 1970s onwards. Policies have focused on deregulation, structural adjustment and productivity improvement, examples of which include deregulation of the dairy industry, privatisation of the former Australian Wheat Board and changes to regulatory arrangements for the wool industry.

The language of policy statements, however, does not necessarily match the reality of policy implementation and policymakers are not averse to appealing to agrarian sentiment when explaining decisions that might otherwise appear inconsistent with stated policy direction. Within the rural policy community there is no identifiable watchdog for what might be characterised as agrarian values; the main players have for more than two decades pursued neo-liberal policy objectives (Botterill 2005). The absence of a visible agrarian interest, however, has not meant that these values have disappeared from policy. They remain an important socio-cultural phenomenon and appear to have an important role in protecting rural policy from rigorous critique, thus facilitating the emergence of inconsistencies in approach between rural and non-rural policies. These inconsistencies are disguised either by rhetoric that reflects overall government policy direction while hiding the reality of implementation or by the use of values-based language to justify inconsistencies when they are obvious. The National Party has been particularly effective at using agrarian imagery for this latter purpose and in defence of its position as part of the Australian political landscape.

A good example of the gap between the rhetoric and the reality is the National Drought Policy (NDP). Agreed by Commonwealth and state governments in 1992, the NDP was a watershed in government responses to drought. It followed the removal of drought from the natural disaster relief arrangements and was based on the principle that drought was not a disaster but part of Australia's climate. The NDP was based on principles of self-reliance and risk management and argued that drought was a risk to be managed by farmers like any other risk facing the farm business. The policy included a series of programs aimed at improving farmers' risk-management skills and introduced tax-effective financial risk-management programs aimed at encouraging farmers to build financial reserves on which they could draw in dry years. The policy included an important caveat: it introduced the concept of 'exceptional circumstances' to describe circumstances that were so extreme that even the best manager could not be expected to cope. In these conditions, further government support to farm businesses would be triggered, however, it was available only to businesses that were considered to have a long-term productive future in agriculture. Policymakers were concerned that drought relief not act as a de facto subsidy to otherwise unviable businesses.

In 1994, the NDP was augmented with the creation of a welfare payment, currently called the Exceptional Circumstances Relief Payment (ECRP), which was linked to exceptional circumstances declarations and this payment changed the whole tenor of the program. The first major shift towards a more agrarian approach was that the viability test did not apply to the welfare payment—so farms that were ineligible for the business support could be eligible for the welfare payment. This altered the incentive structure of the policy as the availability of the welfare payment made attaining an exceptional circumstances declaration more attractive, essentially undermining the objective of self-reliance and risk management. Instead of being motivated to manage a current dry spell, it was more sensible for farmers to make a case that the dry spell they were experiencing was particularly bad in order to access government support. In 1999, ministers went so far as to change the definition of exceptional circumstances drought to elevate the impact of drought on income to the threshold criterion ('key indicator') for a declaration (ARMCANZ 1999:63).

Until 2005, the welfare payment had been paid at the same rate as other income-support payments available to the Australian community—for example, the unemployment benefit. In May 2005, the government announced that it was increasing by $10 000 the amount that a farmer could earn before their drought payment was reduced (Truss 2005), meaning that farmers on drought relief could earn more than twice as much a fortnight as an unemployed person before losing any income support. Farmers are also not subject to any mutual obligation requirements. The May 2005 announcement passed unnoticed by the mainstream media. In its response to the announcement, the NFF continued to use the language of the NDP, noting that 'Australian farmers acknowledged the importance of preparing for, and managing, business climatic risks such as severe drought'. After welcoming the increased level of drought support, the organisation stated:

> EC [exceptional circumstances] assistance is not about handouts or propping up marginal farmers, it is a responsible policy that aims to support viable farm businesses to preserve their natural and productive resource base during periods of severe climatic stress, so that they are in a position to rapidly recover and contribute to Australia's export economy. (National Farmers Federation 2005)

This type of apparent contradiction is not uncommon in rural policy debate—using the neo-liberal language of the NDP while welcoming an inequitable increase in support to farmers that is unrelated to economic outcomes.

The privatisation of the statutory Australian Wheat Board provides a further example of rural policy development that has occurred apparently without reference to broader policy approaches. Deregulation of the wheat market began in 1989 with the removal of the Australian Wheat Board's monopoly over the domestic wheat trade. This change occurred in a climate of general industry deregulation, which had been pursued by the Hawke Labor government from 1984. From 1990, the grains industry started a process of strategic planning that included consideration of the future of export marketing arrangements for wheat. The level of urgency associated with this consideration was increased from 1993 when the report into national competition policy (Hilmer et al. 1993) was published, which included a section on the anti-competitive nature of agricultural statutory marketing arrangements and a chapter on monopolies. In 1995, debate within the grains industry became focused on the future structure of the Australian Wheat Board, with a particular focus on the board's export monopoly—the so-called 'single desk'. Discussions and debate about the structure took place largely independently of government with the main players being the peak industry body, the Grains Council of Australia, and the Australian

Wheat Board. The Department of Primary Industries and Energy had a place in the discussions but did not advocate a strong position. This was consistent with the approach taken by consecutive Ministers for Primary Industries and Energy, Senator Bob Collins (Labor) and John Anderson (National). The final model was developed by industry and implemented through two tranches of legislation in 1997 and 1998. The outcome was a privatised body, AWB Limited, which essentially retained the single desk. The government did not drive the privatisation process, the Department of Finance did not have a central role in the process and the objectives for the privatisation were set by the grains industry, not by government. There is little indication that the government took strong action to protect the public asset associated with the export monopoly, marking the process as a 'very peculiar privatisation' (Aulich and Botterill 2007).

The grains industry continued to be treated differently when the legislation that embodied the export monopoly, the Wheat Marketing Act 1989, came due for review under the National Competition Policy (NCP). While the usual practice for NCP reviews was for the Productivity Commission to undertake the review, the Wheat Marketing Act was reviewed by a committee that included the former president of the Grains Council of Australia (Irving et al. 2000). The Productivity Commission made two submissions to the review (Productivity Commission 2000a, 2000b) in which it argued the case for the repeal of the export monopoly. The NCP review, in contrast, recommended that 'the "single desk" be retained until a scheduled review in 2004 by the Wheat Export Authority of the privatised AWB's operation of the "single desk" arrangement' (Irving et al. 2000:8), although it also stated that 'the main purpose and implementation of this scheduled review should be changed so that it provides one final opportunity for a compelling case to be compiled that the "single desk" delivers a net benefit to the Australian community' (Irving et al. 2000:8). The Commonwealth Government rejected this last recommendation. The National Competition Council subsequently found that 'the Government's review of the Wheat Marketing Act was open, independent and rigorous', however, it concluded that 'the Commonwealth Government had not met its [competition principles agreement] clause 4 and 5 obligations[1] arising from the Wheat Marketing Act' (National Competition Council 2003:1.8).

The single-desk arrangements for the wheat industry have come under more general public scrutiny since the Cole Inquiry into the Oil for Food Program and the revelations of AWB Limited's bypassing of the Iraqi sanctions regime (Cole 2006). It is, however, arguable that the interest in this scandal by the mainstream media and commentators was prompted by the possibility that senior ministers were aware of the behaviour rather than a considered critique of the rural policy underpinning the existence of an export monopoly in the hands of a private company.

## Agrarianism, politics, policy and the National Party

An important beneficiary of agrarianism is the National Party of Australia, which first entered Australian politics in the early 1920s as the Country Party of Australia. Set up as a voice for rural Australians, the party grew out of farm interest groups that had been established from the mid nineteenth century. Richmond (1978:104) argues that '[m]any country people objected to the Labor Party and its talk of socialisation of land; but they also objected to the city domination of the larger non-Labor parties'.

The early Country Party therefore set out to establish itself as a third force in Australian politics. This position was clearly illustrated by the words of the first Country Party leader in the Commonwealth Parliament, W. J. McWilliams, on 10 March 1920:

> The Country Party is an independent body quite separate from the Nationalists and the Labor Party. We occupy our own rooms. We have appointed our own leader and other officers. We take no part in the deliberations of the Ministerialists or of the Opposition. We intend to support measures of which we approve and hold ourselves absolutely free to criticize or reject proposals with which we do not agree. Having put our hands to the wheel we set the course of our voyage. There has been no collusion; we crave no alliance; we spurn no support; we have no desire to harass the government, nor do we wish to humiliate the opposition. (McWilliams 1920:250)

In spite of these protestations of independence, the party was, by 1922, in coalition with the Nationalists and it used its role in subsequent coalitions very effectively to gain cabinet positions and policy influence out of all proportion to its electoral performance. With dominance of the agriculture and trade portfolios, the National Party has managed to pursue farmers' interests effectively. Through the interventionist years, agrarian objectives were pursued openly. More recently, these values have been protected less transparently while still being drawn on rhetorically to retain National Party support. Apart from a general inclination to look after rural interests, specific National Party policies are not easy to identify. Woodward (1985:61) has described National Party policy as 'a strange blend of conservatism coupled with support for radical government intervention in certain economic and social areas'. In recent years, the dominance of the neo-liberal paradigm across government policy has blunted the party's capacity to deliver largesse to its constituency, however, it has achieved some expensive concessions to buffer the impact of these policies. For example, deregulation of the dairy industry in 2000 was accompanied by a $1.74 billion structural adjustment package, funded by a levy on milk, which provided 'substantial adjustment payments' to dairy farmers (Truss 2000). This was augmented with packages to assist communities in dairy-farming areas. A further

$159 million was added to the package in 2001. The Australian National Audit Office (2004:14) reports that 'some 30 000 farmers were granted [Dairy Structural Adjustment Program] payment rights, with an average payment right of $54 300'. A further $100 million was allocated to 7735 farmers (Australian National Audit Office 2004:16) under a Supplementary Dairy Assistance Package. This supplementary package was introduced to provide 'an additional one-off payment to eligible dairy producers who were severely affected by deregulation, and whose eligibility for DSAP was unintentionally limited' (Australian National Audit Office 2004:26).

While the National Party's rhetoric continues to present its objectives in terms of being the sole true representative of farmers and rural people, in recent years that claim has become less convincing. Verrall et al. (1985:9) observe that 'the National Party has by no means a monopoly of the conservative rural vote' and they suggest that 'National Party seats are not typically rural and indeed...there is no typical National Party electorate' (p. 11). Nevertheless, the National Party's web site (<http://www.nationals.org.au/About/values.asp>) makes the claim that '[w]ithout [t]he Nationals, government policy would be determined by a substantial majority of city-based parliamentarians'. The implication is the very agrarian notion that city folk do not understand the 'bush' and cannot be trusted to protect rural interests. As has been argued elsewhere (Botterill 2006), while farmers and their representatives are not reticent about engaging in debates about non-farm policy, they are quick to cast doubts on the views of rural policy commentators who do not have direct ties to the bush. The Nationals also reflect the idea expressed in Aitkin's view of country-mindedness that what is good for the bush is good for the country. As Jaensch (1997:299) has argued:

> As populists, the members of the party believe fundamentally in the virtue of rural people, rural interests and rural morality, not only for rural areas, but as a model for the whole country. It logically follows, then, that any actions which will protect, support and bolster rural people and interests are justified for the good of the nation.

The National Party taps into these sentiments very effectively. Nelson and Garst (2005) have looked at the role of values-based communication 'as a means to signify political identity and establish community with audience members'. They describe this as a 'social purpose of values-based language' and explore the impact this language has on the listening audience. They argue that 'values, like political parties, serve as important foundations for a citizen's political identity' (Nelson and Garst 2005:490). Brewer (2001) has also examined the issue of value framing in political communication and the links between value-based political messages and core values. He argues that:

> value frames...share a feature that sets them apart from other sorts of messages: [t]hey associate an issue with a core value. Thus, a value frame

> may shape opinion in a more subtle way as well: [i]t may encourage audience members to form opinions on the basis of the specific value invoked by the frame. (Brewer 2001:45)

In his study of parties and party systems, Sartori (1976:329) described the use of imagery in party promotion, noting that 'parties communicate to mass electorates via party images and...much of their electoral strategy is concerned with building up the appropriate image for the public from which they expect votes'. While the effectiveness of the National Party at engaging its supporters is not surprising, this chapter argues that the broader community shares the values being drawn on—thus generating support from a wider constituency than the party's small electoral base would suggest. The National Party is very effective at using images in its political messages that tap into agrarian values, among its own supporters and across the wider community. In Parliament, National Party representatives play up the urban–rural divide. Verrall et al. (1985:8) see this rural–urban cleavage as 'an essential and key notion in understanding Australian politics' and it has been used regularly as a basis for attack on the Nationals' political opponents. In a press release, Agriculture Minister, Peter McGauran (2006b), began his attack on the opposition spokesman with '[t]he Shadow Minister for Agriculture, Fisheries and Forestry has today reminded rural and regional Australia how little the Labor Party knows about drought'. Later in the same release, he again made the point that Labor was ignorant about rural Australia, stating: 'If Mr O'Connor had any idea of rural and regional Australia, he would know only too well that this region is part of the South West Slopes and Plains EC declaration' (McGauran 2006b). In apparent contradiction to this statement, but still playing on the city–rural divide, the minister had responded earlier in the year to the failure of O'Connor to win preselection for his seat with the following statement:

> The forced exit of Labor's Agriculture spokesman, Gavan O'Connor, from Federal Parliament will be a serious loss to rural and regional Australia, the Minister for Agriculture, Fisheries and Forestry, Peter McGauran, said today.
>
> Mr McGauran said that, as a former dairy farmer, Mr O'Connor was the only member of the Labor Opposition to have a practical understanding of farming.
>
> 'Mr O'Connor has been a lone voice for farming inside a city-centric and union-dominated Labor Party,' he said.
>
> 'His dumping at the hands of factional bosses will rob Labor of the only practical understanding of farming and regional policy it has.
>
> 'It highlights Labor's disregard for farmers by so unceremoniously sending its only ally into the political wilderness.' (McGauran 2006a)

Another National Party Senator described O'Connor as 'the quintessential city slicker. He rarely gets out of Melbourne, unless he is coming to Canberra, and he is trying to tell this place that he cares about rural and regional Australia!' (Nash 2005:97). Consistency of argument is clearly not important but appeal to the agrarian value frame is.

Although the long-term future of the National Party has been the subject of continuing speculation and discussion (see, for example, Aitkin 1973; Green 2001; Jaensch 1997; Malcolm 1989; Richmond 1978), the adoption of agrarian imagery by other political parties would not be a simple undertaking. Although the Liberal and Labor Parties have held and continue to hold rural-based electorates, they cannot simply pick up the National Party's mantle as the representatives of rural interests. Research by Nelson and Garst (2005) suggests that it is risky for a party to appeal to values with which it is not generally associated. They suggest that values-based political messages are persuasive but these messages are not well received if they come from an unexpected quarter. The research found that '[r]ival party speakers...were punished when they used unexpected language' (Nelson and Garst 2005:510). Brewer (2001:59) also cites research that finds that 'citizens may reject a frame when they perceive that it originates from the "wrong" side of the ideological or partisan fence'. This suggests that Labor Party politicians who use agrarian language are more likely to evoke suspicion and hostility than a positive response. The Coalition has tapped into this on occasion. For example, in a parliamentary debate in 1996, a Liberal member of the newly elected Howard Government stated:

> I am pleased to see that the [M]ember for Hotham [Simon Crean] is here too, because he had a time as the Minister for Primary Industries and Energy, as some of you may well remember. They bought him a pair of moleskins and some elastic sided boots, and got him a Driza-Bone, with the tag still hanging off the back of it after six months. (Ronaldson 1996:669)

This imagery is effective at closing down debate. If you are not a farmer, you don't understand farming; ergo you are unqualified to comment on farm policy. When this is coupled with a general sympathy for farmers anchored in a residual agrarianism in the broader community, it creates an environment in which there is no political advantage to be gained from criticising farm policy and thus policy settings receive little analysis.

## Conclusions

Williams (1979:26–7) argues:

> To be able to infer causal sequences from values to other items, we need some evidence that the value or value system was present prior to or simultaneously with the explicandum, that its presence is associated

with a heightened frequency of the phenomena to be explained, and that there is a theoretically compelling connection.

The existence of agrarian values in Western culture is well established. These values have a long history and, although they have been used flexibly to support different objectives, their basic components are well documented. More research is needed on the causal link between agrarianism and policy outcomes, particularly in Australia, where the link is not explicit; however, the frequent reference to agrarian imagery by the National Party suggests the values are influential and, as Hutcheon (1972:184) suggests, deeply held values might 'not [be] themselves amenable to direct observation and measurement' and might be identifiable only by inference. A plausible explanation of the inconsistencies between rural policy and other analogous areas of government policy is the lack of analytical attention given to the former, which allows some areas of farm policy to develop with limited reference to broader government policy approaches. This chapter provides the examples of the provision of income support to farmers on a more generous basis than to other groups in the community and the unusual privatisation and subsequent National Competition Policy Review of the AWB. There is scope for further theoretical consideration to be given to the influence of deep socio-cultural values on policy.

This chapter has argued that Australian rural policy is influenced by agrarian sentiments that are common to many Western societies. At times in Australia's history, this agrarianism has been explicit. In recent years, as other paradigms have dominated policymaking, agrarian influence has been less obvious; however, it remains evident. Agrarian imagery is used in political debate and is important in differentiating the National Party from its electoral competitors, including its coalition partners. It is also effective in limiting critical analysis of policy settings. The public policy literature discusses the policy process as a balancing act, with decision makers confronting conflicting values that they must weigh up in arriving at policy positions. This literature generally assumes that values are explicit and that they are represented in the process by advocates such as interest groups or political parties. It is argued that this interpretation is too limited and does not recognise the influence of deep socio-cultural values that are so embedded in the community that their existence is not necessarily recognised. Agrarianism in Australia is such a value.

## Bibliography


Aitkin, D. 1973, 'The Australian Country Party', in H. Mayer and H. Nelson (eds), *Australian Politics: A third reader*, Cheshire, Melbourne.

Aitkin, D. 1985, '"Countrymindedness"—the spread of an idea', *Australian Cultural History*, no. 4, pp. 34–41.

Agriculture and Resource Management Council of Australia and New Zealand (ARMCANZ) 1999, *Record and Resolutions: Fifteenth meeting Adelaide 5 March 1999*, Commonwealth of Australia, Canberra.

Aulich, C. and Botterill, L. 2007, A very peculiar privatisation: the end of the statutory Australian Wheat Board, Australasian Political Studies Association Conference, Monash University, 25–27 September.

Australian National Audit Office 2004, *The Commonwealth's administration of the Dairy Industry Adjustment Package*, Audit Report No.36 2003–04, Commonwealth of Australia, Canberra.

Berry, W. 1977, *The Unsettling of America: Culture and agriculture*, Sierra Club Books, San Francisco.

Beus, C. E. and Dunlap, R. E. 1994, 'Endorsement of agrarian ideology and adherence to agricultural paradigms', *Rural Sociology*, vol. 59, no. 3, pp. 462–84.

Botterill, L. C. 2004, 'Valuing agriculture: balancing competing objectives in the policy process', *Journal of Public Policy*, vol. 24, no. 2, pp. 199–218.

Botterill, L. C. 2005, 'Policy change and network termination: the role of farm groups in agricultural policy making in Australia', *Australian Journal of Political Science*, vol. 40, no. 2, pp. 1–13.

Botterill, L. C. 2006, 'Soap operas, cenotaphs and sacred cows: countrymindedness and rural policy debate in Australia', *Public Policy*, vol. 1, no. 1, pp. 23–36.

Brewer, P. B. 2001, 'Value words and lizard brains: do citizens deliberate about appeals to their core values?', *Political Psychology*, vol. 2, no. 1, pp. 45–63.

Chifley, J. B., the Rt Hon. 1946, A rural policy for post-war Australia, A statement of current policy in relation to Australia's primary industries, Bureau of Agricultural Economics, Canberra.

Cole, T. 2006, *Report of the Inquiry into Certain Australian Companies in Relation to the UN Oil-for-Food Programme*, Commonwealth of Australia, Canberra.

Easton, D. 1953, *The Political System: An inquiry into the state of political science*, Alfred A. Knopf, New York.

Feldman, S. 1988, 'Structure and consistency in public opinion: the role of core beliefs and values', *American Journal of Political Science*, vol. 32, no. 2, pp. 416–40.

Finkelstein, J. and Bourke, L. 2001, 'The rural as urban myth: snack foods and country life', in S. Lockie and L. Bourke (eds), *Rurality Bites: The social and environmental transformation of rural Australia*, Pluto Press, Annandale, pp. 45–51.

Flinn, W. L. and Johnson, D. E. 1974, 'Agrarianism among Wisconsin farmers', *Rural Sociology*, vol. 39, no. 2, pp. 187–204.

Grant, W. and MacNamara, A. 1995, 'When policy communities intersect: the case of agriculture and banking', *Political Studies*, vol. XLIII, no. 3, pp. 509–15.

Green, Antony 2001, 'Bush politics: the rise and fall of the Country/National Party', in S. Lockie and L. Bourke (eds), *Rurality Bites: The social and environmental transformation of rural Australia*, Pluto Press, Annandale, New South Wales, pp. 61–71.

Griswold, A. W. 1946, 'The agrarian democracy of Thomas Jefferson', *The American Political Science Review*, vol. 40, no. 4, pp. 657–81.

Halpin, D. and Martin, P. 1996, 'Agrarianism and farmer representation: ideology in Australian agriculture', in G. Lawrence, K. Lyons and S. Momtaz (eds), *Social Change in Rural Australia*, Central Queensland University, Rockhampton, pp. 9–24.

Hilmer, F. G., Rayner, M. R. and Taperell, G. Q. 1993, *National Competition Policy*, Report by the Independent Committee of Inquiry, Australian Government Publishing Service, Canberra.

Hutcheon, P. D. 1972, 'Value theory: towards conceptual clarification', *The British Journal of Sociology*, vol. 23, no. 2, pp. 172–87.

Irving, M., Arney, J. and Lindner, B. 2000, *National Competition Policy Review of the Wheat Marketing Act 1989*, December 2000, Commonwealth of Australia, Canberra.

Jaensch, D. 1997, *The Politics of Australia*, Second edition, Macmillan Education Australia, South Melbourne.

Lawrence, G. 1987, *Capitalism and the Countryside: the rural crisis in Australia*, Pluto Press, Sydney.

Lindblom, C. E. 1959, 'The science of "muddling through"', *Public Administration Review*, vol. 19, pp. 79–88.

Lloyd, A. G. 1970, 'Some current policy issues', *Australian Journal of Agricultural Economics*, vol. 14, no. 2, pp. 93–106.

Makeham, J. P. and Bird, J. G. (eds) 1969, *Problems of Change in Australian Agriculture*, University of New England, Armidale.

Malcolm, L. R. 1989, 'Rural industry policies', in B. W. Head and A. Patience (eds), *From Fraser to Hawke*, Longman Cheshire, Melbourne, pp. 132–58.

McGauran, P. 2006a, Labor gives farmer the boot, Media release by Federal Minister for Primary Industries and Energy, DAFF06/23PM, 8 March 2006, <http://www.maff.gov.au/releases/06/06023pm.htm>

McGauran, P. 2006b, Labor wrong on drought...again, Media release by Federal Minister for Agriculture, Fisheries and Forestry, DAFF06/156PM, 18 October 2006, <http://www.maff.gov.au/releases/06/06156pm.html>

McKay, D. H. 1967, 'The small-farm problem in Australia', *Australian Journal of Agricultural Economics*, vol. 11, no. 2, pp. 115–32.

McWilliams, W. J. 1920, 'Supply Bill (No. 4) 1919–20 No Confidence Amendment: in committee of supply', *Parliamentary Debates Session 1920–21*, vol. XCI, 10 March 1920.

Mill, J. S. 1893, *Principles of Political Economy. Volume 1*, D. Appleton and Company, New York.

Milton, R. 1979, 'From individual to institutional values: with special reference to the values of science', in M. Rokeach (ed.), *Understanding Human Values: Individual and societal*, The Free Press, New York, pp. 47–70.

Montmarquet, J. A. 1989, *The Idea of Agrarianism*, University of Idaho Press, Moscow, Idaho.

Nash, S. F. 2005, 'Matters of public importance: Telstra', *Senate Hansard*, 7 September 2005.

National Competition Council 2003, *Assessment of Governments' Progress in Implementing the National Competition Policy and Related Reforms: 2003. Volume two: legislation review and reform*, AusInfo, Canberra.

National Farmers Federation 1981, *Farm Focus: the '80s*, National Farmers Federation, Canberra.

National Farmers Federation 2005, Government recognises severity of ongoing drought, National Farmers Federation media release NR 66/05, 30 May 2005.

National Farmers Federation 2007, Commonsense wins out in farmers' free NZ holiday offer, National Farmers Federation media release MR 11/07, 1 March 2007.

Nelson, T. E. and Garst, J. 2005, 'Values-based political messages and persuasion: relationships among speaker, recipient, and evoked values', *Political Psychology*, vol. 26, no. 4, pp. 489–515.

Ockenden, J. and Franklin, M. 1995, *European Agriculture: Making the CAP fit the future*, Pinter, London.

Productivity Commission 2000a, Productivity Commission submission to the National Competition Policy Review of the Wheat Marketing Act 1989, July 2000, <http://www.pc.gov.au/research/subs/wheat1/wheat1.pdf>

Productivity Commission 2000b, Productivity Commission supplementary submission to the National Competition Policy Review of the Wheat Marketing Act 1989, November 2000, <http://www.pc.gov.au/research/subs/wheat2/wheat2.pdf>

Richmond, K. 1978, 'The National Country Party', in G. Starr, K. Richmond and G. Maddox (eds), *Political Parties in Australia*, Heinemann Educational Australia, Richmond, Victoria.

Rokeach, M. (ed.) 1979, *Understanding Human Values: Individual and societal*, The Free Press, New York.

Ronaldson, M. 1996, 'Excise Tariff Amendment Bill 1996: second reading debate', *House of Representatives Hansard*, 8 May 1996.

Sabatier, P. 1988, 'An advocacy coalition framework of policy change and the role of policy-oriented learning therein', *Policy Sciences*, vol. 21, pp. 129–68.

Sartori, G. 1976, *Parties and Party Systems. Volume one*, Cambridge University Press, Cambridge.

Smith, M. J. 1992, 'The agricultural policy community: maintaining a closed relationship', in D. Marsh and R. A. W. Rhodes (eds), *Policy Networks in British Government*, Clarendon Press, Oxford, pp. 27–50.

Stehlik, D., Bulis, H., Gray, I. and Lawrence, G. 1996, Rural families and the impact of the drought of the 1990s, Australian Family Research Conference: Family research—pathways to policy, Brisbane, 27–29 November.

Thacher, D. and Rein, M. 2004, 'Managing value conflict in public policy', *Governance*, vol. 17, no. 4, pp. 457–86.

Truss, W. 2000, $1.74 billion dairy assistance package introduced, Media release by Federal Minister for Agriculture, Fisheries and Forestry, AFFA00/18WT, 17 February 2000.

Truss, W. 2005, More support for drought affected farmers, Media release by the Federal Minister for Agriculture, Fisheries and Forestry, DAFF05/152WT, 30 May 2005.

Verrall, D., Ward, I. and Hay, P. 1985, 'Community, country, party: roots of rural conservatism', in B. J. Costar and D. Woodward (eds), *Country to*

*National: Australian rural politics and beyond*, George Allen and Unwin, Sydney, pp. 8–22.

Williams, R. M., jr, 1979, 'Change and stability in values and value systems: a sociological perspective', in M. Rokeach (ed.), *Understanding Human Values: Individual and societal*, The Free Press, New York, pp. 15–46.

Woodward, D. 1985, 'The federal National Party', in B. J. Costar and D. Woodward (eds), *Country to National: Australian rural politics and beyond*, George Allen and Unwin, Sydney, pp. 54–67.

## Endnotes

[1] Clause 4 of the competition principles agreement refers to structural reform of public monopolies and Clause 5 addresses legislation review and reform.

# 4

# Wildlife, wilderness and the politics of alternative land use: an Australian ethnography

**Adrian Peace**


## Abstract

As long-established (settler) farming practices become increasingly unviable in Australia's marginal areas, it is widely argued in governmental and other circles that the extension of wilderness areas that are then populated with native wildlife should be actively encouraged. From a developmentalist perspective, this policy is considered to offer up a number of seemingly incontestable benefits: alleviating the pressure on environmentally marginal areas, creating new employment opportunities, consolidating national biodiversity, and so on. From an anthropological vantage point, however, the prospects generated by this kind of development are by no means so clear cut. In the past five years or so, a state-supported initiative to reintroduce a particular species of wallaby to Innes National Park at the foot of Yorke Peninsula, South Australia, has generated a political conflict that raises a number of salient questions about this kind of alternative rural development and its relation to conventional agriculture. This chapter is based on ethnographic research conducted in 2005 and explores the significance of the conflict from academic and policy vantage points.


## Introduction

The review and reorganisation of long-established settler land-use practices is going to be one of the more urgent and positive outcomes of the current Australian drought and the wider climatic changes of which it is a significant part. While it has taken not just an agricultural crisis but a societal one to bring the situation about, even the short to mid-term prospects of intensive farming in marginal locations are already under review from agricultural organisations, governmental bodies, environmental agencies and related policy-oriented institutions. Inasmuch as the sheer sustainability of settler agriculture in marginal areas is the subject of review and debate, a range of future land-use practices will increasingly become the focus of regional and national political discourse.

The proposal of this chapter is that anthropology's contribution to this debate is to spell out to decision makers and, more importantly, to those who have decisions imposed on them what are the likely difficulties and hazards of embarking on certain types of rural reform by detailing relevant case studies of recent provenance. I argue that anthropology can provide salutary warnings about rural reforms that appear, at first sight, to be heading in the right kind of environmental direction, but, in the event, encounter a number of hidden and substantial obstacles that are best explored through the tightly focused ethnographic work that still characterises the discipline. In this regard, a major initiative in the past five years to reintroduce an extinct wallaby subspecies to a national park in South Australia becomes an instructive case study.

As settler agriculture in marginal rural areas becomes increasingly non-viable, so the prospect of private land being bought up by the State and transformed or incorporated into national parks and wilderness areas is increasingly mooted, not least because there are many wholesale and piecemeal precedents for doing so in most Australian states. From a diversity of policy-oriented institutions and agencies, the idea that such areas be allowed to 'revert to nature', to 'let nature take its course' or to 'become wilderness once again', seems by many to be an attractive prospect. It is variously argued that it will lead to reduced pressure on scarce water resources, greater landscape diversity, a stay on excessive fertiliser usage and new employment opportunities through tourism. Above all, the strategy can be sold on the strength of preserving and enhancing regional biodiversity since the reintroduction of original flora and fauna is always integral to this kind of rural reform. Bringing back trees and shrubs to places where they once were and restoring mammals and birds to localities from which they have long been extinct become appealing prospects to politicians and public servants, to conservation scientists and environmental advisors, who are variously able to acquire political kudos and cultural capital from their public implementation.

In Australia, we can expect a proliferation of proposals on these lines in the near future. The mantra of biodiversification alone will ensure this to be the case as formal reactions to climate change are promulgated by the political elite before elections, by industrial managers as they spruce up their environmental credentials and by state-based environmental agencies as they consolidate their command over official environmental discourse. It is the response from below that promises to be more unpredictable, for local populations weigh up a wide range of economic and social factors when specific proposals for the rural future are imposed on them from above. It is this array of folk considerations—by no means all of them specifically about land use—that can be detailed by ethnographic inquiry. This is the prospect in principle that is open to anthropological research. In practice, how local farmers and their families respond to a conservation initiative to restore an extinct wallaby species to their rural area is what we are immediately concerned with.

## The proposal from above

It was the conservationist concern with the promotion of biodiversification that ensured that the tammar wallaby relocation project had a lot going for it from the outset. Especially in South Australian conservation circles, it was well known that the mainland tammar subspecies had been eradicated sometime during the 1930s when farmers and government officials had designated it a rural pest. What was not known until their presence there was rediscovered by a research team of CSIRO scientists in Canberra was that the same subspecies had thrived on a small island in New Zealand, to which a small number had been transported in the 1860s.

The publication of a research paper (Poole et al. 1991, later detailed by Taylor and Cooper 1999 and Taylor et al. 1999) on this unexpected finding more or less coincided with protection of the continent's biodiversity becoming central to the Commonwealth's environmental policy. Designated wilderness areas were specified as appropriate locations for the protection of biodiversity to be established and managed, and this emphatically included the reintroduction of lost species. It became part of the Federal 1996 Action Plan for Australian Marsupials and Monotremes to relocate the tammar wallaby back in its original habitat (Maxwell et al. 1996). From there, the proposal progressed to being enshrined in the Commonwealth's Environment Protection and Biodiversity Conservation Act 1999 (EPBC Act).

The mainland tammar wallaby was the only animal subspecies specified for salvage under the EPBC Act and so, not all that surprisingly, not only the conservation scientists in South Australia's Department of Environment and Heritage (DEH) but the state's leading politicians, including the Minister for the Environment and the Premier, saw substantial opportunities and benefits in this potentially high-profile contribution to preserving the continent's biodiversity. There was an immediate downside that had to be addressed with some urgency. For a second time in its recent history, the tammar had been officially declared a pest due to be eradicated, but on this occasion it was to be exterminated from Kawau Island at the behest of New Zealand's leading environmental authority. It was therefore necessary to transport a breeding population to South Australia as soon as possible. This was to be executed by a small and dedicated network of government scientists in the DEH's Science and Conservation Directorate.

Before the tammars' return home, as it was increasingly referred to, conservation scientists had chosen the relatively small Innes National Park (9322 hectares) at the foot of Yorke Peninsula as their final destination. It was a location that more than lived up to the stereotype of a wilderness area; it seemed particularly suited to the reintroduction of its original wildlife after more than half a century's absence. Since it was known to be part of the subspecies' mainland habitat on the lower Yorke Peninsula—albeit a habitat greatly transformed in the intervening period, of course—this was where the tammars would be considered properly in place once again. It was also especially appropriate, at least on paper, to the larger ambitions of the conservation scientists who proposed to eventually spread the subspecies across the peninsula, because the tammars would be able to migrate north and east from the national park through 'natural corridors' of parcels of privately owned land already set aside for conservation. Additionally, a second release site would be established elsewhere on the peninsula so that a minimum of two 500-strong tammar colonies would be achieved. At this point, under the EPBC Act, the tammar wallaby subspecies would be relieved of its current status of 'extinct in the wild' and considered a viable population that had returned to its natural habitat.

This conservation project was therefore an ambitious one aimed at making a significant contribution to regional biodiversity, not least because it would generate a good deal of new scientific knowledge over a number of years. From the moment they arrived in South Australia, the breeding population was to be closely monitored; the animals were to be kept in captivity in the regional zoological pack for quarantine and veterinary purposes. They were then to be subject to a strictly controlled breeding program that would maximise their reproductive capacity by using a different subspecies of readily available wallaby as surrogate mothers. Once released in Innes National Park, all animals were to be fitted with radio collars emitting signals that would be picked up by mobile tracking towers built specifically for use in park conditions. Finally, from time to time, tammars released from captivity into the wild, or born in it, would be captured in order to monitor their weight, determine their gender, assess their health and reproductive condition, and so on, along with the prime considerations of detailing where they were migrating to and in what numbers.

Since the relocation project was going to be a costly endeavour, the conservation science behind it was carefully spelled out from the beginning in submissions for financial support; to some of this, I will return below. What was not addressed in anything like the same detail were its social and cultural aspects, despite the obvious fact that the project's success hinged on the tammars moving out of the park wilderness and onto the intensely cultivated agricultural land that dominated the whole peninsula. It would be fair to say that, because the biodiversity credentials of the relocation project were so compelling, it was assumed that if any major questions were raised by the local people, they could be dealt with. At the least, the social and cultural impacts of the project were sparsely attended to in contrast with the depth of the scientific investment.

It therefore came as something of a surprise when, as soon as information about the project leaked out, the DEH officials found they had a major problem on their hands. Despite having intended a careful, public relations-controlled release of information to the general public, word got out as a result of a park ranger ill-advisedly mentioning the project to a young local farmer whose family property shared a long boundary with Innes National Park and would likely be the tammars' first staging point once they moved off-park. The farmer and his father were instantly alarmed at the prospect of 'the wallaby pest' among their grain crops and, as news spread through customary gossip channels, so too were their immediate neighbours and other farm families further afield. Before too long, the media also picked up on the story, and the first headline on the wallabies' return from New Zealand in South Australia's sole daily newspaper read: 'We'll take the "pest" nobody else wants' (The Advertiser, 13 September 2003).

## Conservation science versus commonsense knowledge

For the next 18 months or so, the conflict that developed between the DEH and its conservation scientists on the one hand, and the local people of lower Yorke Peninsula on the other, turned on the plausibility of the former's natural science versus the validity of the latter's local knowledge. Although there were multiple aspects to the relocation, the critical issue became to what extent the size and the spread of the wallaby population once established could be controlled by a scientifically modelled manipulation of the fox population, which was already in place. From this point onwards, the state government scientists from the city aimed to persuade the farm population on the peninsula that their worst fears of a wildlife invasion, which could threaten their rural way of life, were ill founded.

To say that this official pitch would prove an uphill struggle would be an understatement because: first, this exercise in persuasion emanated from the state capital; second, it came from a government body; and third, it was parlayed to the periphery by professional scientists. On all three counts, local farmers and their families were inclined from the outset to be circumspect and cynical at best, suspicious and dismissive at worst. The idea of a shifting boundary of foxes, a pest with which they were extremely familiar, being able to control an encroaching invasion of tammars, a pest with which they had no prior acquaintance, consistently ran counter to the local knowledge and commonsense on which rural folk prided themselves.

The central focus of debate quickly became the *Draft Translocation Proposal: Reintroduction of mainland SA tammar wallabies to Innes National Park*, a substantial document on which the conservation scientists had spent a great deal of time and effort. One of the more intriguing (and never quite explained) aspects of this and similar projects was that it did not have to be subject to an environmental impact statement. In lieu of this, the draft proposal could almost pass muster, since it provided a reasonably thorough introduction to the project's background, the selection of the release site, the acquisition, transportation and quarantining of the breeding population, through to the circumstances under which the tammars would be released, monitored and managed in the wild. It also specified the criteria for the project's success, as well as its short-term budget.

Undoubtedly the key section of the draft proposal was entitled 'Population management' and it was replete with scientific detail. The section was devoted to demonstrating how it was possible to scientifically model the rate at which the tammar population could be expected to increase, once it gained a foothold in the park wilderness. Superimposed on these data was the likely pattern of fox predation on the tammars, which could be manipulated through baiting practices undertaken by local farmers and/or contract pest controllers with experience of the region. Five possible scenarios were detailed in intricate graphs, which, at least to a layman, were not immediately comprehensible—but the major claims being made were clear enough. As the tammar population increased, fox baiting would be reduced, with the result that more foxes would be in place to pick off the wallabies: as the tammar population fell away, fox baiting would be intensified, and the wallaby population would then be able to increase and spread further. The distribution of the tammars could thus be effectively regulated through the manipulation of fox numbers: the farmers' long-established pest could be deployed in order to keep control over a potential one. This would be all the more effective, evidently enough, if farmers who were resident on the physical boundary between national park and agricultural land cooperated with the conservation scientists and the park rangers who would implement the science on the ground. A number of additional variables that might affect the rate of wallaby expansion beyond Innes National Park were factored into the scientific modelling. Again, however, the general point being made was that the local population's fears of an uncontrolled and destructive invasion of their grain fields were found to be at odds with the scientific evidence.

As is usually the case with such documents, the draft proposal was meticulously presented and systematically argued. The most likely counterarguments concerning the possibilities of risk and threat from the relocation project were anticipated and headed off by the welter of scientific discourse. It was a very thorough presentation, which was precisely what made all the more conspicuous the document's imbalances; the proposal ran to 66 printed pages, but only two of these were given over to 'Social and economic considerations'. What merits emphasis is that this kind of imbalance reflected the *modus vivendi* of the wider institutional body of the DEH. In addition to the practice of natural science being the everyday business of the DEH, its leadership was devoted to spreading its commitment to a pervasive scientism among the general public. Inasmuch as it did this with fervour and zeal, any kind of critical response from below that was not conspicuously informed by the culture of natural science was given short shrift, or remorselessly contested by yet another body of scientific evidence.

## The view from below

The local people who made up the frontline of opposition to the relocation proposal were, in contrast, deeply imbued with the culture of rural life that predominated throughout Yorke Peninsula. They were long established, moderately well off and organised in such a way as to maximise the profitability of the family farm, and the codes of self-help and self-reliance were ones that fully informed the practice of their everyday life. The only consideration to qualify the emphasis on family self-reliance was a sense of responsibility to the wider community, but there was never much prospect that the integrity of the former might be compromised by the demands of the latter, which was regularly translated into such contributions as membership of the community fire service, the township association and representing the region in agricultural, fishing, commercial and sports organisations. To be known simply as a good neighbour or stalwart community member was quite sufficient public recognition for most people.

Well before the relocation project was imposed on the community at Innes and its environs, the DEH, in contrast, was considered a poor neighbour with little regard for the collective interests of local folk. The Parks and Wildlife Service, the branch of the department responsible for its national parks, was widely considered deleterious in the maintenance of the Innes National Park boundary: it failed to prevent invasive weeds from spreading to the surrounding farmland or to curb the movement of large wildlife from park terrain into land under wheat and barley. One subject of constant complaint was the rising population of kangaroos that thrived in the national park while regularly feeding outside its limits. Another was that Parks and Wildlife officers were too reliant on the 'book learning' acquired at city-based colleges and were loathe to augment the formal information they had with local knowledge hard won through extracting a living from the soil.

Above all other differences, though, it was the dispute about the part to be played by fox predation in controlling wallaby numbers that symbolised the cultural divide between the conservation scientists and the region's farmers. For while the scientists were assured and confident about their ability to manipulate the fox population, the farmers scoffed at such inflated and hubristic claims, and counterpoised against them their own local knowledge and commonsense.

The fox problem was undoubtedly a major one for all farmers in this area who combined the production of grain with raising cattle and sheep. They spoke uncompromisingly about the toll that fox predation took annually. It was, however, generally taken to be 'a fact of life' that could never be greatly changed but rather had to be rendered tolerable or manageable. If a farmer believed that the fox problem was out of control on his land and adjacent properties, a handful of young men would go out spotlighting for a few nights and kill several score—more if the effort and expense were felt to be worthwhile. A 'big hit', which combined intense baiting and shooting, was usually organised in the weeks before the lambing season, and for a while fox sightings would be negligible. It was, however, still recognised that throughout the year the fox problem was one to be lived with instead of somehow resolved.

It was to be expected, then, that farmers and their dependents were generally sceptical when the conservation scientists from the city or park rangers at Innes claimed that the fox population could be carefully modulated, and even that this could be represented diagrammatically. The cleverness and conceit thus being displayed were symptomatic of the cultural divide that local people had encountered in previous circumstances when city-based bureaucrats steeped in 'book learning' attempted to impose their schemes at the rural periphery.

I emphasise here that the local men and women at the forefront of opposition were well versed in the interpretation of tables, charts and the texts of documents from government sources. As representatives of the local community on a range of regional committees and boards, they were used to perusing and picking up on policy details that would impact on them most. Their critique of the *Draft Translocation Proposal* was no knee-jerk reaction. Further, they clearly acknowledged that one of their major problems was that the full impact of the wallabies' return to the mainland would not be felt for several years, even decades; no one, themselves included, could accurately predict such a distant prospect. In this light, there was one section of the proposal that especially concerned them. For the foreseeable future, the reintroduced tammar would be classified as an 'endangered species' and therefore protected by law from any kind of aggressive response from local farmers and others. In the draft proposal, however, it was acknowledged that where the tammar population was not effectively controlled by fox predation as scientifically predicted, permits might be issued 'to reduce tammar abundance'. This would, however, be allowed only where their adverse impact on farmers' valuable crops had been clearly established. This open admission was taken to epitomise the indifference of the DEH and its scientists to the circumstances of local agriculturalists. In addition to it here being acknowledged that 'tammar abundance' was a real possibility, the wallabies would have to seriously impact on local crops before the farmers could legally cull them.

Opposition to the project drew on much more than local knowledge specific to production on the peninsula and the problem with foxes. It drew also on regional knowledge relating to the disastrous environmental situation prevailing on Kangaroo Island, a mere 60 kilometres to the south-east and across Investigator Strait. On this island, a different but closely related species of tammar wallaby had long ago attained pest status; especially for farmers with agricultural land proximate to the island's national parks, the economic consequences were dire. Not only had successive state governments failed to tackle the tammar problem, the island's koala population had expanded to the point at which eucalypt stocks were exhausted and, despite a considerable body of scientific research that called for a severe reduction in koala numbers, no serious government response had ensued for fear of adverse publicity that might impact on the profitable tourist trade from Japan (see, for example, Lunney and Mathews 1997; Stratford et al. 1999).

In the estimation of the farmers closest to Innes National Park, there was a real prospect of the relocated tammar wallabies likewise becoming a significant pest, but then being protected by the 'cute and pretty' image that, before too long, would be traded on by the tourist industry. In order to explore these evident parallels and turn them to political advantage, the most vocal critic of the proposal, a middle-aged farmer resident in Warooka, spent a few days on Kangaroo Island making a video in which several beleaguered landowners and their wives detailed their travails, ranging from the loss of valuable sweet crops (lucerne, lupins and cereals) through to the gruesome task of shooting the tammar pest in large numbers. Armed with his home video, the farmer then arranged a public meeting at Warooka (the main settlement closest to Innes National Park) under the auspices of the South Australian Farmers' Federation in order to mobilise public support for the cause. Some 55 members turned up, evidently representing a substantial proportion of agriculturalists in the area. The response to several motions from the floor indicated the depth of regional support for concerted opposition to the relocation project. At much the same time, letters to regional newspapers and *The Stock Journal* signalled much the same strength and depth of community opinion.

From late 2003 and throughout 2004, the local folk who had taken the lead from the outset maintained their strident public opposition, but at the same time they had little option but to be drawn into the bureaucratic process of cooptation that the rituals of community consultation were designed to effect. The rituals of consultation are precisely that in situations in which the incomparable resources of the modern State are arraigned against a numerically insignificant grassroots population. Unless they are able to mount a substantial and well-resourced grassroots movement that can not only seriously contest but present viable alternatives to proposals emanating from state institutions, local populations are relatively powerless in these modern times. Ordinary folk have little alternative but to accept the rhetoric, engage with the mechanics of democratic consultation and thereby work for minor changes that necessarily leave the significant parameters of any proposal intact. Faced with the overwhelming resources of the DEH and the unqualified commitment to the project from the government in power, the grassroots network had no option but to try to wrest whatever they could from the consultative committee.

In the event, their success on this score was negligible, despite the enormous energy and time they invested in it. The main demand they put forward was the provision by the State of financial compensation should the tammar wallaby population take off and invade the grain fields belonging to themselves and their neighbours, a threat that might eventuate only in the long-term but nevertheless had to be prepared for. Particularly in the light of what had happened on Kangaroo Island and elsewhere in the country where wallaby populations had run out of control, and since various government bodies had proved quite incapable of dealing with such situations, an appropriate compensation scheme became their main concern. The response from above to this and related issues, however, was emphatically negative. The representatives from DEH on the consultative committee were adamant from the outset that any question of compensation arrangements lay well outside the committee's brief. Nor was there any mechanism in place for the issue to be raised at higher levels. In light of this recalcitrance, a delegation of Innes farmers eventually forced a meeting with the head of the DEH. He did no more, however, than reinforce the blanket refusal with which the proposal had been received lower down the institutional hierarchy. He was adamant that neither the DEH nor the government to which it was responsible would have a bar of compensation arrangements that would establish a precedent with far-reaching consequences for many other spheres of economic life.

## Conclusion

It was to be expected, then, that a forced engagement with the rituals of community consultation eventually reinforced local people's view of the DEH and the politicians behind it as distanced, arrogant and uncompromising. At best, the consultation process was considered a waste of time and effort; at worst, it was a sham and a deceit.

The most significant outcome of this intense and protracted politicking was that when the first batch of tammar wallabies was finally released inside the park, the farm families who had a boundary with it were as hostile as ever to the project. Further afield, it was regarded with circumspection and concern for the long-term consequences. Subsequently, when the rangers put on a small celebration to signal the achievement of the tammar relocation inside the national park, the still stridently opposed farmers and their families were conspicuous by their absence. This stand-off meant that precisely the local folk who could have been of most use to the project were the ones most alienated from it. In no sense was this a fatal setback to the overall project. It will be recalled, however, that the close cooperation of neighbouring farmers, wherever the tammar wallabies were to be introduced, was written into the proposal from the outset as a highly desirable, if not imperative, requirement if the exercise was to be given the best chance of success.

The point that has to be reinforced at this juncture is that the tammar wallaby relocation scheme was, from the outset, an important and innovative prospect. For the dedicated team of conservation scientists, it was a major challenge to their scientific professionalism and one from which they could gain extensive and unique experience. For the upper echelons of the DEH, the project held out a good deal of prestige and publicity in that the return of extinct wildlife to its original wilderness would create an extremely favourable public image. For the state's politicians, especially the Minister for the Environment and the Premier, the return of the tammars could be presented as a highly symbolic contribution to the preservation of Australia's biodiversity, and therefore well indicative of the state government's increasingly important environmental credentials.

Inasmuch as it seems likely that the preservation and enhancement of biodiversity on the Australian continent are going to be central to the way in which rural futures are thought about, there are some salutary lessons to be gleaned from this case study. The first is that a range of social and cultural considerations can influence, if not determine, how grassroots populations respond to initiatives from above—and by no means are these entirely dependent on the intrinsic significance of the policy or proposal. The people of lower Yorke Peninsula had no problems with the overall goal of preserving and enhancing their region's biodiversity, and thus contributing to the national scene. As with so many other rural occupations, the region's agriculturalists considered themselves true environmentalists whose credentials easily outstripped the membership of any city-based green group. These same local folk were, however, frequently cautious, circumspect and pessimistic when external institutions bore down on them with preconceived policies and programs that would impact on their rural way of life. And the more external agencies supplemented their arguments in the same discursive terms with which they began, the more intransigent local people were likely to become.

Circumspection and suspicion about the motives of government institutions and their associated agencies are in no sense restricted to the people of lower Yorke Peninsula. They are considered judgments that are commonplace in the cultures of rural Australia, which is why any official policy or program for the rural future ignores them at their peril. It is not appropriate, therefore, for a major institution such as the DEH to approach 'social and economic considerations' as if they are of secondary or minor consequence, for the straightforward reason that to do so stores up further problems for the future rather than according them proper consideration from the outset. To many people, and certainly to an anthropological audience, this point might be self-evident. As I hope is evident from the above account, however, that was by no means the case with the tammar relocation project, and although the consequences were not disastrous, they would assuredly have been best avoided, if at all possible.

The second cautionary point is that institutions such as departments of the environment cannot be left to determine on their own account the extent and the degree of community involvement in such major areas as the protection and advancement of biodiversity, for their institutionalised scientism means that they respond with outright indifference or heavily qualified attention to non-scientific knowledge claims. Broadly speaking, departments of the environment approach community consultation as a problem to be dealt with and, if necessary, to be circumvented altogether, rather than the source of an alternative, valid and relevant body of knowledge. They function as if their stock definition and body of knowledge are the only ones to be consistently prioritised, yet this occurs at precisely the time at which more and more people in societies such as Australia become increasingly aware of the limitations of natural science and the wide-ranging problems that a previously uncritical dependence on it has generated and compounded. Circumspection towards science, and cynicism towards institutions that privilege it as a source of knowledge above all others, are by no means restricted to the local population of lower Yorke Peninsula. They are significant political developments in Australian society at large, and therefore ones that departments of the environment ignore at their peril.

The third point is that, notwithstanding points one and two, as an anthropologist, I am less convinced than most that continuing dialogue and exchange of views between conservation scientists and local populations are the ways in which differences can be resolved and productive ways forward generated. In the comparative literature, mainly drawn from experience in the United States, where the aims of conservation science and the concerns of local landowners have come into open conflict, sociological analysis generally concludes that the different parties have to continue their dialogue, they have to persist with their continuing exchange of views, and so eventually arrive at a working compromise (for example, James 2002; Norton 2000; Peterson and Horton 1995; Wondolleck and Yaffee 2000).

The main problem with this kind of conclusion is that it fails to address the uneven distribution of power, which not only characterises such relations, it generates the conflict between them in the first place. An emphasis on continuing dialogue and exchange of ideas infers a degree of equivalence and equality between partners to the conversation that is, in reality, quite mythical. In the South Australian case, as in comparable others, the discourse of conservation science was informed and backed by an institutional and political structure of enormous influence and power. Whatever the credibility and legitimacy of those who opposed the tammar relocation project from below, the conservation scientists from the DEH had only to persevere with their major ambitions in order to finally realise them. This is, more or less, the current situation. The project was somewhat delayed by local community opposition, a number of costs were incurred that would otherwise not have materialised and the local support from farm families that would have been far preferable was not forthcoming. None of these costs, however, was overwhelming for the elementary reason that institutional resources provisioned by the State far outweighed anything that the local opposition could possibly muster. As Australia's rural future becomes increasingly linked to major environmental goals such as the preservation of biodiversity and therefore the politics of conservation science, a major requirement will be how to accord proper recognition and authority to those who privilege and build on non-institutionalised, even commonsensical, bodies of knowledge and the folk discourse that gives public voice to them.

## Bibliography

James, S. M. 2002, 'Bridging the gap between private landowners and conservationists', *Conservation Biology*, vol. 16, no. 1, pp. 269–71.

Lunney, D. and Mathews, A. 1997, 'The changing roles of state and local government in fauna conservation outside nature reserves: a case study of koalas in New South Wales', in P. Hale and D. Lamb (eds), *Conservation Outside Nature Reserves*, Centre for Conservation Biology, University of Queensland, Brisbane, pp. 97–106.

Maxwell, S. et al. 1996, *Action Plan for Australian Marsupials and Monotremes*, Australian Marsupial and Monotreme Specialist Group and IUCN Species Survival Commission, Wildlife Australia, Canberra, Australian Capital Territory.

Norton, D. A. 2000, 'Conservation biology and private land: shifting the focus', *Conservation Biology*, vol. 14, pp. 1221–3.

Peace, A. 1996, '"Loggers are environmentalists too": towards an ethnography of environmental dispute, rural New South Wales 1994–1995', *The Australian Journal of Anthropology*, vol. 7, no. 1, pp. 43–60.

Peace, A. 1999, 'Anatomy of a blockade: towards an ethnography of environmental dispute (Part 2), rural New South Wales 1996', *The Australian Journal of Anthropology*, vol. 1, no. 2, pp. 144–62.

Peterson, T. R. and Horton, C. C. 1995, 'Rooted in the soil: how understanding the perspectives of landowners can enhance the management of environmental disputes', *The Quarterly Journal of Speech*, vol. 81, pp. 139–66.

Poole, W. E. et al. 1991, 'Distribution of the tammar, *Macropus eugenii*, and the relationships of populations as determined by cranial morphometrics', *Wildlife Research*, vol. 18, pp. 625–39.

Recher, H. F. 1994, 'Why conservation biology: an Australian perspective', in C. Moritz and J. Kikkawa (eds), *Conservation Biology in Australia and*

*Oceania*, Surrey Beatty and Sons, Chipping Norton, New South Wales, pp. 1–15.

Stratford, E. et al. 1999, 'Managing the koala problem: interdisciplinary perspectives', *Conservation Biology*, vol. 14, no. 3, pp. 610–18.

Taylor, A. C. and Cooper, D. W. 1999, 'Microsatellites identify introduced New Zealand tammar wallabies (*Macropus eugenii*) as an "extinct" taxon', *Animal Conservation*, vol. 2, pp. 41–9.

Taylor, A. C., Sunnocks, P. and Cooper, D. W. 1999, 'Retention of reproductive barriers and ecological difference between two introduced sympatic *Macropus spp.* in New Zealand', *Animal Conservation*, vol. 2, pp. 195–202.

Wondolleck, J. M. and Yaffee, S. L. 2000, *Making Collaboration Work*, Island Press, Washington, DC.

Yaffee, S. L. and Wondolleck, M. 2000, 'Making collaborations work', *Conservation Biology in Practice*, vol. 1, pp. 15–25.

# 5

# Land tenure and identity in the New Zealand high country

Carolyn Morris

## Abstract

People and places are mutually constitutive, and so the particular ways in which people attach and are attached to place have implications for both. A significant aspect of attachment is mode of tenure, with different forms of land tenure allowing for very different imaginaries and practices of self and land. As such, transformations in tenure will have significant implications for land use and subjectivity.

Until recently, farmers leased 2.37 million hectares of pastoral land in the South Island from the Crown and, since 1948, leaseholders have had the right of perpetual renewal. In the mid 1990s, the Crown (with the broad support of farmers, environmental and recreation interests) moved to reorder its relationship with farmers and a process of tenure review was initiated. As a result of tenure review, land with significant conservation and landscape values is being transferred to the Department of Conservation, in return for which farmers are gaining freehold title of lower land, land with production potential. For the people of the high country, relationships to the land are central to the formation of subjectivity, and it is the highest and most remote land, the very land that farmers stand to lose under tenure review, that has the greatest significance for identity. As one informant said, 'Tenure review means that we would become valley farmers', no longer high country farmers. With tenure review in process, the matrix that produces high country farmer identity has been disrupted. As such, it provides a moment in which the simultaneous processes of production of person and place are revealed as differently positioned actors struggle to control the future of the high country.

## Introduction

In many of the so-called developed countries, rural places and conceptions of ruralism appear to be undergoing radical transformation. Historically, in Anglo traditions, high moral value has been attributed to ruralism, and notions of the rural idyll have deep histories (Williams 1973; Schama 1995), an enduring aspect of which is the idea that rural regions are sites for the production of national goods—economic and cultural. In these traditions, ruralism and agrarianism have been often considered synonymous (suppressing the brute realities of agricultural life), but in recent decades this link has begun to be uncoupled. In many European countries, in America and in Australia, the number of people involved in farming has declined and rural production forms an ever-smaller part of national economies. The decline in the economic importance of rural areas, however, has not necessarily resulted in a concurrent diminishment of cultural significance. Instead, the notion of the rural idyll has been reconfigured, in this iteration divorced from agricultural production: rural areas are more and more becoming sites and objects of consumption (for example, Ching and Creed 1997).

The effects of these broad transformations are significant. Transformations of ruralism are simultaneously transformations of landscape, of lived lives in place, of imaginaries and of subjectivities. What we see, as the idea of ruralism is reworked, is a transformation of the place of ruralism in imaginings of place, community, the nation and the self. Though the general trajectory of change might be common across nations, as anthropological approaches to globalisation commonly demonstrate, such processes manifest differently in different places and the outcome of any trajectory of change is always contingent (for example, Inda and Rosaldo 2002). As such, to understand rural change it is necessary to explore particular types of ruralism. As Bourdieu (1998:2) writes, 'the deepest logic of the social world can be grasped only if one plunges into the particularity of an empirical reality, historically located and dated'.

New Zealand presents an unusual case of rural change. In New Zealand, as in other developed nations with strong Anglo heritages, ruralism has loomed large in the national imagination and is understood as the fount of the country's identity, the reservoir of national morality (Bell 1996). On the other hand, though allegedly a developed country, New Zealand's economy is unusual in its continued reliance on primary production: 'agricultural and forestry products earn more than half of New Zealand's export income' and 'farming and forestry employed about 8.5 percent of employed people aged over 15 years in 2001' (Statistics New Zealand 2002). Despite this, however, and in contrast with policies of subsidising agricultural production and supporting farmers regardless of their waning economic significance in other developed nations, since the mid 1980s and the implementation of wide-ranging neo-liberal reforms, the agricultural sector in New Zealand has received no government support or subsidy whatsoever (Sandrey and Reynolds 1990; Gouin et al. 1994). Notwithstanding the centrality of primary production to the economy, in New Zealand as elsewhere, we see a process whereby consumption values have come to trump production values in relation to ruralism, and the 'natural' link between agrarianism and rurality is being severed.

Just as there are significant differences between nations with regard to the place of ruralism, so there are differences within nations. Recent decades have seen profound alterations in the agricultural sector in New Zealand: 'with fewer sheep, more dairy cows, more trees, burgeoning vineyards and spreading avocado orchards and olive groves' (Statistics New Zealand 2002), New Zealand no longer lives on the sheep's back. Between 1994 and 2002, there was a 20 per cent decline in sheep numbers to 39.5 million and an increase in dairy cow numbers, from 3.9 million to 5.2 million. There were dramatic increases in grape plantings in the same period, rising from 7200 hectares in 1994 to 17 400ha in 2002 (Statistics New Zealand 2002). These changes have radically reordered life in particular localities, with profound impacts on ruralism as symbol, landscape and community, and on possible rural futures. This chapter considers one particular case of rural change in New Zealand: pastoral sheep farming in the South Island high country. Because of the symbolic stature of the high country, this case also speaks to the place of ruralism in New Zealand's imagining of itself as a nation. As such, I simultaneously address rural futures and the future of ruralism.

Cohen (1985) argues that when communities perceive themselves to be under threat, they mobilise to assert their distinction from others, drawing from a collective repertoire of discourses and symbols to articulate who they are in order to achieve certain ends. The situation I will describe is just such a case. It is very much in flux, with outcomes uncertain. As such, this analysis attempts to capture a particular moment in what is a continuing process. In such instances of disruption to the previously taken for granted order of things, the effects and processes of rural change become visible, as social actors struggle to secure their land, their communities and their selves.

## Place and subjectivity

The link between place and subjectivity has been established theoretically and empirically by a number of authors (for example, Altman and Low 1992; Hirsch and O'Hanlon 1995; Feld and Basso 1996; Low and Lawrence-Zúñiga 2003), and in relation to farming has been explored in most detail by Gray (2000, 2003) in Scotland and Dominy (1992, 1993, 2001) in the New Zealand high country. The ethnographies of Dominy and Gray focus on the ways in which farmers come to selfhood through an experiential and embodied knowledge of the land they farm. There has, however, been less attention paid to other aspects of the formation of farmer subjectivity. Things such as policy and regulation, legal structures and politics tend to be constituted as context, as shaping what farmers might do, but essentially as external to their selves. In this chapter, I focus on land tenure. Rather than thinking of tenure as an element of context, however, I will argue that tenure is in fact one of the building blocks of farmer subjectivity. As McNay (2000:76) writes, 'individuals do not passively absorb external determinations, but are actively engaged in the interpretation of experience, and therefore, in a process of self-formation'. Different forms of tenure attach people to land in different ways, providing different understandings of the relationship between land and people and producing different forms of being in those worlds. As such, changes in mode of tenure will necessarily result in alterations in identity. I explore the ways in which the legal matrix of land tenure is productive of high country farmer identity. Currently, land tenure in the high country is changing from leasehold to freehold. With tenure review, a previous identity, grounded in place and legitimated through a particular relationship with the Crown, is under threat (or is at least being destabilised), as one of the key modes through which that identity has been authenticated is being removed. Changing land tenure, in reordering the connection between farmers and the State, is producing a new form of farmer subjectivity, and an oppositional subjectivity. Farmers are reimagining themselves in relation to the State and to the nation. In turn, this change in tenure is part of a transformation of the place of high country farmers in the polity and the nation.

## High country pastoral farming

The high country is land above 600 metres in altitude that runs the length of the South Island. High country farming is characterised by the extensive grazing of merino sheep on large properties, ranging from approximately 2500ha to 180 000ha, with wool as the major commodity. The high country is a vast area: 6 million of the 27 million hectares of New Zealand's land mass is high country land. About 2.5 million hectares is farmed; the rest is part of the conservation estate (<http://www.highcountryaccord.co.nz/>). Pastoral land, then, constitutes almost 10 per cent of the land of New Zealand. Very little of this land is held under freehold title. Until the late 1990s, 2.37 million hectares were held in Crown ownership, let to 304 farmers as Crown Pastoral Lease. The *Land Act 1948* created leases that were perpetually renewable for a term of 33 years, though there was no right to freehold. Rents were set at between 1.5 and 2 per cent of land value exclusive of improvements. The lessee had many of the same rights as freeholders: trespass rights, rights of exclusive occupation and the ownership of improvements. These leases were, however, pastoral leases only, meaning that leaseholders had only the right to graze the land and had to apply to the Crown agency responsible if they wished to undertake any other activities. This provision of the act thus ensured that the extensive grazing of sheep and cattle remained the dominant land use in the high country. The security of tenure granted by the 1948 act promoted the investment of money, time and self in high country properties and a strong sense of belonging to the high country developed in run-holders. From the perspective of high country farmers themselves, and for writers such as Dominy (2001), a unique high country 'culture' emerged, based on the practices of farming that land. As one high country farmwoman put it: 'We're only second generation, but we still have a firm cultural attachment to the land. We have cultural, spiritual and historical connections' (Karen Simpson, *The Christchurch Press*, 22 November 2003).

The 1948 act made possible a particular mode of attachment to the high country. As the land remained in Crown ownership, a relationship of stewardship was available—the idea of the leaseholder as guardian and caretaker of the land. As one farmer said: 'We're custodians. Nobody ever owns it, we're just passing through and trying to enhance it for the next generation' (Andrew Simpson, *The Christchurch Press*, 22 November 2003). This imagining of the relationship between farmer and land differs from that of other farmers, because the land is leased. And it was, in part, through the 1948 act that the potential for stewardship subjectivity, rather than ownership subjectivity, was generated.

Expressions of belonging and attachment to place are mobilised by particular groups at particular times for particular reasons. At the Ngai Tahu Claim hearings before the Waitangi Tribunal in the late 1980s,[1] anthropologist Michele Dominy (1990:13–14), presenting evidence of run-holder attachment to place, stated: 'Material affinity is expressed in the value runholders place on their sense of ownership in the land they farm and inhabit. It is also expressed in the value placed on long term security of tenure.' In this context, when control of the leases was at stake, a discourse of ownership rather than stewardship was deployed. Current assertions of attachment must, then, be viewed in the same light: as strategic deployments by interested actors.

## The tenure review process

In the mid 1990s, the Crown instituted a process of tenure review, considering that the system of pastoral leases had outlasted its usefulness as a means of protecting land and promoting agricultural development (Clayton 1982:65). Tenure review aimed to 'achieve...productive economic land-use and conservation outcomes in the South Island high country' (<http://www.linz.govt.nz/home/index.html>). Tenure review was widely supported by farmers, recreation and environmental groups (Brower 2006:27). Farmers and environmentalists had different reasons for wanting tenure review, but there was general agreement that it was required:

> High country lessees wanted to have the management and investment flexibility that comes from freehold title. The Crown wanted to get out of the uneconomic business of being a landlord. And the Environmental pressure groups, along with the Crown, wanted land with significant inherent values (SIVs) to go into the conservation estate. (<http://www.highcountryaccord.co.nz/>)

Under the terms of the 1998 *Crown Pastoral Lands Act*, leaseholders have the opportunity to convert to freehold part of their land—that considered to have economic values—in return for which land with significant historic, scientific, ecological or cultural characteristics is restored to full Crown ownership, and, in reality, to Department of Conservation (DoC) management (<http://www.linz.govt.nz/home/index.html>).

Tenure review is initiated by individual leaseholders and, through consultation with the Department of Conservation, Fish and Game,[2] *iwi* [3] and the general public, individual properties are divided into freehold and conservation land. Tenure review is a voluntary process and leaseholders or the Crown can withdraw at any time (<http://www.linz.govt.nz/home/index.html>). The results of tenure review will vary by property. In some cases, all of the land of a particular lease might go to conservation and, in others, all of the land might be converted to freehold (<http://www.linz.govt.nz/home/index.html>). As of August 2007, 47 lessees had settled with the Crown, with another 13 in the final stages, and 115 properties had not entered the process (<http://www.linz.govt.nz/home/index.html>). To date, about 162 000ha of land have been converted to freehold and about 117 500ha have been added to the conservation estate, with an additional 45 500ha being bought outright from lessees (<http://www.highcountryaccord.co.nz/>). Officials estimate that, by the end of the tenure review program, 50 per cent of pastoral lease land will become freehold and 50 per cent will become conservation land (<http://www.linz.govt.nz/home/index.html>). To date, the split has been closer to 60/40 in favour of farmers (Brower 2006:3).

At present, tenure review seems to be stalling. Farming, conservation and recreation groups have begun to voice serious doubts about the outcomes of tenure review and are lobbying hard to change the outcome. Tenure review has become contentious because what is at stake is not just ownership of land, or even conservation, but control over the way in which the high country and New Zealand as a nation is imagined. Two web sites, produced by farmer lobby group High Country Accord (<http://www.highcountryaccord.co.nz/>) and conservation/recreation lobby group Stop Tenure Review (<http://www.stoptenurereview.co.nz/>), give insight into how the different groups understand the issues and the discourses they deploy to make their respective cases.

## The high country and New Zealand identity

Ruralities and nature are central elements in New Zealand's imagining of itself as a nation (for example, Bell 1996; Sturm 1998; King 1999; Dominy 2001:68; Jutel 2004) and in the construction of the New Zealand national subject. Despite a very high degree of urbanisation (85.7 per cent of the population was classified as urban, according to the 2002 census),[4] a '[n]ational identity based on physical geography, and on idealisation of lifestyles within nature, is persistently used as our claim to fame' (Bell 1996:34). According to Jutel (2004:54–5), three landscapes have particular significance: 'dramatic volcanic topography, the pastoral farmland, and the exotic "otherness" of the native bush are located at the centre of New Zealand national identity constructs'. These landscapes are iconic and stand for the nation. Such imaginings are widely disseminated and have continuing salience. For example, White (2006), writing in *North and South*, a monthly magazine for, in the words of the magazine's web site, 'thinking New Zealand', wrote of the high country:

> The empty inner expanse has been the backdrop of pioneer legend and in inspiration to everyone from Samuel Butler, to Brian Turner, Grahame Sydney to Speight's marketers. Autumn musters; the desiccated Otago tors; the Mackenzie Country's tawny tussock carpet; the remote corrugated iron huts with names of sheltering shepherds scratched in their rafters; the 'red-gold cirrus/Over snow mountain shine' of James K. Baxter are part of a cultural heritage we all share and celebrate, no matter how deep in suburbia we dwell. (White 2006:42)

Not only does the land of the high country carry immense symbolic weight, so does (or perhaps so has) the high country farmer, because of his intimate connection with the high country landscape. In the popular (and farmer) imagination, this iconic land has forged an iconic subject, a subject who embodies all that is best in the national character. The high country farmer subject position is constituted through discourses of pioneering. As McAloon (2002:109) noted, the pioneer subject position was established from the early days of the colony: as early as 1890, 'the pioneer myth...was becoming increasingly evident in the account rich settlers gave of themselves'. High country farmers continue to constitute themselves through this discourse: 'in many respects the "high country farmer" is an image of yesteryear, a portrayal of the early settler battling against the elements to earn a living' (Cushen 1997:78). Pioneering people are hardworking, thrifty, resilient, flexible, independent and self-reliant; they are possessed of what Wevers (1980:244) calls the stoic virtues. These are the characteristics of the New Zealand national subject, embodied in national heroes such as the late Sir Edmund Hillary (conqueror of Mount Everest), Charles Upham and Bill Apiata (winners of the Victoria Cross) and countless All Blacks captains. Likewise, they are possessed by the high country farmer. Moreover, high country farmers have played a significant role in building the nation's wealth (Gardner 1981; Bremer and Brooking 1993).

It is because of the place of the pioneering high country farmer in the foundation myths of the nation, the iconic stature of the land they farm and their economic contribution that high country farmers have become established as central to New Zealand's national identity and as guardians of the nation's physical and cultural heritage. Farmers considered that their interests paralleled the nation's interests because of the natural moral superiority of ruralism and because they produced the wealth of the nation: '[m]ost other groups seemed parasitic in comparison with family farmers who constituted the "backbone of the economy"' (Bremer and Brooking 1993:108). This status translated into a dominant cultural and political position in the affairs of the State, with successive governments supporting agriculture: '[t]he history of New Zealand farming is in a real sense the history of New Zealand. Until the Second World War all life here was powerfully conditioned by what happened in the country' (McLauchlan 1981:11). Also, until the 1980s, '[s]tate economic policies exhibited a clear bias in favour of the farming community' (Bremer and Brooking 1993:108). Considerable rewards accrued to farmers as a result. Brooking argues that 'the image fostered of the pastoralist as a "natural" part of a romantic high country, as the guardian of a way of life, has helped legitimise their claim to control huge tracts of land leased from the state at peppercorn rentals' (Brooking in Cushen 1997:74–5).

The place of high country farming and farmers in the national imaginary, however, is being transformed. What I suggest is happening through tenure review is that farmers are being dislodged from their position of national subject and are being replaced by the environmentalist (understood as urban greenie), and an unspoiled nature is replacing a productive ruralism as the morally correct relationship to the high country.

## High country farmer identity

High country farmer subjectivity is, as all research and all of the writings by high country farmers themselves indicate, inextricably bound up with the land. Dominy's work demonstrates in most detail the 'mutuality of spatiality and cultural identity' in the high country, how land is a site of 'intense cultural activity and imagination—of memory, of affectivity, of work, of sociality, of identity' (Dominy 2001:3). Not all of the land, however, on a high country station carries the same symbolic weight. It is the land that is the highest, the most remote—the tops, the back country—that bears the greatest symbolic load. It is the possession of *this* land that forms the foundation of high country farmer subjectivity, and farmers are aware that its loss will necessarily transform identity.

In interviews conducted in 2003 about the impact of tenure review (Akers 2004; Morris and Akers 2004), interviewees expressed concern about what tenure review would mean for the future of the high country. High country people articulated a deep sense of attachment to high country farming as a way of life, as in the words of one young woman: '[I]t's just everything to me. It's just absolutely everything, it's my whole life. It's more important than boys, school [university] and everything' (see also Dominy 2001; Morris 2002). Whether they had entered the process or not, and whether they considered that they would personally do well out of tenure review, farmers expressed deep concern about the impact of changing land tenure on being in the high country. They were concerned that there was a desire for the removal of farmers from the high country altogether: 'We're the thorn in their side, the greenies. They want home [the station]...they would love to get their hands on everything' (Morris and Akers 2004). This, farmers say, would result in the destruction of the high country, physically and culturally:

> In the worst case scenario the high country will still be there but the high country will transform because the vegetation type, the land use type, it'll revert back to where it came from. The local, indigenous[5] people will disappear because it will become uneconomic to live in these environments, so they'll disappear. (Morris and Akers 2004)

Though it is unlikely that farming will disappear entirely from the high country, with the transfer of the highest country from farmer to DoC control, *high country* farming could do so. True high country farming requires particular kinds of country (extensive, rugged, isolated, high-altitude tussocks with snow risk; Dominy 2001:42), and the loss of such land will mean that particular properties might no longer qualify. In response to a question about what tenure review would mean for their property, one farmer responded:

> Yeah, it's still high country, it's still a high country place. A lot of places aren't probably. We still will be 'cause we'll still have some high bits of land, real tussock, you know, real rugged stuff. But a lot of places won't be, I suppose, when they [DoC] cut what they want out. (Morris and Akers 2004)

This farmer will remain a high country farmer because he will retain real high country land, but is not likely to be the case for everybody. For those who lose the highest country, the high country farmer subject position will no longer be available. In the words of one woman: 'We are an endangered species.' High country farmers will become instead 'valley farmers', sheep farmers like any others, no longer unique.

Significantly, it is the possession of the very same land that is the goal of environmental and recreation groups. The high country is central to *their* identity projects as well, projects they increasingly successfully constitute as New Zealand's project, just as farmers, until recently, have been able to do.

## Recreation and environmental interests in the high country

People who do not live in the high country consider that they have rights in relation to it because of its iconic nature and because it remains in Crown, and therefore in some sense public, ownership. Farmers are not the only group interested in the outcome of tenure review. As the process evolved and a number of reviews were completed, environmental and recreation interests became increasingly vocal in their criticism, resulting in the formation of a lobby group called Stop Tenure Review.

From the perspective of this group, and others such as Forest and Bird, tenure review will result in the privatisation of the high country, with negative implications for conservation, recreation and landscape. They argue that too much land is being converted to freehold, land with significant natural and recreation values that should be included in the conservation estate, and that farmers are benefiting from tenure review at the expense of the New Zealand public. Eugenie Sage of Forest and Bird, for example, says the high country is being given away in 'the biggest wave of privatisation…since Roger Douglas'. She says she fears that iconic landscapes will pass into private hands to become 'McMansion subdivision sprawls' (<http://www.highcountryaccord.co.nz/>). These groups note that under tenure review farmers give up their least productive land and in return receive land of much greater value, and in some cases cash settlements as well: 'So far high country farmers have received agricultural and real estate development rights worth tens of millions of dollars from the Crown AND an average of $186,000 extra compensation per deal' (<http://www.stoptenurereview.co.nz/>). Like the farmers, Stop Tenure Review argues that what is being lost is not just land, but 'identity':

> Ever since European settlement, 150 years ago, the South Island high country has been owned by the Crown. But we are not concerned just about land ownership. It's also about protecting a spiritual landscape and an environment that is an indelible part of our collective heritage. It's more than just our land, it's part of who we are as New Zealanders. So while the government is handing over Crown land and taxpayers' money to a small group of high country farmers, it is also alienating our identity. (<http://www.stoptenurereview.co.nz/>)

These groups draw attention in particular to the privatisation of lakefront land: under the Mt Burke review, 35km of Wanaka shore was converted to freehold and 9km of Lake Tekapo frontage was converted to freehold under the Richmond review (<http://www.stoptenurereview.co.nz/>). The group cited cases in which land converted to freehold under tenure review was subsequently subdivided and sold by farmers for massive profits. For example, the Closeburn lessee paid $158 000 for 930ha of land on the shores of Lake Wakatipu, close to the tourist hub of Queenstown; in 2006, a 1.2ha section of Closeburn Station land was on the market for $3.9 million (White 2006:46–7). In 2006, Fulbright Scholar Anne Brower published the results of her research into tenure review in a report called *Interest Groups, Vested Interests, and the Myth of Apolitical Administration: The politics of land tenure reform on the South Island of New Zealand*. In this report, Brower argues that the Crown is being exploited by farmers who are making massive financial gains at the expense of the Crown and the New Zealand public.

This report, and the furious response from farmers, brought tenure review to the public's attention. In November 2006, the magazine *North and South* published an article titled 'High country hijack'. This article leads with the Brower and environmentalist perspective and suggests a conspiracy:

> It's a process whereby 10 percent of New Zealand's most remote but most beautiful country, owned by the Crown, is being divided up, with much of it effectively given away to farmers, who until now have only leased this land. It's called tenure review and it's been going on for 15 years but it's only now people seem to be understanding what's really happening, how many iconic landscapes are under threat—and what's already been lost. Warning. This is a complex story. It's been made complex—or nobody involved with it has tried to make it simple—perhaps so that people like you won't become interested in it, let alone get involved. (White 2006:42)

## Farmers' perspectives

It is not only environmental groups who are unhappy with the outcomes of tenure review; so, increasingly, are farmers. In 2003, a high country lobby group called the High Country Accord was established, aiming 'to seek a change in government policy relating to the Land Tenure Reform Process' (<http://www.highcountryaccord.co.nz/>).

In opposition to Stop Tenure Review, the High Country Accord denies claims that farmers are the beneficiaries of tenure review:

> Forest and Bird has been creating a perception that the public is somehow being ripped off. There is a clear implication that individual farming families are somehow guilty parties. It has all become very unfair and unpleasant...By ignoring [the] facts and playing to an old prejudice that high country farmers are unfairly privileged people, Forest and Bird have finally managed to attract the urban media to take an interest in what has been happening in the high country.
> (<http://www.highcountryaccord.co.nz/>)

Rather, they argue, it is farmers who are doing badly. From the perspective of the High Country Accord, tenure review is unsatisfactory because too much land will be lost from production. Farmers argue that much of the land that is earmarked for conservation is necessary for the viability of stations and high country community life:

> Most of this land is suitable for long-term sustainable economic use. But it is going to be locked away in [the] conservation estate forever. As high country farmers we are particularly concerned, because we will lose most of the tussock rangeland which we need for summer grazing. Without access to this land, most high country farms will not be viable...The creation of government-owned parks and reserves should

> not be at the expense of the families who farm this land sustainably. (<http://www.highcountryaccord.co.nz/>)

Indeed, the impact on the merino industry is likely to be significant. A report by Lincoln agricultural economist Glenn Greer estimates that tenure review will result in the 'loss of 663,000 stock units from the high country—a 31% reduction on current numbers. The estimated loss of gross economic output at the farm gate per year will be $33 million' (<http://www.highcountryaccord.co.nz/>). The accord estimates that one in five properties will become economically unviable, with the loss of 70 to 80 families from high country farming (<http://www.highcountryaccord.co.nz/>). The accord argues that this will destroy farming as a way of life and, in doing so, will destroy New Zealand's heritage:

> In seeking to nationalise 60 per cent or more of pastoral lease land, the Crown has failed to recognise the value to the nation of the productive effort and commitment to these lands by existing farming families for over 150 years...we are a self-reliant community in which concern for the safety of neighbours and visitors is part of the culture...We live in this landscape 24 hours, 7 days a week and we understand the risks and how to manage them. It's a very different culture from that which the government would have us replaced with—that of the transitory visitor, supported by a seasonal and possibly itinerant workforce. As high country farmers we are managers of the landscape and part of it. We are part of a living heritage which most New Zealanders and tourists value. (<http://www.highcountryaccord.co.nz/>)

Although, as in this statement, farmers position themselves as the rightful guardians of the high country, a delicate discursive strategy is needed here, because it is the deployment of the discourse of guardianship rather than ownership that is one of the things that has allowed other New Zealanders to mount compelling claims to participate in decision making about the future of the high country. As a result, the High Country Accord has begun to argue that leasehold tenure almost amounts to freehold:

> [L]eases give farmers exclusive occupancy rights to their property, as well as a perpetual right of renewal. In these respects, the leases have a status which is very similar to freehold title...The lessee's financial interest in a typical High Country farm is 85 per cent of the capital value. The Crown's interest is the remaining 15 per cent...we are not talking about rental agreements for state houses.
> (<http://www.highcountryaccord.co.nz/>)

The High Country Accord argues that farming and conservation are not incompatible. Indeed, they suggest, farmers are better able than the State to be environmental managers:

> [M]ost of the land being targeted by the Crown could be protected while still remaining in private hands. There is no evidence to show that the Crown is a better land manager than farmers. In fact, there are many examples of land in Crown ownership which is poorly managed. Scientific research shows that most tussock rangeland is being sustainably managed by farmers. The fact that the land still has conservation values after 150 years of grazing is a testimony to their stewardship. (<http://www.highcountryaccord.co.nz/>)

In arguing their case, the accord positions farmers in opposition to the State but as having parallel interests with the New Zealand public (that is, the nation): 'Accord members are privileged to farm some of New Zealand's most magnificent landscapes. We accept that our fellow New Zealanders want the right to enjoy these landscapes too' (<http://www.highcountryaccord.co.nz/>). What they object to is the extent of the proposed conservation estate, which they constitute as the aim of the government, not, by implication, the aim of the public:

> Our objection is to the scale of the government's plans. Basically, we think the government is going overboard. Instead of establishing a handful of parks in key areas, it plans to set up 22. About 1.3 million hectares will be involved. That's a huge area—it's more than Fiordland National Park. (<http://www.highcountryaccord.co.nz/>)

Again, they position themselves and their interests with the public and against the government:

> Ultimately New Zealanders need to ask whether they want more than half the land area of the South Island locked into Crown ownership and management indefinitely. The techniques used by the government to acquire this land amount to an abuse of property rights. Every New Zealander who owns land, shares or other investments should be concerned that such a precedent is being set. (<http://www.highcountryaccord.co.nz/>)

The accord suspects that the ultimate aim of the Crown is to remove farmers from the land in the name of the retention of a 'natural' landscape, which farmers assert is in fact produced (and sustained) through their farming practices.

## Farmers, the State and subjectivity

Two kinds of transformations in farmer subjectivity are being produced through tenure review. First, a steward subjectivity—in which the interests of the State and farmers coincide, and through which farmers are positioned as guardians of the nation—is no longer easily sustainable. Farmers attempt to deploy this discourse at times, but it has lost the power it once had. Second, as farmers find themselves in opposition to the policies of the State, a resistant subjectivity is produced. This represents a radical change from times when farmers were considered to be the economic and symbolic backbone of the nation. Farmers and farming are no longer understood in this way. Increasingly, they are regarded as an ecological threat to the nation (their gas-emitting cows are contributing to global warming, fertiliser run-off is polluting rivers and lakes and so on) or as simply businessmen, motivated purely by profits, with discourses about farming as a morally superior way of life increasingly ringing untrue.

The unravelling of the close relationship between farmers, the State and the nation has its roots in the 1980s and the neo-liberal policies of the fourth Labour Government. In the 1980s, in a very short time, all supports for farming were removed and the sector was deregulated, exposing New Zealand agriculture to the full brunt of market forces (Sandrey and Reynolds 1990; Johnsen 2003). This resulted in profound crisis for farmers—economic and symbolic. If the historical extent of government support for agriculture signalled farmer's iconic status, the removal of that support signalled its loss. Farmer power was further undermined with the 1996 electoral system change to MMP, a system of proportional representation. Under the new system, smaller parties have a greater voice, and one of the new parties in Parliament is the Green Party. Greenies are the traditional enemy of farmers, representing interference from outside and the imposition of alien values. Farmers are concerned that the power of such interests (constituted as urban) will increase (Cushen 1997:5). And, it seems, their worries have some foundation. In June 2007, David Parker, the minister responsible for tenure review, announced the withdrawal of the Crown from some 40 tenure reviews to, in his words, 'protect important high country landscapes and diversity values' ('High country tenure review decision welcomed', *Scoop Independent News*, 22 June 2007). These properties are those with lakeside frontages—precisely the kind of land that farmers have the most to gain from converting to freehold. This effectively means that this land will remain in Crown ownership, though whether it will continue to be farmed or become conservation estate is not clear. Stop Tenure Review welcomed the decision, farmers deplored it: '[o]ptions for High Country farmers are becoming increasingly limited by a government which seems determined to force them from their leasehold land', said Donald Aubrey, chair of the High Country group of Federated Farmers ('Another blow for the high country', *Scoop Independent News*, June 2007).

Though high country farmers continue to assert that their interests are the nation's interests, this claim is no longer persuasive. No longer guardians of the nation's heritage, high country farmers are being dislodged from their position as national subject and keeper of a national morality; they are being replaced by the urban environmentalist.

## Conclusion

Tenure review, it seems clear, will lead to fundamental changes in the high country, in terms of land use, landscape and social system. Some possible futures are indicated in areas where reviews have been completed. Central Otago, for instance, is now known for pinot, not merino, and for adventure tourism, and sheep farming and farmers no longer dominate. This is a new high country, increasingly a site, and object, of consumption. Tenure review is also fundamentally challenging farmer subjectivity. Some have embraced the change, constituting themselves as businessmen, while others hold on to the ideal of stewardship. The sense of loss and anger among farmers evoked by the loss of the high country, the loss of their place as guardians of the nation and their inability to control the outcomes of tenure review can be understood as a version of what Hage (1998:218ff.) calls the 'discourse of Anglo decline'. As Park et al. (2002:527) write of farmers in Northland, '[p]akeha [European] pastoral farmers, key protagonists in a white managerial fantasy, are experiencing themselves as no longer in control of, or as central to, national life as they were'.

These rural transformations also signify a shift in the place of ruralism in the imagining of New Zealand. The land of the high country remains an important feature of the national imaginary, but it is now imagined as a landscape to be viewed or a space of leisure; pastoral farming and pastoral farmers are no longer automatically synonymous with the high country.

## Bibliography

Akers, A. 2004, 'Valley farmers': place attachment and challenges to high country identity from the tenure review process, Unpublished dissertation, Anthropology Program, University of Canterbury, Christchurch.

Altman, I. and Low, S. M. (eds) 1992, *Place Attachment*, Plenum Press, New York.

Bell, C. 1996, *Inventing New Zealand: Everyday myths of pakeha identity*, Penguin Books, Auckland.

Bourdieu, P. 1998, *Practical Reason: On the theory of action*, Stanford University Press, Stanford.

Bremer, R. and Brooking, T. 1993, 'Federated Farmers and the State', in B. Roper and C. Rudd (eds), *State and Economy in New Zealand*, Oxford University Press, Auckland.

Brower, A. L. 2006, *Interest Groups, Vested Interests and the Myth of Apolitical Administration: The politics of land tenure reform on the South Island of New Zealand*, Fulbright New Zealand.

Ching, B. and Creed, G. W. (eds) 1997, *Knowing Your Place: Rural identity and cultural hierarchy*, Routledge, New York.

Clayton, W. G. 1982, *Crown Pastoral Leases and Leases in Perpetuity: Report of the committee of inquiry*, Government Printer, Wellington.

Cohen, A. P. 1985, *The Symbolic Construction of Community*, E. Horwood, Tavistock Publications, Chichester, London and New York.

Cushen, J. 1997, Images of the interior: landscape perceptions of the South Island high country, Master of Arts thesis, University of Otago, Dunedin, New Zealand.

Dominy, M. 1992, 'Knowing this place I learn to know myself': toponymy and topographic representation on New Zealand sheep stations, Paper presented to the 91st annual meeting of the American Anthropological Association, San Francisco.

Dominy, M. 1993, '"Lives were always, here": the inhabited landscape of the New Zealand high country', *Anthropological Forum*, vol. 6, pp. 567–86.

Dominy, M. 2001, *Calling the Station Home: Place and identity in New Zealand's high country*, Rowman and Littlefield Publishers, Lanham.

Feld, S. and Basso, K. (eds) 1996, *Senses of Place*, School of American Research Press, Santa Fe, NM, distributed by University of Washington Press, Seattle.

Gardner, W. J. 1981, 'A colonial economy', in W. H. Oliver and B. R. Williams (eds), *The Oxford History of New Zealand*, Oxford University Press, Wellington.

Gouin, D.-M., Jean, N. et al. 1994, *New Zealand Agricultural Policy Reform and Impacts on the Farm Sector*, Agribusiness and Economics Research Unit, Lincoln University, Lincoln.

Gray, J. 2000, *At Home in the Hills: Sense of place in the Scottish Borders*, Berghahn Books, New York.

Gray, J. 2003, 'Open spaces and dwelling places: being at home on hill farms in the Scottish Borders', in S. Low and D. Lawrence-Zúñiga (eds), *The Anthropology of Space and Place: Locating culture*, Blackwell, Malden, Mass.

Hage, G. 1998, *White Nation: Fantasies of white supremacy in a multicultural society*, Pluto Press, Sydney, and Comerford and Miller, West Wickham.

Hirsch, E. and O'Hanlon, M. (eds) 1995, *The Anthropology of Landscape: Perspectives on place and space*, Clarendon Press, Oxford.

Inda, J. X. and Rosaldo, R. 2002, *The Anthropology of Globalization: A reader*, Blackwell Publishing, Malden, Mass.

Johnsen, S. 2003, 'Contingency revealed: New Zealand farmers' experiences of agricultural restructuring', *Sociologia Ruralis*, vol. 43, no. 2, pp. 128–53.

Jutel, T. 2004, '"Lord of the rings": landscape, transformation and the geography of the virtual', in C. Bell and S. Matthewson (eds), *Cultural Studies in Aotearoa/New Zealand: Identity, space and place*, Oxford University Press, Melbourne.

King, M. 1999, *Being Pakeha Now: Reflections and recollections of a white native*, Penguin, Auckland.

Low, S. 1992, 'Symbolic ties that bind: place attachment in the plaza', in I. Altman and S. M. Low (eds), *Place Attachment*, Plenum Press, New York and London.

Low, S. M. and Lawrence-Zúñiga, D. (eds) 2003, *The Anthropology of Space and Place: Locating culture*, Blackwell, Malden, Mass.

McAloon, J. 2002, *No Idle Rich: The wealthy in Canterbury and Otago 1840–1914*, University of Otago Press, Dunedin.

McLauchlan, G. 1981, *The Farming of New Zealand*, Australia and New Zealand Book Company, Auckland and Sydney.

McNay, L. 2000, *Gender and Agency: Reconfiguring the subject in feminist and social theory*, Polity Press, Cambridge.

Morris, C. 2002, 'Station wives in New Zealand: narrating continuity in the high country', *Anthropology*, University of Auckland, Auckland.

Morris, C. and Akers, A. 2004, 'Valley farmers': land tenure review and subjectivity in the New Zealand high country, Paper presented at the ASAANZ Conference, Auckland.

Park, J., Scott, K., Cocklin, C. and Davis, P. 2002, 'The moral life of trees: pastoral farming and production forestry in northern New Zealand', *Journal of Anthropological Research*, vol. 58, pp. 521–44.

Sandrey, R. and Reynolds, R. (eds) 1990, *Farming Without Subsidies: New Zealand's recent experience*, MAF & GP Books, Wellington.

Schama, S. 1995, *Landscape and Memory*, A. A. Knopf, New York, distributed by Random House.

Statistics New Zealand 2002, *Agriculture Statistics 2002*, viewed 7 August 2007, <http://www.stats.govt.nz/analytical-reports/agriculture-statistics-2002/the-agricultural-industry.htm>

Statistics New Zealand 2008, *Defining Urban and Rural New Zealand*, <http://www.stats.govt.nz/urban-rural-profiles/defining-urban-rural-nz/default.htm>

Sturm, T. (ed.) 1998, *The Oxford History of New Zealand Literature*, Oxford University Press, Oxford.

Wevers, L. 1980, 'Pioneer into feminist: Jane Mander's heroines', in P. Bunkle and B. Hughes (eds), *Women in New Zealand Society*, George Allen and Unwin, Auckland.

White, M. 2006, 'High country hijack', *North and South*, November 2006, Auckland.

Williams, R. 1973, *The Country and the City*, Chatto and Windus, London.

## Endnotes

[1] The Waitangi Tribunal was established under the *Treaty of Waitangi Act 1975* as a forum for hearing Maori grievances in relation to violations of the Treaty of Waitangi. In 1986, Ngai Tahu, the dominant South Island tribe, lodged a claim. As partial remedy, they sought ownership of high country pastoral leases. High country farmers, arguing that pastoral leases should not constitute part of any remedy, asked anthropologist Michele Dominy, who was working in the area at the time, to make a submission on their behalf to the tribunal about their economic, cultural, spiritual and historical links to the land. In their submissions, they drew parallels between their attachment and Maori attachment to land: 'Kevin O'Connor, Professor of Range Management at Lincoln College, has called this affinity [with the land] "landship" and compares it with *turangawaewae*, in Maoridom' (Dominy 1990:14). They also asserted that they were the indigenous people of the high country: 'A committee member in writing to me said that in their evidence high country people would stress the historical importance of the land to them and "how we feel as though we are the indigenous people of the high country"' (Dominy 1990:14). Indigenous status and a strong spiritual attachment are central to Maori claims of attachment to place and to their claims before the Waitangi Tribunal. In this context, farmers drew on parallel discourses to assert their own claims.

[2] Fish and Game represents hunting and fishing interests and has 'a statutory mandate to manage New Zealand's fresh water sportsfish fisheries and gamebird hunting' (<http://www.fishandgame.org.nz>).

[3] *Iwi* are Maori tribes.

[4] Settlements with a population of 1000 people or more are classified as urban for census purposes (Statistics New Zealand 2008).

[5] Note that the indigenous people referred to here are high country farmers, not Maori.

# 6

# Moving to the country for a graduated retirement: constructing new meaningful lives

**Lesley Hunt**

## Abstract

It is assumed that anything to do with 'the rural' is in decline but no account has been made of the flow of 'older' people into the countryside—those people who after successful careers elsewhere are moving to rural locations to set up new, supposedly less stressful working lives. In this chapter, I explore the way in which some couples in New Zealand are creating new and meaningful lives by growing kiwifruit, an activity that fits well with those who seek an active and graduated retirement.

These people saw orchards as actors capable of a moral exchange: 'if we make an orchard like this then it will reward us by giving us indications of our care'. Two different orchards were constructed. One was an orchard that was so wild that it needed to be made tidy and productive and the other was an orchard that was so needy it required nurturing. Are these 'new' orchardists really creating new lives or are they creating orchards that represent their old identities but in a different medium? What are the implications of their practices for the resilience of the environment, the countryside and the kiwifruit industry?

## Introduction

We see a lot on television and in books (for example, Mayle 1992) about baby boomers starting a new life in the country, people, who, after stressful but successful professional careers in the city, are able to use their accumulated wealth to buy land. There they are, talking or writing enthusiastically about producing their own wine, olives, avocados or whatever, and about the merits of getting out of the rat race to live the idyllic life that the country provides. As one of the women in the research reported on here said: 'Other trees around—yeah, we've got persimmons, avocados, tamarillos, fejoas, guavas—bits and pieces. I like trees. I like space. I like the space. I love this. I've always wanted more than a quarter acre, so now I've got it' (Woman, organic).[1]

In New Zealand, it is not only wealthy people who have lived in the cities who are moving to more intensive, smaller landholdings. Some dairy farmers are doing it too as they escape from the early morning milking routine and being tied to the farm seven days of the week for much of the year. One of the popular options for ageing New Zealanders is to become a kiwifruit orchardist. In practice, the people I interviewed who had moved into kiwifruit after a career elsewhere were rather more 'ordinary' than those seen on TV and in books! Taking on a kiwifruit orchard could be as much of a risk as they are prepared to take, as earning a living is still important to them. They might not have amassed a lot of capital and might require a mortgage to start their new manner of living.

Growing kiwifruit is a way of life very suited to people who wish to move towards retirement in a graduated way:

> [T]he vision for me, for my future? Spending the rest of my days here. I'm now sixty-two but I would see us staying in this home. We have no plan to move or downsize to a retirement village...and the beauty of orcharding is that you can do as much or as little as you choose...[With] us getting older, we are stepping back—like I've got contractors...[to] come in this winter and do two blocks of pruning for us. [My wife] won't be pruning anymore. She'll just do some of the tying down which is a lighter job and I'll continue to do the pruning while I can and then I would say a few years down the line, the contractors'll be doing more than what I'm doing, and if I'm not able to do too much at all I may just sit on the tractor and mow the orchard, and I might lease the orchard out to one of the packhouse facilities to run the orchard. So my business can continue to operate, I can oversee it. Probably I wouldn't be too popular with the lessees but—keep an eye on things and just step back. So it's a lifestyle that we're deliberately aiming for—yes. And being relatively mortgage free these days we can take that luxury I suppose and if there's [sic] downturns in the industry, we're not too exposed. (Man, organic)

As the orchardist above has described, the kiwifruit industry is well structured to support a lifestyle that involves as much work as a person is prepared to do, with it being possible to do the rest on contract, by leasing the orchard or handing its management over to someone else. This distinguishes these people from 'lifestylers' who wish to move to the country for its lifestyle while commuting to the city to earn their 'real' incomes. Kiwifruit grow well in locations that are very desirable places to live. They thrive in a temperate climate with cool winters and warm summers. In New Zealand, this means that the main growing areas are in the lush and beautiful Bay of Plenty, situated on the east coast of the North Island, close to stunning beaches. This contrasts with the iconic landscape of high country farming in Chapter 5 of this volume. The identities of those who grow kiwifruit, a symbolic New Zealand product, are associated with their landscapes in quite different ways from those of farmers as described by Carolyn Morris. Kiwifruit orchardists are able to create their landscapes whereas high country farmer identity is attached to the more 'natural' landscape of mountains.

Macnaghten and Urry (1998:4) have observed that 'the "social" dimensions of nature have been significantly under-examined', and Shucksmith and Hermann (2002:39) advocate the importance of studying 'farmers' own ways of seeing the world'. Burton (2004:212) goes further, saying it is important to investigate farmers' behaviour when thinking about future change by taking greater account of social and cultural factors—especially identity and symbolic meaning. He is critical of quantitatively based research that finds attitudes but does not explore the real meaning behind the adoption or rejection of what are assumed to be friendly, environmental practices.

This chapter takes up the challenge posed by these writers to examine a largely unexamined phenomenon: the movement of older people into the horticultural industry. There is an increasing amount being written about the intensification of land use, biodiversity, sustainability and resilience, but no-one has thought about the values and motivations of this particular group and how they could impact on the countryside of the future. To do this, I draw together two strands of thinking to explain how these people, through their relationships with their orchards, construct identities of 'good' selves, living meaningful lives. They do this by conferring agency on non-human actors (orchards) and then developing a moral economy of exchange relationships with these non-human actors. This is not, however, the only dimension of this chapter. It also explains how relationships constructed in this way can determine the nature of production landscapes and the implications for the future of older people taking up rural lives.

A kiwifruit orchard can be seen as a rural space, 'lovingly cultivated and controlled nature' (Macnaghten and Urry 1998:179). It could be considered a 'careful and long-term construction of the tame, which includes domesticating and commodifying nature' (Buller 2004:132) in order to produce kiwifruit for the global market. How do kiwifruit orchardists relate to their orchards in order to do this and to make their lives meaningful? I observed an 'embedded and implicit' (Gray 1998:342) relationship between an orchardist and their orchard in the talk of orchardists about their practices. No particular theoretical positioning informed my gaze in this matter—that came later, as I grappled with making sense of what I was observing.

## A moral economy of exchange between orchardists and their orchards

### Agency and orchards

At first, I was interested in orchardists' representations of a 'good' or ideal orchard as implied in their response to interview questions. I found that many described their orchard as pushing or encouraging them to interact with it in certain ways. Orchardists can develop an intimate relationship with their orchard—caring for it by mowing, pruning, controlling weeds, protecting it from frosts and fertilising the soil. These practices embed orchardists in the place of the orchard through the embodiment that arises from really doing something rather than gazing on it as an observer. As a result, the idea that an orchard could be thought of as an 'active' participant by orchardists evolved, just in the way that Jones and Cloke (2002) through the medium of ANT write about trees as actors in the landscape in their book *Tree Cultures: The place of trees and trees in their place*. They describe how practices to do with trees in different situations, such as on farms, in cemeteries and in orchards, have developed over time through relationships between people and trees.

### Social exchange

Mauss (1990:83) makes the case that exchange relationships are a universal characteristic of any society: 'There is no other morality, nor any other form of economy, nor any other social practices save these.' Accordingly, there is no such thing as a free gift. A 'free' gift is one that supposedly does not entail a response from the recipient. As far as Mauss is concerned, however, any gift incorporates within it a moral implication of, a commitment to, a response of an equivalent nature: 'the unreciprocated gift makes the person who has accepted it inferior' (Mauss 1990:65). A gift is relational. It establishes a relationship and a commitment between the giver and the receiver (Douglas 1990:ix). There are no independent individuals, only social beings with connections (Douglas 1990:x).

Social exchanges do not operate just in the economic dimension. Exchange for work or goods is usually expressed in economic returns in our society, but exchange also operates in the legal, moral, religious, aesthetic and other domains (Mauss 1990:79). Therefore, orchardists who see themselves in an exchange relationship with their orchard are acknowledging their continuing commitment to their orchard: a continuing relationship of giving and receiving on the part of each. Every exchange can be assumed to have a moral dimension; there is an expected reciprocity. Although the relationship of orchard and orchardist encompasses a relationship with nature and with the land, it is not seen purely in those terms because the relationship is also an economic one: an orchard is a workplace (Clark and Lowe 1992).

An orchard acts primarily as an enabler, an intermediary or a provider. In a manner similar to other forms of paid employment, orchardists are able to obtain what they want through their orchard: 'If I do this and this then the orchard will enable me to get this and this.' Hence, by responding to their orchard in a particular way, orchardists expect to get certain rewards.

## The nature of the rewards of exchange

In Bourdieu's (1998, 1990) notion of capital in his theory of practice, a theory of social exchange (Bourdieu 1998:vii–viii), rewards can be viewed as capital of a symbolic nature through other people's recognition and acknowledgment of particular symbols that give people status in their eyes. Through their habitus, or 'disposition to act', people have learned from their life experiences the 'right thing to do' (Bourdieu 1998:8), thus habitus becomes embodied through the practices of everyday lives (Adams 2006:514–16; Lau 2004:374–6; Thompson 1992:12–17). Actions in the world are structured around fields that have particular rules that structure the game that must be played to increase or exchange capital. Capital comes in three basic forms—economic, social and cultural—and it is the cultural I wish to concentrate on. Cultural capital can be seen as having three components: the capital acquired through education, possession of 'things' that give status and the acquisition of qualities associated with habitus (Burton et al. 2008). The last two are of relevance here. The way in which an orchard is physically presented can provide status, but 'for a symbolic exchange to function, the two parties must have identical categories of perception and appreciation' (Bourdieu 1998:100). In other words, in order to comprehend what these physical aspects mean, orchardists must share a common understanding of the symbolic significance they have within the fields of the kiwifruit industry and the local and wider communities in which they live. I posit that alongside status, meaning could also be acquired as an orchardist's identity is reinforced and maintained.

## A moral economy

Out of these insights emerged the realisation that what I was noticing was a 'moral economy' (Tanaka 2005; Robbins and Sharp 2003; Park et al. 2002). If an orchardist behaved in a particular way towards their orchard, they believed the orchard would not only reciprocate but was obliged to reciprocate because of the mutuality of exchange relationships. It would do this by producing a product that would enable the orchardist to have a livelihood and a lifestyle according to their hopes and expectations (apart from the constraints of the market).

Any action is usually associated with a moral judgment. Someone or some group is doing something that is considered good or bad from the perspective of some other person or group. As Matless (2001:522) has said, 'the conduct of particular groups or individuals in particular spaces may be judged appropriate or inappropriate, and the ways in which assumptions about the relationship between people and their environments may both reflect and produce moral judgments'.

Many actions aim to make something 'better' than it was before, such as in assisting a plant to bear 'better' fruit or making the land 'better' by making it productive, as these orchardists in this study said:

> [I]f I could leave them [farms/orchards/land] in a better condition than I found it then I was improving the land. And that didn't necessarily mean spraying the hell out of it. (Man, green)
>
> We have to make things better. (Man, organic)
>
> Obviously being organic we do more...than a lot of people towards the environment, and we're aware of it more. (Woman, organic)
>
> I think it has made us more aware of the environment and looking after it, really. We're really only caretakers of it, you know, while we've got it, and the idea is that you leave it better than you found it. (Man, organic)

Some explanations for real farming practices are described in terms of the 'good farmer' or 'good farming' (Setten 2004; Burton 2004; Silvasti 2003). The particular model of concern to many is that of the 'productivist' approach to farming in which farm practices are oriented to producing more of a farm product such as meat or a crop rather than practices that care for the environment or produce so-called 'environmental goods'.

## The kiwifruit industry in New Zealand

In New Zealand, the kiwifruit industry is dominated by ZESPRI, the single-desk marketer and exporter of New Zealand's kiwifruit. Rather than rewarding high productivity, the Taste Zespri program rewards high dry-matter fruit. It is very consumer focused. All export fruit from the more than 2000 kiwifruit growers has to meet the requirements of the GlobalGAP (formerly EurepGAP) audit system (in which GAP stands for good agricultural practices) and growers of organic fruit are certified by BioGro. To quote from the GlobalGAP web site (<www.globalgap.org>): 'The GlobalGAP standard is primarily designed to reassure consumers about how food is produced on the farm by minimising detrimental environmental impacts of farming operations, reducing the use of chemical inputs and ensuring a responsible approach to worker health and safety.'

GlobalGAP and BioGro carry out a process of certification of a product from farm inputs and all on-farm practices until it leaves the farm. Once certified, a farm is audited annually.

To indicate the degree of the issue this chapter is describing, I provide here some of the relevant demographic details of kiwifruit orchardists in New Zealand. The average age of green orchardists was fifty-nine years, fifty-six for gold and fifty-eight for organic in 2006 (Fairweather et al. 2007:18); about 80 per cent lived on their orchard (Fairweather et al. 2007:18; Colmar Brunton 2007); 65 per cent were in households with no children; 72 per cent of orchards were owned and operated by the orchardist and his/her partner; and 83 per cent of orchardists were male (Colmar Brunton 2007). In 2006, 23 per cent said that they would be retired or have the orchard leased or managed within the next five years (Fairweather et al. 2007:21). All of these figures demonstrate the predominance of older orchardists in the kiwifruit industry.

## Method: the ARGOS program and this research

This research has been carried out under the auspices of the Agricultural Research Group on Sustainability (ARGOS). It has a mandate from the Foundation for Research Science and Technology (FRST)[2] to examine the environmental, social and economic sustainability of New Zealand farming systems through studies comparing organic systems with conventional (and sometimes integrated) systems in the kiwifruit, sheep/beef and dairying sectors (see <www.argos.org.nz>).

For the research program, I conducted interviews with 35 kiwifruit participants from May to November 2004. For the purposes of this chapter, however, only those orchardists who have come into orcharding after other careers and who live on their orchard have become subjects of interest. This whittles the number used as a resource for this work to six ZESPRI green, six certified organic green and three ZESPRI gold orchardists. Four of the green and two of the gold orchardists had been dairy farmers, while five of the organic orchardists had formerly lived and worked in towns or cities. The interviews consisted of semi-structured questions in which orchardists were asked about their visions for themselves and their orchard; what they thought would be possible indicators for the measurement of economic, environmental and social wellbeing; and what was going well and what was difficult for them in their management of the orchard (see Hunt et al. 2005). I also observed the orchards and have photographs of them.

The interviews were transcribed and the transcripts analysed using qualitative research methods (for example, Tolich and Davidson 1999) to understand what meaning orchardists gave to their lives in order for me as interviewer and researcher to 'abandon all previous judgements about what is objective, factual, natural or scientific, against what is subjective, historical, cultural or religious in order...to conceptualize the view...held by each farmer, not only as spoken in words, but also as interpreted in daily practice' (Kaltoft 1999:41).

According to Morris (2004:281): 'A key contribution of ethnography to the study of processes often glossed as globalisation, is the attention such work pays to the micro-practices of the constitution and reproduction of identities in everyday life, for it is here that people work to achieve subjective stability.'

I will now outline the things that I found were important to the orchardists studied. This leads into a description of the sort of orchards that resulted from the expectations of the exchange between orchardists and their orchards.

## The importance of 'doing'

It was 'unthinkable' (Bourdieu 1990:52–65) for these orchardists not to be 'doing' something for the rest of their lives. One green orchardist who used to be a dairy farmer said it was a 'lifestyle choice'. He and his wife used to work 'seven days a week for 23 odd years...we're both still working full-time. I can't see us ever...stop doing completely. You gotta retire to something you can't retire from—that's my belief anyway' (Man, green).

An exchange between an orchardist and myself on this subject went like this:

> Interviewer: And when you say you like doing things, what do you mean by doing?
>
> Orchardist: Well just mowing and repairing and...Well, just maintenance really. Instead of sitting around doing nothing, you've gotta do something. (Man, green)

A former teacher spoke of his desire for his future: 'It's lifestyle, it's wanting something that will carry us from teaching through to a productive retirement...and we don't imagine that we will retire and do nothing' (Man, gold).

Another spoke of his orchard in this way: 'It's an asset that can earn...a reasonable sort of income for us when we retire, and even perhaps...semi-retire, as I can't see myself staying here till sixty-five and stop working. I'll be needing to be doing something, and both physically and mentally' (Man, green).

An element of 'doing' is that it is an indication that these orchardists will still be working hard. They made comments about how their city friends had the idea that kiwifruit orcharding would provide a nice lifestyle in which the orchardist did very little and sat around sipping wine, but 'a relatively small block of land can mean an awful lot of work' (Man, gold). Another spoke of his first impressions and how wrong they were:

> I'm an ex-engineer—[from] Auckland. I came down in '91 to visit my partner's father who's got [an] orchard down at Pangaroa. [I] [l]iked the place. And saw these old boys sitting on their backsides and all the fruit was growing and I thought, that's a good life. And they sucked me in

> nicely, didn't they? I haven't worked so many hours, for such a long time, in my life. (Man, organic)

## The rewards of doing

These are orchardists who are serious about what they 'do'. It is not a 'game' or a hobby. They still feel that they have a need for income: 'You've got to have an interest...keeps you occupied...but at the end of the day it's what you get, the bottom line, the net figure' (Man, green). Or, as another person said, 'You've got to be realistic, you've got to make a dollar' (Woman, organic).

Other rewards come in the form of the symbolic capital gained from the appreciation of visitors to the orchard—and some of them are unexpected, as this orchardist described:

> And I guess it's the response of people that visit. They come here and I don't want to be bragging in any way but people that come and visit the orchard, in their own way they are expressing the ambience of the place and if we get them sitting outside here, and it's just a nice atmosphere—even the tradespeople that we've had currently working on the house, the plumber and the pretty rough stone man that was in here, remarked how lovely it was and how nice and it was unusual to get that sort of response from people that I didn't think were sensitive to environmental type things. (Man, organic)

For some, the observation and protection of wildlife brings pleasure:

> [I]n our four canopy hectares we'd have well in excess of a hundred birds' nests in the spring time out there. So we respect them, and we give way to them. If there's pruning to be done near the nest, well it doesn't get done...and in return we get the pleasure of seeing the chicks on the nest. (Man, organic)

For a couple (green), taking up a kiwifruit orchard was returning to a more carefree lifestyle. They called themselves 'recycled teenagers'. Another orchardist reflected on his working life: 'I've fished, I've trucked, I've owned a bar, and they're just nothing compared to this' (Man, green). The ex-teacher emphasises, not surprisingly perhaps, the fun of learning new things:

> So, it's quite multi-skilled multi-tasked and, very interesting. Hell of a lot of fun...There's always the...financial side of things—you know—budgeting, record keeping, coming to terms with things like EurepGAP and...the Future Fed. certification we needed for selling in the local market, attending workshops and keeping up to date technically speaking, gaining qualifications for things like the Grow Safe qualification for doing your own spraying. And yeah, it's been a thoroughly enjoyable learning exercise—still is. (Man, gold)

Another orchardist found growing organically a rewarding challenge:

> I think there's a little bit of scepticism round the place [about being organic]—they were wondering how long it would be before we'd sort of bail out. That's probably still there a little bit but it's probably one of the things that makes me dig my toes in...Quite a few of us are proving that it can be done and it can be done economically...we've still got a long way to go but there's [sic] things that we're learning all the time—new products, new ways of doing things...Those of us that are in it now, I suppose you could say, are the pioneers of organics in kiwifruit growing, just because it is relatively new...it's always a challenge and just learning more and more about it. (Man, organic)

The orchard also provides a form of continuity, providing possibilities and meaning for the future and links to the past:

> [O]ur vision really—because it's my wife's as well—is for it to be...able to provide a good lifestyle for us through into our retirement years. So it should provide money. It should also provide a healthy lifestyle. And we want to do that in the most ecologically friendly fashion we can, keeping in mind the demands of the markets for our fruit, and our own philosophies. (Man, gold)

> I'm proud of this little place because it may not seem anything very spectacular to an outsider, but I know what it was eight years ago. So, it gives me, I suppose, a sense of satisfaction, to live here and be able to enjoy what I have done so far and plan what I'm going to do next. (Woman, green)

> [T]he last two years we've been going up in crop...when you see that's happening you feel like you're doing, enjoying it—you know? And I enjoy doing something, so, yeah, the trays have gone from 14 800 the first year; the second year we got 28 700; and this year—we haven't done a tally—but we should be around 34 this year. But we should be able to do 40. (Man, green)

## Linking the doing and the rewards

There is an indication the reward from the orchard is in exchange for the 'doing' and that this is not just a monetary exchange. It is also an expectation of a moral exchange, a social contract between the orchard and the orchardist, as the two following quotes demonstrate:

> [I]t's what you put into the orchard you get out type thing...I mean, you can go to orchards and you can tell that people don't do much on them because they're blinkin' terrible. And they've got terrible fruit. The

> pruners don't like them, the pickers don't like them, nobody likes working for them. (Man, green)
>
> [W]e've worked really hard all our...working life so far...we have denied ourselves a lot to bring up a family and we'd like to think that OK, there will come a time when the income stream from the orchard will support a nice house, a good car, comfortable living conditions, a healthy work environment, and the opportunity to go overseas or have really good holidays. (Man, gold)

## The signifiers of the rewards of doing and caring

There were two basic ways in which these orchardists saw their relationship with their orchard and these were signified by quite contrasting constructed landscapes. In the first landscape, the degree of care was demonstrated by how tidy the orchard looked, whereas for the second, care was demonstrated by the number of living things that were able to take refuge there. These orchards, however, were landscapes made through the particular way in which the orchardist thought of the agency of their orchard.

### The wild orchard: signified by tidiness and control

The visual feedback provided by the 'look' of an orchard gave feedback to an orchardist that their management practices were correct. Tidiness was equated with orchard health, as the following two quotes indicate: 'I'd like to see the canopy...a pruned canopy...with nicely spaced canes...that certainly looks tidy...a good orchard looks healthy' (Man, green). And, 'I've got a vision that when it's all up and running, that all the shelter's nice and trimmed and it's even...being tidy is important to me...as well as...performing. And that's part of the health of the place, I believe' (Man, green).

Creating a tidy orchard brings with it the implication of the need for control: '[It] became a giant mess with different weeds and stuff getting in there, but it's reasonably tidy looking [now]...we keep it under control with the sheep' (Man, organic).

Unless the orchard is controlled, it will become wild and out of control. It will become recalcitrant and not do what an orchard 'should' do, which is produce lots of fruit. As one green orchardist said, 'There's [sic] a lot of young five year olds in there, which still need a bit of training.' Hence, I have called this a wild orchard because that is how the orchardist portrays its agency.

In this kind of orchard, the orchardists place an emphasis on production, making the land useful. This means that all available land is planted with kiwifruit vines, as this orchardist illustrates when he describes how they decided where to position their house: 'we needed a house...so we sort of plonked this one here. We've been here ever since [laughs]. But no, that's why we're...in the orchard—there's nowhere else you could put a house—unless we start cutting vines out and I didn't really wanna do that' (Man, green).

When I interviewed this man in his house and looked out the window, I found myself looking straight into the kiwifruit vines! For this next orchardist, by drawing on the knowledge he obtained from his experiences as a dairy farmer, he was able to totally reconstruct his orchard landscape by starting with a large amount of earth moving. As he explained to me while drawing a map of his orchard:

> [I] did a lot of planning and drawing and whatnot from the dairy farm development work. This has all been contoured in here. That drain has actually been shifted...We brought it as close to the existing kiwifruit as we can. Eventually I'd like to tidy this area up and plant that out. No point in having that like it is. And some of the ground here we'll extend the canopy a wee bit on this row just to make use of the available space and tidy it up. (Man, green)

For another orchardist, his orchard was 'basically a wasteland' (Man, green) until he came along and made it useful.

The desire that orchardists have to keep their land 'neat and tidy' is not restricted to New Zealand, though it has been documented for farmers rather than those working in the horticultural sector. Others have drawn attention to this in England (Burton 2004; Burgess et al. 2000; McEachern 1992), the central plains of the United States (Nassauer 1997), Austria (Schmitzberger et al. 2005) and Finland (Silvasti 2003). As Burgess et al. (2000:121) express it, rough land is 'an anathema to farmers' sense of their professional identity and expertise'.

Beyond their practical application, these views contain a moral dimension: it is 'good' for an orchard to be helped to produce the best fruit it can, hence plants need to be guided, controlled or manipulated to produce, to be made better—more useful, more domestic—by controlling the fertility and growth of the vines and keeping the weeds and pests away so that all the available resources from the soil and plant will go into fruit production. It is good that every bit of available land is used to produce as much as possible.

The wild orchard that has become tidy fits all the descriptions of a 'good farmer'. The habitus of these orchardists is acted out on the orchard where a tidy, clean orchard signifies a good orchardist, the hard work that is needed to keep such a wild thing under control and in production and a person who cares about their orchard. Its tidiness, due to the weekly mowing and elimination of weeds, and its productivity are symbols that the orchardist is doing the 'right thing'; 'untamed and untended land represents decline and disarray' (Silvasti 2003:146). Tidiness is also a reflection of attitudes towards the land imbued from the days of New Zealand's colonisation, when land was broken in and control exercised over the 'wildness' (Egoz et al. 2001; Brooking 1996). It falls down, however, on one crucial point, which demonstrates how the moral economy approach enriches the understanding of orchards and orchardists. While paying attention to productivity, it is not necessarily the raison d'être for these orchardists. The reward they expect for attending to their orchard is a transition to a comfortable retirement lifestyle living alongside their orchard. As this process to a graduated retirement is worked through, often all an owner will do on their orchard is the mowing and weed control, hence these might be the only ways in which an orchardist can stamp their identity on the orchard. Regular mowing and weeding parallel the care that is taken of a garden. It is an example of an orchardist giving in to the 'urge to garden' (Brook 2003), creating a place where the orchardist feels 'at home'. A tidy orchard looks like a well-manicured garden: 'the economic as well as the aesthetic status of rural areas is generally predicated upon the exclusion of the wild' (Thomas 1983). This orchard is a demonstration of solidity and reliability and careful stewardship for one's future and of one's investment. 'This is a safe countryside where humanity nurtures and is, in return, nurtured by an accessible, appropriated and unthreateningly recognisable nature' (Buller 2004:132).

## The needy orchard: creating a haven

The other kind of orchard is constructed by orchardists from their understanding of their orchards as needy—needing to be cared for, loved and nurtured—as the following quotes illustrate:

> You can soon walk into an orchard and see if it looks stressed or anything like that...the colour of the leaves, the size of the leaves...same with any farm. You can work on a farm and soon tell whether it's lacking something or hungry. You might not know what [it is]. [If] you consistently produce...big crops and don't put the inputs in then eventually you're gonna have a reserve system...that you're gonna deplete. (Man, green)
>
> Under the organic regime, we try and nurse the soil. (Man, organic)
>
> Man: We do know that the high producing orchards are the ones that are run by the owners.
>
> Woman: [A]nd they're out there every day, pruning and titivating.
>
> Man: Doing it for love. (Organic)
>
> In fact, these orchards did not look needy. The orchardists owning needy orchards responded to their orchards by creating a haven for as many living things as they could as long as these things did not threaten the orchard.

> I might mow here three times a year. I give the neighbour this side [a hard time]. He's just got a new mower and it's like a bowling green…got an hour to spare and he's out killing the place. But to me, the longer grass—there's [sic] creatures in it as well—bugs and birds and bits and pieces running round out there. (Man, organic)

> [W]e could see there are advantages to the neighbours in that…we don't have to worry about using aggressive chemicals near to where people live, and worry about what the wind is doing—that kind of thing…It's an organic orchard alongside them…I actually feel happier walking around this place than I do some other orchards…[In the] HiCane[3] season the neighbours bring over their dog for walks…the neighbour on the other side quite often brings her horse for a walk and a bit of a chomp on the grass too…the neighbours have got 65 chooks [chickens]…which spend most of their time on our orchard. (Woman, organic)

This woman provided a refuge for her neighbour's hens, which had a practical side:

> We have taken some from [the] neighbour as well, 'cause once they go off the lay a bit he just chops their head off. But we'll put them into the pension box over there…and we use the poo and I go down the orchard with a barrow load and just scatter it round the orchard—it's a little bit of nutrient for the plants as well. (Woman, organic)

The orchard was regarded as a haven that was an escape from suburbia. For example, one orchardist (Man, organic) criticised his neighbour for building a metal driveway the full length of his orchard. He said, 'That's bad—it's suburban…commercial industrialisation.' For some, this attitude extended to creating a less industrial space by making the orchard look like a garden:

> Woman: The orchard's an extension of our garden…[at] the end of the rows and corners we've got various other shrubs and bits and pieces…just to make it look a bit sort of less clinical…it just breaks up the monocultures in there.
>
> Man: And [it] keeps the bees in the [orchard all the time] and the bumble bees are lovely too—such gentle giants in the bee world and yeah—I haven't been stung by one yet.
>
> Woman: Bumble bees work in the rain. (Organic)
>
> The way in which all the things in the orchard worked together was expressed often, as in the quotes above and in the following. There is an essence that such orchardists are working with nature rather than seeking to control it.

> [In] October and November, the bees come in and do their bit. So in my case, four hectares, I have a million workers come on site and pollinate the crop. That's critical to getting both [the] size of kiwifruit and the yield as well. So the weather at that time is really important, the bees only fly in the good weather. And then we move into three months of summer pruning intensive work again, which I find quite enjoyable. And because of the nature of the canopy that we've organised for our convenience the vines start leafing up as the summer weather comes on, and working under the vines in the summertime, I say it's a large airconditioner, because the plants are transpiring moisture. Ah, they're taking the latent heat away from the canopy and underneath the canopy is actually cooler—not just because it's in the shade—but it's actually the latent heat is being extracted by the vines so we work in a wonderfully comfortable environment. The height's right—we don't have to reach unduly or bend over—it's designed at six feet and it's a good working environment there for us, so when the hot sun is out we've got the umbrella up. (Man, organic)

Overall, however, the orchard is performing a much higher purpose: by creating such a haven, the orchardist has contributed to making the world a better place: 'Oh it's just, I guess, being very satisfied [that] what we're doing is good for the world...and that we are not destroying the environment—we're actually contributing to it' (Man, organic).

The needy orchardist runs the risk of being called lazy by wild orchardists because for them tidiness implies hard work (Nassauer 1997; Burgess et al. 2000; Oresczyn and Land 2000; Egoz et al. 2001). Some 'needy' orchardists demonstrated an awareness of this risk by comparing themselves with wild orchardists. As Burton (2004:209) points out, however, 'an untidy farm is not necessarily an unprofitable farm...Therefore, "untidy" farmers may not be lazy farmers from an economic perspective'. Needy orchards are also viable businesses.

Thus, all orchardists described here have constructed orchards that represent their response to the agency they have attributed to their orchard and the care that they are taking of it. This care, however, is indicated in two different ways, resulting in tidy orchards and orchards that are teeming with life.

## Discussion and implications

I now wish to examine what I have written thus far in two different ways: one rather more esoteric, the other pragmatic. First, I will consider the framework I have used: that of a constructed moral economy of exchange between two agents. How does this contribute to our understanding of how this group of people is constructing new and meaningful lives as kiwifruit orchardists making their way to retirement? Are they really forming new identities? Second, I will ponder the implications for the future of this movement of older people into rural life.

## Creating identity: living meaningful lives

It is clear from the illustrations I have used that this group of people has come from an upbringing and life experience in which it is deeply ingrained that you do not get something for nothing and so it is important to be 'doing'. By implication, retirement, as in 'doing nothing of consequence', is not an option. This identity related to the work ethic becomes one of the values of the field of the communities in which these people live or have their friends, and has to be demonstrated by their orchard for themselves and other people to see. The orchard has to be a symbol of hard work and disciplined caring for the wild/tidy orchardists and of extravagant 'caring' and nurturance for the needy orchardist. There are, however, three moral issues also implied here. First, to be a good person one has to be working/doing, living a 'useful' life. Second, each orchardist in their own way is striving to make the orchard 'better'. For the wild orchardist, the orchard is better because it is under control, domesticated and no longer 'wild'; it is doing what an orchard should be doing: producing good fruit. For the needy orchardist, the orchard is no longer needy because the orchardist has fed it and made it into a haven where everything is welcome, creating an environment that not only produces wholesome fruit but is an example of care for the environment. Finally, there is reciprocity involved. If one 'does', there is the expectation of a return. As a reward for making it better, the orchard has to demonstrate its response to the actions of the orchardist. By attributing agency to their orchards, orchardists are able to accept as rightfully theirs the rewards the orchards produce because the rewards are in exchange for what they have done, thus reinforcing their identities as good people living meaningful lives. This could be very important to people on the way to retirement as they supposedly exchange an old identity maintained by work in another place and context to a new one. Otherwise, who would they be?

Are these people just creating a landscape like home (Brook 2003) and/or an identity that really is the same as it was in the past but just in a new setting? Bourdieu's theory of practice (1998) is usually seen as a theory of continuity (for example, Shucksmith and Hermann 2002; Setten 2004), but it can also help in the understanding of change (Raedeke et al. 2003:79) and identity (Adams 2006). Critics of Bourdieu consider his notion of habitus deterministic and restrictive (for example, Silber 2003), claiming that it limits an individual's capacity to act (Widick 2003:688; Jenkins 1992:77, 272). On the other hand, proponents of Bourdieu's approach argue that while habitus reduces possibilities for action through its deeply instilled ways of 'practising', many possibilities remain (Adams 2006:515). All of the orchardists in this study come from somewhere other than where they are now living. Therefore one has to ask how their past working experiences are affecting their expectations of and practices in their orchards. It is apparent that those in the ARGOS program taking up kiwifruit growing after experience in the primary sector in dairying are more likely to have a wild/tidy orchard than those from 'the city', who are more likely to have a needy orchard and are also more likely to take up organics. Ex-dairy farmers and some of the city folk might be happy to create an 'industrial' ordered environment—reflected by one of the quotes in which one person is rebelling against this concept. The kiwifruit is an exotic species—it has moved out of orchards to become classified by the Department of Conservation as a noxious weed—so it has an alien nature that people might wish to domesticate or keep suppressed and one way of doing so is to impose tidiness in a ruthless fashion. In contrast, those with urban backgrounds might be creating a less-ordered garden—for example, the same woman who is planting garden plants and shrubs in the kiwifruit orchard will encourage biodiversity but it will not look like a monoculture orchard, growing only kiwifruit.

There also appears to be a gender influence. I interviewed whoever chose to be interviewed, so in some instances there were couples and in others a single person, usually a male. Wherever there was a woman involved in the orchard work, she usually participated in the interview. Hence it seems more likely to be a couple involved in the needy orchard, whereas on the tidy orchard the woman is more likely to lead her own life and not participate in on-orchard work. Also, the emphasis placed on mowing the orchard is reflected in the literature. Some writers think there is an association between men and lawns, particularly between men and lawnmowers. In a book called *The Grass is Greener: Our love affair with the lawn*, Fort (2000) asserts that keeping a lawn 'right' is all about 'one-upmanship: how national pride, social status, even sexual identity can be bound up in the greenness and smoothness of the grass'. He shares the view that 'men love lawns because, like dogs, they repay love and attention' (Woolfrey 2000). One person he consulted thought the impulse to mow lawns 'sprang from a deeply imprinted desire to control and domesticate nature' (cited in Woolfrey 2000). The orchardists who are planning their retirement paths see mowing the grass in the orchard as the last thing they will give up. As stated earlier, this would then be the only way in which an orchardist could stamp their identity on the orchard.

What role does meeting the audit requirements of the GlobalGAP system play in the life of these orchardists? Tidy orchardists were more likely to complain about the book work associated with this. 'Doing' book work was not associated with on-orchard work, whereas the needy orchardists were more likely to accept the requirements—often already associated with BioGro if they were using organic practices—but they would complain about where this paperwork doubled up. (This has since been dealt with by making this information-providing process more streamlined with less redundancy.) Perhaps book work is more acceptable to people who formerly worked in offices. Meeting audit requirements is something that everyone in the kiwifruit industry has to do so it cannot be a distinguishing feature that differentiates one orchardist from another. Hence it is less likely to have much currency except in the way that it separates out New Zealand kiwifruit in the international marketplace, which can be a source of pride for all kiwifruit growers.

So, are these people changing their identities? I suggest that these people are using kiwifruit orcharding as a medium to maintain the continuity of their identity from past lives. For example, the teacher who values learning is still able to learn, and for all, the need to do something useful is still fulfilled. The orchard (and its economic return) provides further evidence and support for this identity. The orchard also provides a form of differentiation from other orchardists. In spite of the many constraints experienced by orchardists and the fact that they all grow a similar product, there are many ways in which their orchards can differ. In other words, the constraints of ZESPRI, meeting audit scheme requirements and meeting the expectations of neighbours and communities have not limited the choices of kiwifruit orchardists in the way they relate to their orchards and the influence of this on the orchard landscape.

## Issues for rural futures

What are the implications of this movement of older people into the countryside, a place usually assumed to be the best for bringing up children? The demographic implications of countryside with an increasing proportion of older couples are intriguing. It raises questions about the impact of a very mobile, reasonably wealthy group of people on the local rural communities. I raise this as an issue for thought. I do not have any answers here except that it will obviously not do anything to increase the decline in the numbers of rural schools. Also, this is a group without long experience in orchards, therefore they will have greater needs for knowledge pertinent to this work. This leads nicely into the next issue.

Burton and Wilson (2006) have scrutinised the farming styles literature to develop themes which they say cover all the identified 'types'. They came up with four:

> (1) 'Traditional'—a conservative productivist farmer who maintains cultural notions of stewardship; (2) 'Agribusiness person'—a farmer who concentrates on agricultural production to the extent that the profit motive dominates and stewardship concerns are lessened; (3) 'Conservationist'—a farmer who focuses on environmental and lifestyle concerns; and (4) 'Entrepreneur'—a farmer who is shifting the focus away from standard agriculture towards non-agricultural sources of income. (Burton and Wilson 2006:101)

It can be seen that the orchardists of a wild orchard are a mix of Burton and Wilson's first and second theme and the orchardists of needy orchards fit their conservationist theme. In other work, I have identified a challenging orchard whose orchardist is entrepreneurial and likes to take risks and try new things while staying within the orchard (see Hunt and Rosin 2007). This sort of orchardist, however, is not present in this study of 'older', 'new' orchardists and this could be a source of concern. Every industry needs its entrepreneurs—the people who try things out and introduce successful practices to the mainstream. They play an important part in the resilience of the system by introducing change and being prepared to try things even if they fail. In the future, the industry will need to make sure it continues to be attractive to such people. In the meantime, the needy orchardists add resilience to the kiwifruit industry by providing ways of growing kiwifruit without chemicals and with a greater care for environmental biodiversity, and the wild/tidy orchardists are guarantors of a steady and reliable supply of quality kiwifruit. As these people are new to the industry, however, and are ready to become more knowledgeable about it, when they learn they will be learning the latest practices. As the kiwifruit industry is renowned for how quickly it is able to change, this aspect will only enhance this ability, as long as it is not in conflict with the attributes of orchards and of themselves that this group values.

Maintaining a productive orchard requires periods of intensive seasonal labour. Winter pruning, which can be carried out over a longer period than summer pruning, is often able to be done by the owners. Summer pruning needs to be done quite quickly and more frequently and fruit picking requires only a day or two at the instant when the fruit is deemed to be ready. Contractors can do the spraying. Finding labour, especially skilled labour, is already a big issue in the horticultural industry and, as working orchardists such as those described here give up more and more manual work, this will be exacerbated, particularly as the New Zealand population ages. It also, however, provides a group of people who are likely to continue working after the age of 65 so there are pluses and minuses here.

## Conclusion

Information such as that presented in this chapter could contribute to more resilient and sustainable orchard practices by developing a greater understanding that orchardists do not set out solely to gain materially, nor are all orchardists aiming for the same kind of orchard. Thus, this has demonstrated that the way in which an orchardist relates to their orchard is contested. As Setten (2004:391) states:

> Notions of what is natural and unnatural are notions of morality, and notions of morality surface frequently because different people and groups know and conceive of landscape and nature in differing ways...The cultural meanings of nature shaped by individuals and groups are hence contested, because inherent in shaping the meanings of nature

> are powerful moral judgements as to who is 'right' or 'wrong', 'good' or 'bad', 'natural' or 'unnatural'.

This is a particularly interesting conclusion because for many forms of farming (for example, dairying; Jay 2005) only a single kind of productivist farm is rewarded with symbolic as well as economic capital. Jay indicates that such a farming structure reduces the chance of farmers taking up environmentally sustainable practices. If the land-use practices are to be sustainable and resilient there is a need for diverse models of potential practices so that choices are available to people. This poses less risk to the environment than a singular normative practice model. It also reveals for New Zealand, as in other places, the ways in which nature (as seen here in kiwifruit orchards) and 'social practices and values are inextricably interlinked and...[are] co-constitutive' (Buller 2004:139).

This chapter has explored how the people who have taken up kiwifruit growing as a progression to retirement adapt their orchard landscape so that things important to their identity in their former working lives are maintained. Such people contribute to the stability of the kiwifruit industry but will need to be balanced by the risk takers and supported by the encouragement of seasonal workers.

## Bibliography


Adams, M. 2006, 'Hybridizing habitus and reflexivity: towards an understanding of contemporary identity?', *Sociology*, vol. 40, no. 3, pp. 511–27.

Bourdieu, P. 1990 [1980], *The Logic of Practice*, Polity Press, Cambridge, United Kingdom.

Bourdieu, P. 1998, *Practical Reason: On the theory of action*, Stanford University Press, Stanford, Calif.

Bourdieu, P. and Wacquant, L. 1992, *An Invitation to Reflexive Sociology*, Polity Press, Cambridge, United Kingdom.

Brook, I. 2003, 'Making here like there: place attachment, displacement and the urge to garden', *Ethics, Place and Environment*, vol. 6, no. 3, pp. 227–34.

Brooking, T. 1996, 'Use it or lose it: unravelling the land debate in late nineteenth-century New Zealand', *New Zealand Journal of History*, vol. 30, pp. 141–61.

Buell, L. 2001, *Writing for an Endangered World: Literature, culture and environment in the US and beyond*, Belknap Press at Harvard University Press, Cambridge, Mass.

Buller, H. 2004, 'Where the wild things are: the evolving iconography of rural fauna', *Journal of Rural Studies*, vol. 20, pp. 131–41.

Burgess, J., Clark, J. and Harrison, C. M. 2000, 'Knowledges in action: an actor network analysis of a wetland agri-environment scheme', *Ecological Economics*, vol. 35, pp. 119–32.

Burton, R. J. F. 2004, 'Seeing through the "good farmer's" eyes: towards developing an understanding of the social symbolic value of "productivist" behaviour', *Sociologia Ruralis*, vol. 44, no. 2, pp. 195–215.

Burton, R. J. F. and Wilson, G. A. 2006, 'Injecting social psychology theory into conceptualisations of agricultural agency: towards a post-productivist farmer self-identity?', *Journal of Rural Studies*, vol. 22, pp. 95–115.

Burton, R. J. F., Kuczera, C. and Schwarz, G. 2008, 'Exploring farmers' cultural resistance to voluntary agri-environmental schemes', *Sociologia Ruralis*, vol. 48, no. 1, pp. 16–37.

Clark, J. and Lowe, P. 1992, 'Cleaning up agriculture: environment, technology and social science', *Sociologia Ruralis*, vol. 32, no. 1, pp. 11–29.

Colmar Brunton 2007, Understanding kiwifruit growers and their relationship with ZESPRI, Colmar Brunton Powerpoint presentation.

Douglas, M. 1990, 'Foreword: no free gifts', in M. Mauss, *The Gift: The form and reason for exchange in archaic societies*, W. W. Norton, New York and London, pp. vii–xviii.

Egoz, S., Bowring, J. and Perkins, H. C. 2001, 'Tastes in tension: form, function, and meaning in New Zealand's farmed landscapes', *Landscape and Urban Planning*, vol. 57, no. 3, pp. 177–96.

Fairweather, John, Hunt, Lesley, Cook, Andrew, Rosin, Chris, Benge, Jayson and Campbell, Hugh 2007, *New Zealand farmer and grower attitude and opinion survey: kiwifruit sector*, ARGOS Research Report 07/08, <www.argos.org.nz>

Fort, T. 2000, *The Grass is Greener: Our love affair with the lawn*, Harper Collins, Glasgow.

Gray, J. 1998, 'Family farms in the Scottish Borders: a practical definition of hill farmers', *Journal of Rural Studies*, vol. 14, no. 3, pp. 241–356.

Hunt, L. and Rosin, C. 2007, 'The active kiwifruit orchard: orchard/orchardist interaction', *ISHS Acta Horticulturae*, vol. 753, <http://www.actahort.org/books/753/753_76.htm>

Hunt, L. M., Rosin, C., McLeod, C., Read, M., Fairweather, J. R. and Campbell, H. R. 2005, *Understanding approaches to kiwifruit production in New Zealand: report on first qualitative interviews with ARGOS kiwifruit participants*, ARGOS Research Report 05/01, July 2005, <www.argos.org.nz>

Jay, M. 2005, 'Remnants of the Waikato: native forest survival in a production landscape', *New Zealand Geographer*, vol. 61, pp. 14–28.

Jenkins, R. 1992, *Pierre Bourdieu*, Routledge, London.

Jones, O. and Cloke, P. J. 2002, *Tree Cultures: The place of trees and trees in their place*, Berg, Oxford.

Kaltoft, P. 1999, 'Values about nature in organic farming practice and knowledge', *Sociologia Ruralis*, vol. 39, no. 1, pp. 39–53.

Lau, R. W. K. 2004, 'Habitus and the practical logic of practice: an interpretation', *Sociology*, vol. 38, no. 2, pp. 369–87.

McEachern, C. 1992, 'Farmers and conservation: conflict and accommodation in farming politics', *Journal of Rural Studies*, vol. 8, no. 2, pp. 159–71.

Macnaghten, P. and Urry, J. 1998, *Contested Natures*, Sage Publications, London.

Matless, D. 2001, 'Moral geographies', in R. J. Johnston, D. Gregory, G. Pratt and M. Watts (eds), *Dictionary of Human Geography*, Fourth edition, Blackwell, Malden, Mass., p. 522.

Mauss, M. 1990, *The Gift: The form and reason for exchange in archaic societies*, Translated by W. D. Halls, W. W. Norton, New York and London.

Mayle, P. 1992, *A Year in Provence*, Ulverscroft, Leicester.

Morris, C. 2004, 'The Great Depression and the downturn: narrating continuity in the high country', *New Zealand Sociology*, vol. 19, no. 2, pp. 281–98.

Nassauer, J. 1997, 'Cultural sustainability: aligning aesthetics and sustainability', in J. Nassauer (ed.), *Placing Nature: Culture and landscape ecology*, Island Press, Washington, DC, pp. 67–83.

Oresczyn, S. and Land, A. 2000, 'The meaning of hedgerows in the English landscape: different stakeholders' perspectives and the implications for future hedge management', *Journal of Environmental Management*, vol. 60, pp. 101–18.

Park, J., Scott, K., Cocklin, C. and Davis, P. 2002, 'The moral life of trees: pastoral farming and production forestry in northern New Zealand', *Journal of Anthropological Research*, vol. 58, pp. 521–44.

Raedeke, A. H., Green, J., Hodge, S. and Valdivia, C. 2003, 'Farmers, the practice of farming and the future of agroforestry: an application of Bourdieu's concepts of field and habitus', *Rural Sociology*, vol. 68, no. 1, pp. 64–86.

Robbins, P. and Sharp, J. T. 2003, 'Producing and consuming chemicals: the moral economy of the American lawn', *Economic Geography*, vol. 79, no. 4, pp. 425–51.

Schmitzberger, I., Wrbka, T., Steurer, B., Aschenbrenner, G., Peterseil, J. and Zechmeister, H. G. 2005, 'How farming styles influence biodiversity maintenance in Austrian agricultural landscapes', *Agriculture, Ecosystems and Environment*, vol. 108, pp. 274–90.

Setten, G. 2004, 'The habitus, the rule and the moral landscape', *Cultural Geographies*, vol. 11, pp. 389–415.

Shucksmith, M. and Hermann, V. 2002, 'Future changes in British agriculture: projecting divergent farm household behaviour', *Journal of Agricultural Economics*, vol. 53, pp. 37–50.

Silber, I. F. 2003, 'Pragmatic sociology as cultural sociology. Beyond repertoire theory?', *European Journal of Social Theory*, vol. 6, no. 4, pp. 427–49.

Silvasti, T. 2003, 'The cultural model of "the good farmer" and the environmental question in Finland', *Agriculture and Human Values*, vol. 20, pp. 143–50.

Tanaka, K. 2005, 'Redefining the moral responsibilities for food safety: the case of red meat in New Zealand', *Rural Sociology*, vol. 70, no. 4, pp. 470–90.

Thomas, K. 1983, *Man and the Natural World*, Allen Lane, London.

Thompson, J. B. 1992, 'Editor's introduction', in P. Bourdieu, *Language and Symbolic Power*, Polity Press, Cambridge, pp. 1–31.

Tolich, M. and Davidson, C. 1999, *Starting Fieldwork: An introduction to qualitative research in New Zealand*, Oxford University Press, Melbourne, Australia.

Widick, R. 2003, 'Flesh and the free market (on taking Bourdieu to the options exchange)', *Theory and Society*, vol. 32, nos 5–6, pp. 679–723.

Woolfrey, Celia 2000, 'One man went to mow', *The Guardian*, 16 September 2000, viewed 21 October 2008, <http://www.guardian.co.uk/books/2000/sep/16/houseandgarden.features>

## Endnotes

[1] These are quotes taken from interviews with orchardists as described later in the 'method' section. Eighty-six per cent of kiwifruit orchardists grow the green-fleshed Hayward variety of kiwifruit, 21 per cent grow the gold-fleshed variety and 5 per cent grow fruit organically (Colmar Brunton 2007). (These figures do not add to 100 per cent because some orchardists grow gold and green kiwifruit.) Hereafter, the orchardists will be referred to as green, organic and gold.

[2] The government organisation assigned the task of allocating funding to research that meets government goals.

[3] A bud break spray.

# 7

# Intergenerational transitions in rural Western Australia: an issue for sustainability?

**Daniela Stehlik**

## Abstract

Towards the end of the past decade, signs were emerging as to future challenges associated with impending intersections between the ageing of global rural populations and their impacts on agricultural production and food safety. In a landmark paper for the Food and Agriculture Organisation (FAO), Iaquinta et al. (1999) made a strong plea for additional research in the field and developed a schematic highlighting the linkages between ageing, land tenure, intergenerational change and agricultural production for developing countries. The link to sustainability within this schematic was implied rather than highlighted and the importance of the issue for the developed world was glossed over. This chapter argues that this is a vital challenge for Australia now at the end of the first decade of the twenty-first century, as the country ages and the transition of knowledge from the 'baby boom' generation impacts at all levels of Australian society. It draws on continuing research being undertaken in Western Australia as part of an international research group focusing on sustainability and conservation. It takes up the schematic as designed by Iaquinta et al. and highlights the key issues for land tenure, the impact on rural values, natural resource management and future sustainability with specific focus on the south coast region of the state.

## Introduction

Rapid transition from rural to peri-urban settlement in coastal southern Western Australia, combined with the potential changes in climate, demographic growth and intergenerational transitions, are creating potential future policy challenges. This has emerged as an issue for research within the context of the natural resource management (NRM) sector in the region and the concept of 'transitions' of knowledge and capital as Australia ages.

In a discussion about 'rural futures' for the developed world, a landmark paper written in 1999, which focuses on the issue for the developing world, offers some frameworks for discussion. This chapter draws on this framework to highlight key issues. It begins with a statement of the issue and some reflections from the literature; it then gives a snapshot of the region in question and of the evidence gathered to date, summarising some aspects of the framework and concluding with some questions for future research.

## Statement of the issue

There has been recognition for more than a decade of the ageing of the farm workforce in Australia. As most reports point out, this is not simply because of an increased number of older farmers, but, importantly to our discussion, it is a result of decreased numbers of younger people entering or remaining in agriculture. The transition of farms and land management has a long history—for example, Foskey (n.d.:3) found evidence of intergenerational arrangements among landholders dating back to the Middle Ages. Barr et al. (2005), in their report to Land and Water Australia, point to the 'pattern of agricultural adjustment for many generations'. This chapter suggests that the issue has a more powerful difference as the whole Australian population ages.

There is also the important link with NRM policy in Australia.[1] While risk assessments might highlight the NRM environment risks, they ignore risks associated with demography. For example, the major NRM regional strategy on the south coast of Western Australia (see below) identifies population decline and ageing as a threat on one page (p. 48) and it is never mentioned again.

This chapter is based not on empirical research (which has yet to be undertaken in detail in the region) but on personal involvement in NRM governance and on a close reading of policy documents for the region's future strategic planning. In other words, what I am highlighting here are preliminary signposts for the future, and I am calling for more detailed research. As a nation, we can no longer ignore the demographic trends, nor can we just hope that things will turn out for the best. While there has been a variety of risk assessments undertaken in rural Australia, at the time of writing, a risk assessment as to the impact of the ageing of the rural workforce[2] on rural futures, or to the imminent intergenerational transfers of knowledge and power that are essential to enable a sustainable future, is not under way.

By *transition* here I am not so focused on the land transfer (this is where Voyce's 1999, 1996 work on inheritance sits), but rather on the experience, knowledge, social and cultural capital associated with the passing of one generation and the taking up of future challenges by other generations. Nowhere is this more evident that in the NRM 'sector'. Governance of NRM remains essentially in the hands of the older generation (very evident in my own region) and there is no evidence yet from a detailed literature review that any strategic thinking has taken this matter up as a key issue. There has, however, been much discussion about farm transfers, succession planning that focuses on the transition of the business, technology, stock, equipment and housing—in other words, an instrumental approach as follows:

> Inheritance—legal transfer of ownership of the business assets
>
> Succession—transfer for managerial control over the use of these assets
>
> Retirement—the withdrawal of the present manager from active managerial control. (<http://www.management.edu.ru/images/pubs/2003/11/29/0000135240/075-067-errington.pdf>)

Such a typology captures the essence of the literature to date, specifically the practical and productive nature of any transition. My current research is highlighting a little-explored aspect of the intergenerational shift—the transition of knowledge in governance—an aspect that is crucial for our deeper understanding of rural futures, and the potential impact of the ageing of Australia's population on NRM and food safety into the future.

Four years ago, in its submission to the Department of Agriculture, Fisheries and Forestry (DAFF) on 'Agriculture Advancing Australia' (AAA), the National Farmers Federation (NFF) stated that as the average age of farmers was now close to sixty years, to ensure the long-term prosperity and sustainability of Australian agriculture, effective intergenerational transfer was essential. The report, *Australia's Farmers: Past, present and future* (Barr et al. 2005), examines trends in the demographic structure of Australia's farmer population throughout the period 1976 to 2001 and concludes that there is no looming crisis with Australia's food production capacity, despite the expected continued decline of farmers in broadacre farming regions. The report conceptualises intergenerational transfer as related to farm size and this is explored from the perspective of farm development, innovation and how technology can impact on levels of production. The report argues that protection of the rural environment through farming practices is anticipated to be continued as long as the activities are labour efficient and profitable or if they are required by regulation.

Argent (1999) suggests that the established gender order within Australian farming households is undergoing gradual and uneven change as a familial ideology—in which the maintenance of family living standards is considered more important than the preservation of the family's ties with the land—assumes importance in some young families' adjustment responses. Voyce (1999) explores issues of farming succession with particular reference to the *Social Security and Veterans' Affairs Legislation Amendment (Retirement Assistance for Farmers) Act 1998*.He outlines that this legislation seeks to: 1) maintain political and social control in the rural sector; and 2) foster intergenerational continuity of family farms. He argues that the State's involvement is in 'facilitated and ordered controlled successions' tending to be through the establishment of rural norms or 'responsibilities' between an inheriting son and father (Voyce 1999:22). Foskey (n.d.) discusses two main but opposing trends within agriculture in Australia—farming as a lifestyle and farming as a business—both of which are linked to rural ideology.[3] The ageing of farm populations is a worldwide trend, with the highest rates in the United States, Canada, Europe and Japan. Foskey concludes by highlighting the need to support ageing farmers as they make the transition into retirement and the challenges they face in this, as well as utilising their skills and experience to further enable younger farmers. Errington's 2002 review of the topic in the United Kingdom, France and Canada concludes that there is a sequencing of transition, including major decision making along the process, although in France this seems to be more rapid than in the United Kingdom (<http://www.management.edu.ru/images/pubs/2003/11/29/0000135240/075-067-errington.pdf>).

## A region in context

The chapter now turns to the site of analysis. The south coast region of Western Australia[4] has some of the world's most endangered flora and fauna, is recognised as one of 25 world biodiversity 'hot spots', covers a land mass of some 5.4 million hectares in what is arguably a high-amenity area and is now experiencing rapid change. This is one of the oldest areas of human settlement in Australia, with Aboriginal settlement dated to 40 000 years and European settlement (around the Albany area) to the 1820s. Unlike the Margaret River (south-west) region of Western Australia, it is not yet as well known internationally, although this is changing.

It is the state's second-largest agricultural production region. Despite the historical records showing a 30 per cent decrease in average rainfall for south-west Western Australia, the region had relatively positive rainfall in the 2006–07 season. About 70 per cent of the region's 5.4 million terrestrial hectares is under some form of primary production, the majority being cropped (including wheat, canola, and so on) or under pasture, but with more than 125 000ha under timber plantations and about 4000ha under viticulture and various forms of horticulture (SCRIPT 2005:76). This intensive agriculture has resulted in four identified major environmental challenges for agricultural production:

- soil acidity
- salinity
- excess phosphorous (excess fertiliser usage)
- invasion of weeds and feral animals.

To provide a brief snapshot of the costs associated with such threats, land salinisation offers a salutary lesson. By the late 1990s, 9 per cent of Western Australia's agricultural land was affected by salinity and predictions identified a doubling in the next 15–25 years, with a further doubling in the next decades. The WA *State of the Environment Report* (Government of Western Australia 1998:56) detailed that 'up to 80 per cent of susceptible remnants of native vegetation of forms and 50 per cent on public lands (including nature reserves) could be lost in the agricultural regions of W.A. within the next century'. It has been estimated that the current loss of capital value of WA land to dryland salinity is in the order of $1.445 billion, with a prediction to an escalation of a further $64 million per annum in the next five decades. It is not, however, just the land value that is decreasing; estimates of tourism potential are also impacted, as are the livability and amenity capacities of small rural centres and the potential production of agricultural products.

The south coast region of Western Australia is one of 58 NRM regions in Australia and it is being managed through the South Coast NRM Incorporated. It is also the site of a five-year research project by Curtin University, Sustaining Gondwana, funded through a grant from the Alcoa Foundation (United States). The site was chosen for this research because the region provided an example of the complex interrelationships between place, environment, production and sustainability.

In the 18 months since the start of our project, the pace of change has increased exponentially. For example, in the major western centre of the region, Albany, there has been a 37 per cent increase in the price of housing, with a projected release of more than 2000 new blocks in the next five years. The pressure of demographic change (see Stehlik 2007; Government of Western Australia n.d.) is now recognised as a key issue for future sustainability.

This chapter examines questions of change through what is termed the Albany hinterland, a broad arc surrounding the City of Albany and including the Shire of Denmark. Many of my comments apply to the region as a whole. The Albany hinterland subregion takes in the city of Albany and the towns of Denmark, Mount Barker, Manypeaks and Wellstead. It contains all of the Denmark, Hay and Kalgan River catchments flowing south from the Stirling Range and discharging into Wilson Inlet and Oyster Harbour.

**Figure 7.1 South coast of Western Australia**

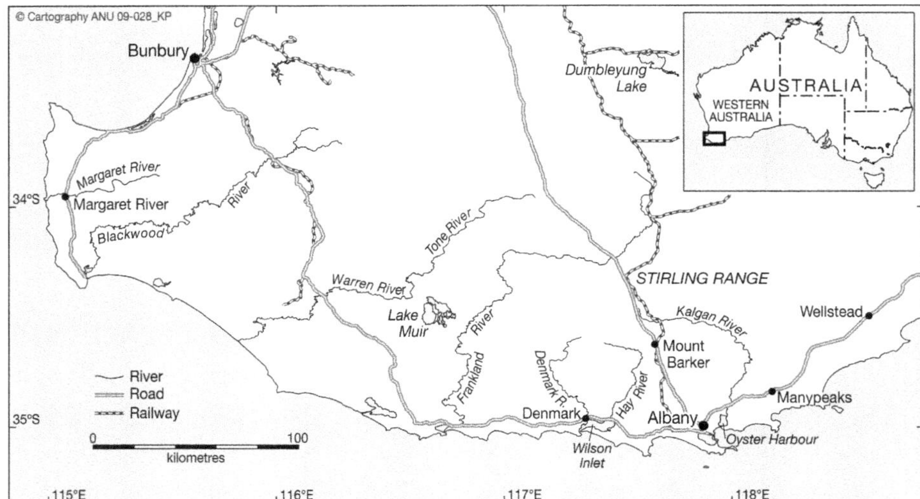


Source: ANU Cartography.

ABS Census data highlight the trend towards the urbanisation of the south coast region, with nearly three-quarters of the population living in the two key urban centres of Albany and Esperance. Consequently, the population in the smaller rural villages—such as Tambellup, Gnowangerup, Jerramungup and Cranbrook—are decreasing (Figure 7.2).

The proportion of the population in the Albany Hinterland of the region as a whole is 62.6 per cent and growing. In this sense, the urban centre of Albany can be seen as acting as a 'sponge city'—pulling services and residents into the urban space, at the cost of the rural outlying communities. There was a reduction of some 7–10 per cent in the populations of the smaller rural centres in the south coast region in the 2001 census and this pattern was expected to be repeated despite some early indications of a 'tree change' housing boom in some centres such as Mount Barker.

**Figure 7.2 Population change, 1996–2006, Albany and Denmark**

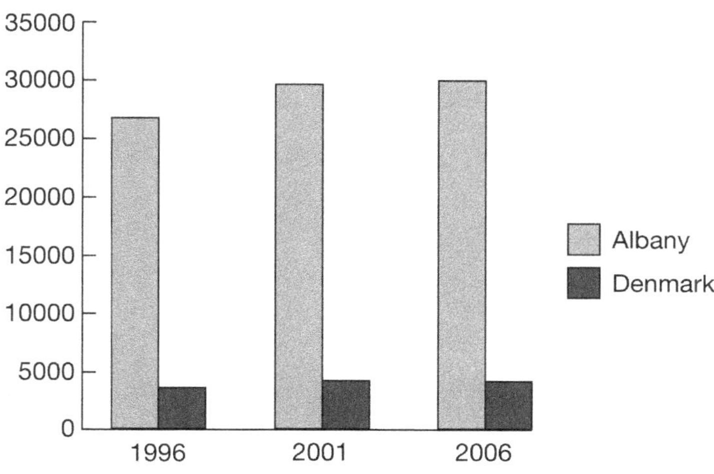


Source: Derived from ABS (2007).

**Figure 7.3 Population aged 55–64 years, 1996–2006, by shire (Jerramungup, Gnowangerup, Tambellup and Cranbrook—Albany hinterland)**

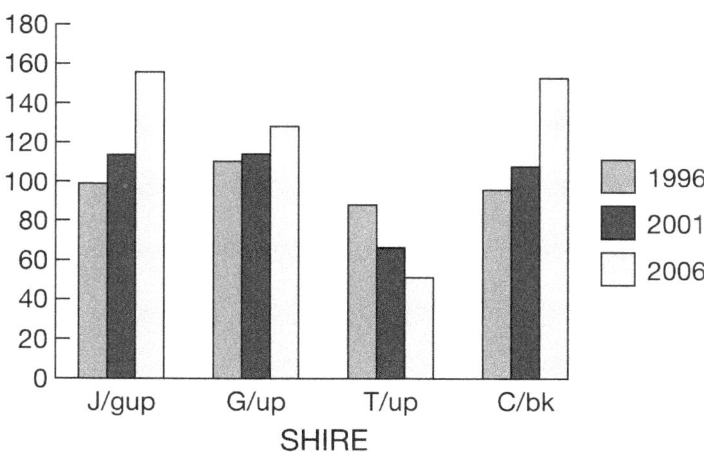

**Figure 7.4 Population aged over 65 years, 1996–2006, by shire (Jerramungup, Gnowangerup, Tambellup and Cranbrook—Albany hinterland)**

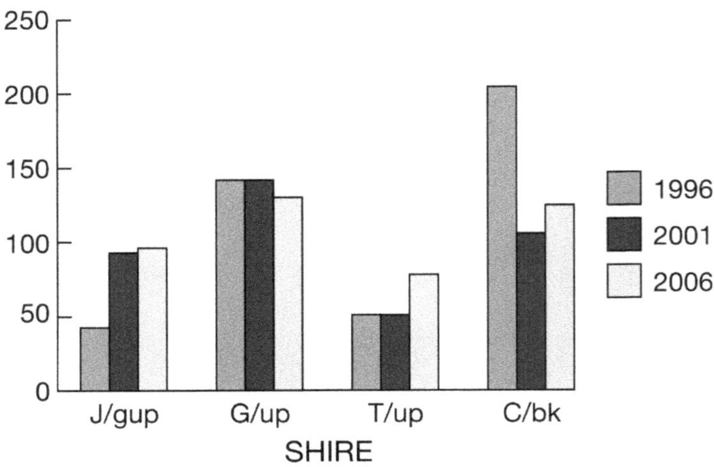


There have been many predictions by the City of Albany that the population will continue to increase at 3 per cent per annum in the foreseeable future, and this in turn is placing increasing pressure on the demand for the release of land. The latest data from the 2006 census have, however, challenged such predictions. Nevertheless, the perception of demographic pressure has in fact changed the land usage in the immediate periphery of Albany: peri-urban land is becoming more urban and less rural.

The other important aspect of our brief demographic analysis is the proportion of those in the population aged more than fifty-five years (see above). In a state that is experiencing an unprecedented resources boom, we are also seeing the direct impact on skills shortages and, in the case of agriculture, even less interest in the sector as a long-term career opportunity. Young people are being led away from the sector and into another sector, which appears to offer more future opportunities as well as more immediate income. The latest ABS data put the proportion of the population aged more than fifty-five in the City of Albany at 27.8 per cent and in the Shire of Denmark at 33.4 per cent—which is high compared with the 24 per cent overall for Australia. In their analysis of the whole Australian population, Barr et al. (2005:1) suggest that 'since the 1991 census the rate of exit of older farmers (aged over 60) has been slowly declining. Retirement is being delayed,[5] possibly in response to the fewer numbers of young persons seeking to take over family farms.'

In the same report, Barr et al. also highlighted that the rate of exit of older farmers (aged over sixty) fell during the 1990s. They make the point that farmers 'are retiring later. This appears to be counterbalancing the continued higher rates of exits of younger farmers, causing the median age of exit to again rise towards 58 years of age' (Barr et al. 2005:17).

## Land use

The south coast region of Western Australia has traditionally been viewed as a 'rural' area. In Australian terms, this means that the majority of economic production has been agricultural. As I will explain shortly, this balance is shifting rapidly. Among other important trends in the past decade, in

> the north-eastern part of the subregion, there is a trend towards fewer, larger broad acre farms focusing on traditional and diversified cropping and livestock industries. In the south-western part of the subregion, landholdings are becoming smaller with more focus on intensive and diverse agricultural systems. New industries that have been established or are evolving in the subregion include viticulture, timber production, farm forestry, olives and fishing. The subregion is also renowned for its tourism, recreational and nature conservation values. (SCRIPT 2005:14)

Table 7.1 provides an explanation of current land use.

**Table 7.1 Albany hinterland land use**

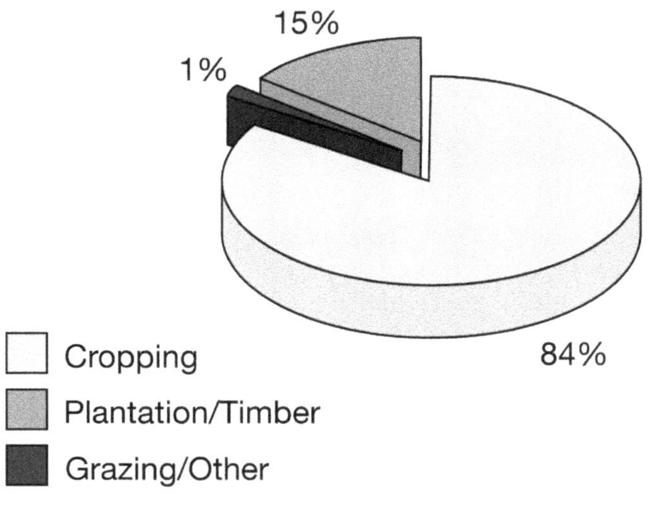


Source: Derived from SCRIPT (2005:78).

The establishment of tree crops in the past decade, particularly in the higher rainfall areas, has marked a significant change in the region's land uses. By far the largest areas have been planted to blue gums. A woodchip plant at Mirambeena, north of Albany, and export facilities at the Port of Albany are now significant contributors to the region's economy (SCRIPT 2005:76).

Some 354 867ha of a total of 617 155ha (57.5 per cent) are in production. It should be noted that in real terms the *value* of agricultural land has remained stable.

There has, however, been a shift, not only in production, but in off-farm activity. In line with the rest of Australia, farmers in the south coast region need to supplement their income, as highlighted in Figure 7.6.

**Figure 7.6 Farm income/off-farm income, south coast region**

| Local Government | Albany | Denmark |
|---|---|---|
| Cropping | 263,311 | 35,841 |
| Dairy | | 321 |
| Grazing | | 3,756 |
| Hardwood | 401 | 250 |
| Plantation forestry | 49,008 | 1,299 |
| Seasonal horticulture | | 22 |
| Softwood | 656 | 2 |

Source: Stehlik (2007).

## A framework for analysis

Having laid out the context, I now turn to an explanation of the framework as proposed by Iaquinta et al. (1999) in their paper for the Sustainable Development Department and the FAO of the United Nations. The purpose of this paper was to establish the effects of demographic ageing on intergenerational transfers of land. It also focuses largely on the developing world, where land tenure is often fragile and not systematised. This framework could assist us in our discussions here and I am therefore going to explain the framework, then use it to discuss the south coast Albany hinterland. Iaquinta et al. (1999) identify six aspects of land and land-associated transfers:

- institutionalisation mechanisms
- property involved
- people involved
- duration of arrangement
- nature of entitlement
- specification of use.

Importantly for our discussion, however, they also identify other types of intergenerational transfers: other 'goods', not just property, which can be transferred between generations. These are important in our intersecting discussion of rural futures, NRM and sustainability. The other types of transfers are:

- ownership and control of non-land resources (such as money, financial investments, water rights, stock, and so on)
- control of information and membership of information networks (social, trade, political, and so on)
- formal and quasi-formal positions in a community.

In regard to the last category, the framework highlights the 'relevant privileges and rights, as far as control over the transfer [of this capital] rests with the current occupant and is not subject to a formal authorisation mechanism [such as elections, and so on]' (Iaquinta et al. 1999:4). I will return to these issues again in the discussion. The authors then discuss the mechanisms through which intergenerational transfers can be affected by the ageing of the population. They have identified 10 categories, and then asked some questions to enable analysis as follows:

- change the timing of the transfer
- change the duration of the transfer
- change the mix of assets transferred
- change the completeness of the transfer
- change the generations involved in the transfer
- change in who makes the decision to transfer
- change the usual recipient of the transfer
- change the value of the goods to be transferred
- change the relevance of the transfer to the intended recipient
- changes in settings where communal lands dominate.

## Intergenerational transitions

I want to highlight a couple of these points for more detailed discussion within the context of the south coast region: changing the timing of the transfer and changing the mix of assets transferred.

## Change the timing of the transfer

Both points are relevant to my argument that it is *more* than the land itself that is transferred. Iaquinta et al. (1999) point out that as life expectancy increases, the transition time changes. In addition, in developed countries, the 'empty nest' and the fluctuations of agricultural production also mean that, in many cases, the next generation has already left the farm well before there is any serious contemplation of transfer. It is often difficult to entice the younger generation to return to the property and, in many cases, current farmers are often reluctant to pass on the stress and uncertainty. Research in Queensland and New South Wales in the mid 1990s highlighted the dilemma that many farmers felt about their role as 'stewards' for their children on the one hand, and the demands and stresses they were themselves experiencing on the other, which they felt reluctant to 'pass on' as an inheritance (Stehlik et al. 1999).

We are already well aware that rural land management tends not to be able to afford employed labour. In the WA south coast region, evidence suggests that any instrumental 'transfer' of property is therefore more likely to be a sale—often to a neighbour[6] —who of course is usually also within the age range that we are considering. This is linked to a trend towards larger properties in the north-western part of the Albany hinterland. The other aspect of timing is that changes in agricultural production—evident in the south coast particularly in relation to plantation timber, grape production for wine and smaller properties with more 'boutique'-style horticulture—appear to be more attractive than traditional broadacre systems, and can, of course, be carried out closer to the regional centres (thus enabling a combining of lifestyle with off-farm income potential). Across the Great Southern region itself, the median size of properties has reduced by about 16 per cent in the past five years. The pressure is on those who are currently on the property to remain there.

Iaquinta et al. (1999) ask: '[H]ow does population ageing influence the ages of donors and recipients? Do the family life stages of persons involve change with population ageing? Is the recipients' life cycle situation important in relation to agricultural production?'

## Change the mix of assets to be transferred

This aspect is of importance if we are considering 'rural futures'. The transfer by the older generation of social and cultural capital—other than financial capital (that is, the farm)—is very important in relation to any sustainability of the rural sector. As we are all now well aware, social and cultural capital are essential to the integration of networks, trust relationships, mutuality and the essential *health* of any community. This has become an overt issue for those who are focusing on research of increased production:

> [A] major challenge in the agricultural industry is maintaining a positive social fabric. Tensions between the achievement of financial and social goals will prompt some farmers to leave the industry while others will adapt in an attempt to achieve both ends, for example fly-in/fly-out farm management. (Professor D. Pannell, cited in the *Great Southern Farmer*, 28 March – 3 April 2007:7)

One of the positive advantages of the Albany hinterland is that it is relatively accessible to Albany and Denmark and the 'drive-in/drive-out' opportunities could well encourage more intergenerational transitions. Nevertheless, at present, the transition is a fragile one, with there being no strategic planning either within agriculture or within the NRM sectors, while the governance of both sectors remains essentially in the hands of the older generation, and the younger generation does not demand its place at the table. Iaquinta et al. (1999:5) ask (in relation to the developing world), '[W]hat could the elderly gain from such protracted transfers?...[Perhaps] to create intergenerational exchanges while keeping back enough to assure that the process will continue and that the quality of life in their own ageing period will not suffer.'

Is there a similar trend in the Albany hinterland? We do not know and will not know unless detailed empirical research is undertaken. We need to ensure that any discussions about rural futures and NRM start taking a good hard look at who is involved and how the transition of knowledge and power between the generations is being promoted and encouraged. This is not only at the level of government policy, but practically at the level of service delivery, extension and research.

Iaquinta et al. (1999) ask: 'Does population ageing influence the composition of assets that are being transferred between generations? Do the exchange relationships change? Does population ageing affect the gender aspect? What is the impact of these on agricultural production?'

## Some preliminary reflections

How does this present us with possible rural futures?

1. The increasing demand within NRM for 'social sustainability/social indicators'—indeed, social anything—is in large part due to the fact that we have tended to ignore the obvious and focus on what appears more 'simple', namely, the environment. As I mentioned earlier, while there have been any number of risk assessments, and by latest count the south coast NRM has funded many millions of dollars into this activity, they are all limited in scope. The human dimensions associated with NRM and rural Australia, while on the agenda, have yet to receive the comparative funding essential to undertake the empirical detailed work that Iaquinta et al. (1999) called for.

2. It remains unclear where the responsibility for this should lie. Demographic change—like climate change—is difficult to 'box in' or 'silo' into one department or one agency. While the WA Department of Agriculture and Food has always taken primary agency responsibility for farmers, it has tended not to focus on their ageing, but rather on their capacity for production. Its main activity therefore remains extension. Once farmers 'retire' they are no longer included. Linkages at the local level between health, community services, local government, and so on regarding intergenerational transitions are very much in the early stages—and everyone is looking for leadership. Where should it come from? The related issue is how can we continue to capture the expertise, experience and knowledge from the older generation?
3. The transitions from broadacre to boutique farming evident in the Albany hinterland are being promoted through activities such as the 'slow food' movement and farmers' markets, as well as through tourism and the hospitality industry. Could this be indicative of a developing differentiation of 'trendy' agriculture and 'non-trendy' agriculture? If so, what does this mean for food safety?
4. The increasing incorporation of off-farm income into farm families' budgeting does not appear to be slowing. Despite the Albany hinterland doing somewhat better than the rest of Western Australia in terms of rainfall, in the period we saw that off-farm income has increased. The proximity of farms to regional centres becomes doubly important—not just for such employment opportunities, but to enable the work/life balance so essential for future social cohesion and social capital. It appears that the increasing sponge-like impact of larger centres will continue.
5. Will the baby boomers ever give up power? What kind of intergenerational transitions will Australia experience in the next 25 years? How will these be played out? What is the importance of 'place' in such transitions? We simply do not know yet.
6. Finally, what impact will these intergenerational shifts have on the assumptions we have made about the governance of NRM in the future? So much of south coast NRM governance is in the hands of the older generation now. We need to be thinking about what transitions will take place.

## Conclusions

Iaquinta et al. (1999), while focusing on the developing world, offer some questions pertinent to our contemplation of rural futures in Australia. From the time of presenting this paper to the seminar to its publication, a new Federal Government has taken office and rural Australia waits anxiously to see what impact the new Labor Government will have on rural policy, NRM governance and the general ageing of the population. In the meantime, the drought along the eastern seaboard has eased after widespread flooding, while drought continues to be declared in the northern half of the West Australian wheatbelt. Western Australia's rural futures are still dependent on the current and continuing resources boom as the skills shortage in the agricultural sector becomes more acute. Australia's rural futures remain unpredictable and vulnerable to the vagaries not only of climate variability, but to rural policies and demographic change.

## Bibliography

Argent, N. 1999, 'Inside the black box: dimensions of gender, generation and scale in the Australian rural restructuring process', *Journal of Rural Studies*, vol. 15, no. 1, pp. 1–15.

Arkle, P. 2003, Submission to the Department of Agriculture, Fisheries and Forestry—Australia (AFFA), Agriculture Advancing Australia (AAA) Review, Policy Manager—Rural Affairs, National Farmers Federation, viewed 10 July 2007, <http://www.nff.org.au/pages/sub/AAA%20Review%20Submission.pdf>

Australian Bureau of Statistics (ABS) 2007, *2006 Census Quick Stats. Denmark. Albany*, Australian Bureau of Statistics.

Barr, N., Karunaratne, K. and Wilkinson, R. 2005, *Australia's Farmers: Past, present and future*, Land and Water Australia, Canberra, viewed May 2007, <http://products.lwa.gov.au/files/PR050941.pdf>

Foskey, R. n.d., *Australian Agriculture, Ageing and Adaptation: At the forefront of a world-wide phenomenon?*, Institute for Rural Futures, University of New England, Armidale, New South Wales, viewed 10 July 2007, <http://netenergy.dpie.gov.au/corporate_docs/publications/word/industry_dev/aaa/australian_ag_ageing_adaptation.doc>

Government of Western Australia n.d., *Indicators of Regional Development in WA*, Government of Western Australia, Perth.

Government of Western Australia 1998, *Environment Western Australia 1998. State of the Environment Report*, Department of Environmental Protection, Perth.

Government of Western Australia 2002, *Population characteristics and trends. Update. Western Australia's seniors*, Topic Sheet No. 1, edn 2, Government of Western Australia, Perth.

Government of Western Australia 2004, *A Profile of Western Australia's Seniors*, Government of Western Australia, Perth.

Iaquinta, D., du Guemy, J. and Stloukal, L. 1999, *Linkages Between Rural Population Ageing, Intergenerational Transfers of Land and Agricultural Production: Are they important? SD dimensions*, Sustainable Development Department, Food and Agriculture Organisation of the United Nations, viewed 18 January 2007, <http://www.fao.org/sd/wpdirect/wpan0039.htm>

SCRIPT 2005, *South Coast Strategy for Natural Resource Management—2004–2009*, SCRIPT, Albany.

Stehlik, D. 2007, *Whose sea-change? Some reflections on transformations in the City of Albany*, Sustaining Gondwana Working Paper Series, Issue 2, April, Curtin University of Technology, Perth.

Stehlik, D., Lawrence, G. and Gray, I. 1999, *Drought in the 1990s. Australian farm families' experiences*, Rural Industries Research and Development Corporation No. 99/14, Canberra.

Voyce, M. 1996, 'Ideas of rural property in Australia', in G. Lawrence, K. Lyons and S. Momtaz (eds), *Social Change in Rural Australia*, Central Queensland University, Rockhampton, pp. 95–105.

Voyce, M. 1999, 'How ya gunna keep 'em down on the farm? Giving it all away: the role of the State in the intergenerational exchange of the farm', *Alternative Law Journal*, vol. 24, no. 1, pp. 22–9.

## Endnotes

[1] NRM implies the legislative and institutional governance of natural resource management activities in Australia.

[2] In the context of the discussion at the symposium, the 'workforce' is predicated on a definition of work as paid and unpaid.

[3] Further discussion of Australian rural ideologies can be found in companion chapters.

[4] All details are drawn from SCRIPT (2005).

[5] Confirmed by a recent University of Tasmania study reported in *The Australian* (12 July 2007).

[6] There is also some evidence that farms are being bought for investment and managed by external companies.

# 8

# Under the regulatory radar? Nanotechnologies and their impacts for rural Australia

**Kristen Lyons and Gyorgy Scrinis**

## Abstract

Nanotechnology is the latest platform technology to capture the imagination of the agricultural and food industries, with applications being adopted across these entire sectors. With companies such as Kraft Foods and H. J. Heinz investing heavily in nanotechnology research and development, industry commentators have suggested that the global nano-agri-food sector will, by 2010, be worth in excess of US$20 billion. While the nano-revolution is well under way, however, the entry of nanotechnologies into paddocks and onto our plates has occurred largely beneath the policy and regulatory radars. As such, agricultural inputs and food items that contain nano-materials are unlabelled, thereby preventing consumers from differentiating between nano-products and their non-nano counterparts. This situation persists, despite a mounting body of scientific evidence pointing to potential health and environmental risks associated with the manufacture of, and exposure to, nano-materials.

While proponents of nanotechnology promise a range of benefits across the agri-food sector, this chapter considers the potential impact of the unfettered introduction of agriculture and food-related nanotechnologies on Australian rural communities. To date, this issue has received little recognition in the emerging debates. Our chapter contributes to these critical discussions by highlighting a range of social issues associated with the introduction of nanotechnology for rural Australia within the context of the development and application of nanotechnologies across the agri-food sector. The chapter also identifies potential human and environmental risks for these communities. We argue that a lack of nano-specific regulations could exacerbate a number of these risks.

## Introduction

Nanotechnologies are a panacea for global social and environmental problems—or so industry and governments proclaim. At the same time, critics argue that nanotechnologies could present a range of new risks to human and environmental health and safety (Friends of the Earth 2006a; ETC Group 2003; International Centre for Technology Assessment 2006). Despite these conflicting views, research and development of nanotechnologies are occurring at a rapid pace, with total global investment in 2005 estimated to be worth US$9.6 billion (Lux Research Incorporated 2005). As a result, products derived from nano-techniques or containing nano-materials are already on the market, despite the absence of nano-specific regulations or labelling requirements. The agricultural and food industries are among those to have embraced nanotechnologies, with leading industry commentators suggesting that the nano-agri-food industry will be worth in excess of US$20 billion by 2010 (Helmut Kaiser 2004).

Even at this early stage, nanotechnologies are being developed for applications from paddock to the plate and promise to bring profound impacts for people and the environment. It is anticipated, for example, that within the short to medium term, farmers will have access to a new range of 'smart' inputs and products, including nano-seed varieties with in-built pesticides that will release by remote control or under specific environmental conditions (ETC Group 2003a). It is anticipated that nano-cochleates and nano-encapsulation techniques[1] will enable consumers to select foods that match their personal tastes and physiological requirements. These applications of nanotechnologies across the agri-food sector will have specific impacts for rural communities. People living in rural communities are, and will increasingly be, directly exposed to nano-agri-food applications, as food producers, residents and consumers.

Despite the potential human and environmental health and safety issues for the whole society, including rural communities, there is an absence of federal nano-specific regulations to oversee research through to the commercial application of nanotechnologies, including those relating directly to the agri-food sector (Marchant and Sylvester 2006; Bowman and Hodge 2007a). As explored in this chapter, however, nanotechnology poses a number of regulatory challenges for rural Australians—challenges that are similarly faced by rural communities globally. In this chapter, we examine the current and projected social, health and environmental impacts associated with the emerging nano-agri-food industry. It is argued that the current regulatory gaps in relation to nanotechnology have the potential to exacerbate potential risks and adverse impacts. Our chapter concludes that there is a clear need for governments, including the Australian Government, to implement nano-specific regulations, which minimise the potential adverse impacts of nanotechnology to humans and the environment, including rural communities, while also taking into account the views and concerns of citizens.

## Technological change in rural Australia

There is a history of technological innovation in agriculture and agri-food production. The latest of these technological innovations include the new genetic and cellular plant and animal breeding and reproduction techniques, information and satellite technologies and the continued evolution of chemical inputs and mechanical technologies. The products of these technological innovations have been diverse: novel seed and animal varieties, new varieties of chemical pesticides, fertilisers and veterinary drugs, the ability to manage ever larger scale farming operations and the reduced dependence on farm labourers for specific tasks (Bonanno et al. 1994; Busch et al. 1991; Goodman et al. 1987). Many new technologies have been promoted with promises of increased productivity, improved efficiency, greater precision, reduced costs for industry and consumers alike, economies of scale and, ultimately, increased profitability for industry. New technologies have also been promoted by some in terms of their claimed environmental benefits, such as the reduction in the use of chemical inputs and water, alongside growing concerns about some specific environmental problems in recent years (Huang et al. 2003). In short, agri-food technological innovations have been continually proclaimed as a social and environmental panacea for rural communities.

Successive waves of technological development have been the primary drivers of change in not only the technical means and practices of production, but in the structures and cultures of production. The increasing scale of production and size of farms, the decline in the number of farm families and rural communities and the increasing control that agri-food input suppliers exercise over farmers have all been facilitated by technological innovation (Lawrence 1987; McMichael 1999). One of the characteristics of this technology-driven mode of production is the technological treadmill that farmers have been on for the past century—whereby farmers and other food producers are compelled to quickly adopt the latest tools and products of innovation to remain competitive—from the mechanical and chemical treadmills, to the genetic and information technology treadmills, and now the nano-treadmill.

While it is claimed that modern biotechnology has been to date the 'latest and perhaps most fundamental innovative technology to be applied to the agri-food sector' (Phillips 2002:504), the convergence of nanotechnology with the food and food-processing sectors is anticipated to further revolutionise agricultural production. Nanotechnology represents a new techno-scientific *platform* that will potentially facilitate technological innovation across all agricultural inputs, practices and products of the agri-food system.

Nanotechnology commonly refers to any engineered materials, structures and systems that operate at a scale of 100 nanometres or less (one nanometre is one-billionth of a metre, or $10^{-9}$). At this scale, nano-materials, relative to the same material at a larger size, have significantly different chemical reactivity, electrical conductivity, strength, mobility, solubility and magnetic and optical properties (Royal Society and Royal Academy of Engineering 2004). In order to exploit these novel properties, nano-scale techniques, equipment and products are being developed and applied across a range of scientific disciplines and technological forms, including chemistry, physics, biotechnology, information technology and engineering. The production of a range of engineered nanoparticles, including tubes, dots and fullerenes, has dominated the first wave of nanotechnology applications, offering aesthetical and functional improvements to conventional products. Nanoparticles have been incorporated into a wide range of everyday products, ranging from paints and cosmetics to electronics and car tyres (Woodrow Wilson 2007). It is anticipated that this 'first generation' will be followed by second, third and fourth generations of manipulating and reconstituting materials and living organisms at the nano-scale, and the construction of objects and systems from the 'bottom up'.

Nanotechnology has captured the imagination of the agri-food sector, with leading food and agri-chemical companies such as Kraft Foods, H. J. Heinz and Syngenta all racing to get a slice of the nano-pie. Established in 2000, Kraft's global research consortium of 15 university and private laboratories, 'NanoteK', reflects the corporate drive behind the nano-agri-food sector (Kuzma and VerHage 2006; Rowan 2004). The ETC Group (2004a) reports that nanotech materials and products being researched and commercialised include seed and animal breeding applications, nano-pesticides, remote sensing and precision farming technologies, as well as food processing, packaging and retailing applications.

A commercially available example of nanotechnology being used in the agri-food sector is a new generation of chemical pesticides or 'nano-pesticides'. These include nano-scale chemical pesticide emulsions and nano-encapsulation techniques. One strategy for producing nano-pesticides is to take an existing chemical pesticide—particularly one that already has received regulatory approval for environmental release—and to reduce the size of the active molecules to the nano-scale. This reduction in scale can give the pesticide new and beneficial properties for pest control, such as increased dissolvability in water, increased stability, the capacity for absorption into plants or increased toxicity to pests. The global agribusiness company Syngenta—with global sales of more than US$8.05 billion in 2006—already retails a number of pesticides with emulsions containing nanoparticles, including Primo MAXX Plant Growth Regulator and Banner MAXX Fungicide (ETC 2004b).

In contrast, nano-encapsulation techniques are utilised to create nano-scale capsules, which are designed to transport chemical substances such as toxins. The nano-scale capsules can be designed to release in specific environmental or physiological environments, such as inside the stomach of an insect. These 'smart' pesticides could provide more precise, controlled and effective use of pesticides, and therefore potentially reduce the overall quantities of pesticide used. Nano-sensors are 'smart' nano-scale particles that are able to be engineered to provide real-time monitoring of situations and for gathering information on the nutrient levels of soils, water availability and the presence of pests and pathogens affecting plant and animal growth. Nano-sensors will provide information to computer-controlled, GPS-guided, precision-farming systems. These nano-sensors could potentially be scattered and distributed widely over farming landscapes.

## Approaches to nano-regulation and its limits

As noted earlier, agri-food nanotechnologies are being promoted with promises of increased productivity, profitability and environmental sustainability. At this early stage in the development and commercialisation of nanotechnology-based products, however, considerable uncertainty exists as to the extent to which these social, economic and environmental claims will be realised, and over what timelines. Scientific uncertainty also exists over the potential hazards posed by engineered nanoparticles (Aitken et al. 2004; Oberdörster et al. 2005), with Maynard (2006:10) noting, for instance, that 'certain nanoparticles may move easily into sensitive lung tissues after inhalation, and cause damage that can lead to chronic breathing problems'. Due to these uncertainties, nanotechnologies must be regulated in such a way that ensures that the supposed benefits are not overshadowed by the potential risks (Bowman and Fitzharris 2007). Bearing this balancing act in mind, this chapter now turns to an examination of how nanotechnologies are currently regulated within Australia. This approach will be briefly compared with regulatory developments occurring elsewhere.

As stated by van Calster (2006:360), 'nanotechnology will never go "unregulated". In other words, it will never be a "lawless" technology. Ordinary principles of law will apply to nanotechnology.' Accordingly, Marchant and Sylvester (2006) and Bowman and Hodge (2007b) have pointed to a range of legislative and regulatory mechanisms for 'regulating' nanotechnology across the various stages of its life cycle, from research and development through to disposal. With the majority of these frameworks having been in existence for some time, however, leading commentators have begun to question the suitability of these regulatory frameworks in relation to nanotechnology. Bowman and Hodge (2006:1068) argue that 'while governments have invested heavily in R&D programs they have been noticeably unenthusiastic about implementing new [nano-specific] regulatory frameworks for risk minimisation'.

The increasing use of the nanotechnology label in commercially available products—resulting in increasing public curiosity about the technology, increased media coverage and greater public debate about associated risks and benefits—would appear to have played an important role in stimulating policy action within the Australian Government about the future of nanotechnology in Australia. As discussed by Bowman and Hodge (2007c), these activities are probably best illustrated by the establishment of the National Nanotechnology Strategy Taskforce (NNST) in mid 2005, in order to devise 'a national strategy for development and regulation of the emerging field of nanotechnology' (Macfarlane 2006). The public release of the NNST's report, *Options for a national nanotechnology strategy*, in September 2006 articulated a nine-point plan designed to secure Australia's future role in nanotechnology. Despite the rapidly expanding nano-agri-food industries as outlined above, the report did not address applications of nanotechnology within the agri-food sector or the specific concerns for rural communities alongside the extension of nanotechnologies across rural landscapes. While it has been suggested that the report 'will help to establish a regulatory framework for the development of nanotechnology applications' (Macfarlane 2006), the report explicitly states that 'there is currently no case for establishing any new, nanotechnology specific regulations, but rather, existing regulations may need some adjustments' (NNST 2006:32). The NNST's emphatic rejection of new, nanotechnology-specific regulations can be contrasted with regulatory approaches that have been adopted by Australian governments in respect to other, earlier 'revolutionary' advances, including genetically modified organisms (GMOs). Since 2001, dealings with GMOs have been regulated through a national regulatory scheme, the Gene Technology Regulator, in coordination with other federal regulatory agencies, and supplemented further by state and territory regulations (Ludlow 2004, 2005). As such, the development of specific regulation for new technologies in Australia is clearly not without precedent. The development of such a scheme for nanotechnology, however, could be somewhat more challenging given the potential scope of the technology.

While the NNST did not articulate which regulatory frameworks or how these current provisions could be adjusted, the Australian Government has subsequently published a request for tender for the 'review of the capacity of Australia's regulatory frameworks to manage any potential impacts of nanotechnology' (DITR 2006:4). As noted in the tender document, the focus of the review will be on the health, safety and environmental (HSE) implications of nanotechnologies for Australia in the next 10 years (DITR 2006). Importantly, it would appear that this review will not be limited to Australia's chemical regulatory framework, but will also include consideration of quarantine, agricultural and veterinary chemicals and environmental regulatory frameworks. While it is unclear whether the findings of the review will be made public, it is anticipated that the final report will provide a basis for deciding how best to govern nanotechnology within the Australian context.

Looking further afield, commentators such as Wardark (2003), Davies (2006), Kimbrell (2006) and Taylor (2006) have highlighted the limitations within existing US regulatory frameworks in relation to nanotechnologies, specifically industrial chemicals (as regulated by the Environmental Protection Agency) and cosmetics and foods (as regulated by the Food and Drug Administration). Across the Atlantic, Chaudhry et al. (2006, 2007) have observed a number of gaps in relation to a range of nanotechnology products and applications in respect to the current UK environmental regulations. As observed by Bowman and Hodge (2007b), commentators including Balbus et al. (2006) and Kimbrell (2006) have suggested that one way in which governments could easily address these gaps is through the introduction of nano-specific provisions within existing national legislation. Others believe that more is needed in order to protect human and environmental health and safety concerns. Bowman and Hodge (2007b) note, for instance, that leading non-governmental organisation Friends of the Earth (2006b) has advocated that a new, nano-specific framework is needed to address the current risks, uncertainties and complexities of nanotechnologies. Others have gone further. Since as early as 2002, the US-based Action Group on Erosion, Technology and Concentration (the ETC Group) has repeatedly called for a moratorium on the commercial production of new nano-materials until an appropriate regulatory framework is implemented (ETC Group 2002, 2003b, 2004b).

Amid these growing calls for regulatory action, in December 2006, the City of Berkeley in California took regulatory action into its own hands by amending the hazardous materials and waste management sections of its municipal code to explicitly include 'manufactured nanoparticles' under its scope (Del Vecchio 2006; Associated Press 2006a, 2006b; Monica et al. 2007). The amendments, which were reportedly in response to the city council's concerns about current occupational practices within two local laboratories, and the potentially hazardous nature of nanoparticles (Del Vecchio 2006), imposed 'comprehensive disclosure requirements on companies that manufacture or use manufactured nanoparticles within the city' (Monica et al. 2007:68). These requirements do not extend, however, to federally funded laboratories within the city's limits, including, for example, the University of California at Berkeley. While the effectiveness of these amendments is unknown at this time, it has been reported that other US cities are currently in the process of reviewing their own municipal codes in order to specifically regulate nanoparticles within their own jurisdictions (Williams 2007; Bowman and Hodge 2007b).

## Agri-food nanotechnologies and their social impacts for rural Australia

While the nano-regulatory debate continues to gather momentum nationally and internationally, Australian rural communities are already engaging with agri-food nanotechnologies. Nanotechnology can be found in paddocks and on plates, exposing rural people to nanotechnologies as producers and consumers. This exposure is likely to increase as investment in agri-food nanotechnologies expands. This chapter now turns to an overview of the current and likely social impacts and the potential human and environmental risks associated with the application of nanotechnologies across agri-food industries. It is argued that there is a fundamental need for the public to be actively engaged and involved in shaping nanotechnology policy, including the development of regulatory responses to address the current limitations within Australia's regulatory frameworks.

As with previous technological innovations, the agricultural and food industries assert sweeping claims about the social benefits that will arise from nanotechnologies. Proponents present nanotechnology as a miracle cure for problems as diverse as world hunger, homelessness and protecting national security. Dunkley (2004:1131), for example, declares that through applications of nanotechnology, '[f]ood could be replicated. Starvation and hunger could be eliminated from the globe.' In a less bold approach, Roco and Bainbridge (2005:3) claim that '[n]anotechnology will help ensure that we can produce enough food by improving inventory storage and the ability to grow at high yield and a diversity of crops locally'. In the nano-agri-food sector, agricultural producers have been made a range of promises related to their uptake of nanotechnologies, including a reduction in the costs of farming and chemical use, alongside an increase in farm productivity, while the promised benefits to consumers include safer and more nutritious food (Weiss et al. 2006).

Despite the promises, there is a conspicuous gap in publicly available data to substantiate these claims. According to Sandler and Kay (2006:679), '[w]hile scientists and industry leaders may be "elite" in their knowledge of the science and business of nanotechnology, this status does not imply that they are "elite" with respect to the SEI [social and ethical issues] associated with nanotechnology'. Research into social and ethical dimensions of nanotechnologies attracts little resources from government and industry, leaving us with little understanding of these complex issues. In their evaluation of the National Nanotechnology Initiative (NNI), Sandler and Kay (2006) found 4 per cent of funding (or US$48 million) was directed towards ethical, legal and social (ELS) research, representing the minimum legal requirement for ELS research under the *21st Research and Development Act* (Public Law 108-153). They also found that social research that was funded through the NNI was directed into building public support and acceptance of nanotechnology, rather than deepening public understanding and engagement in nanotechnology debates, or directing nanotechnology applications towards the public good. This mandated funding of ELS research related to nanotechnologies within the United States could be contrasted with the current situation in Australia. For instance, while the NNST (2006:33) recognised the need to 'support HSE research in Australia and to support involvement in international HSE studies', it did not go as far as suggesting that the Federal Government allocate a specific percentage of all nanotechnology research and development funding towards such research. While there is clearly support within government to support these fundamental areas of research, any such investment in research related to these fields is more likely to occur in an ad hoc manner. Accordingly, it is difficult to understand how rural Australians—and Australians more generally—will be affected by this 'revolutionary' technology.

The Australian Government's inadequate response, including to ELS issues within the nanotechnology research agenda, is likely to limit the capacity to identify and/or address the social impacts associated with the application of agri-food nanotechnologies. The current regulatory arena related to nanotechnologies also inhibits the capacity to effectively identify the extent to which farmers are already engaging with nanotechnologies—including applications in plant and animal breeding, pesticides, precision farming and animal disease protection. While a search of patent databases might provide information related to what companies are researching and patenting, this painstaking process is time consuming and difficult.

Nanotechnologies—including pesticides, seeds and monitoring devices—are likely to exacerbate the cost of farming, by extending farmers' dependence on costly off-farm inputs. Australian farm families frequently suffer financial hardship, which is accentuated by declining terms of trade, rising oil prices and long-term drought conditions (Almas and Lawrence 2003). The extension of nanotechnologies into the agri-input sector has the potential to exacerbate some farmers' financial burden. While early adopters of nanotechnologies might experience a reduction in farming costs, other farmers could suffer increased costs—in the form of new inputs and technologies. While smaller producers might struggle to manage these increased input costs, leading multinational agri-chemical companies such as Syngenta, which has positioned itself at the forefront of nanotechnology research and development, appear to have already begun reaping the profits from the burgeoning nano-agri-food industry. For instance, while current regulatory frameworks do not recognise reformulated nano-pesticides as 'new' products for the purposes of risk evaluation, it would appear that national intellectual property regimes might consider such products as 'new' for the purposes of patent production. The ETC Group (2004a) has argued, for instance, that the reformulation of a product to nano-scale could enable a company to extend the patent protection period for the pesticide, thereby providing the company with exclusive rights over the product for up to another 20 years. In short, the uptake of agri-food nanotechnologies is set to concentrate economic power among corporate actors in the agri-food industry, while providing new financial burdens for farm families (Scrinis and Lyons 2007).

At the same time, the uptake of nano-agri-inputs—including pesticides and seeds produced via the convergence of nanotechnologies and genetic engineering[2] —appears destined to further entrench chemical and genetic systems of agriculture. The nano-treadmill reduces the options for low-input (cost-neutral) and organic farming systems. At the farm level, the application of nanotechnologies will appropriate space that could otherwise be cultivated utilising low external input or organic farming techniques. Farmers could be constrained from adopting low-input or organic farming by a range of controls, including patents and licensing fees that could lock them into using nanotechnologies. This could be similar to genetic engineering (GE), in which intellectual property rights have locked many farmers into the purchase of GE seeds each planting season, rather than relying on traditional seed-saving techniques. In addition, intellectual property rights require farmers to ensure they do not 'illegally' obtain privately owned GE—and now nano—material through pollen drift, cross-species transfer, and so on; while in terms of research, investment in nano-agri-food applications will likely occur at the expense of research into alternative—low-cost and low-input—farming systems (see Jones 2004).

Ownership of nano-agri-inputs by the corporate sector is also privatising new forms of agricultural and farming knowledge. Nanotechnologies will enable corporate actors to hold and control new forms of specialist knowledge, including capabilities to detect pH levels, moisture, pests and disease. This could in turn displace farmers' traditional knowledge and techniques (Miller and Kinnear 2007). At the same time that nanotechnologies could marginalise farmers' knowledge and skills, the transformation of farm work through the uptake of nano-agri-inputs could also reduce the importance of farmers and farm workers (Crow and Sarewitz 2001). For example, the integration of nanotechnology with information technology and geographical positioning systems could enable farm management to occur off-site. The ETC Group claims that such technologies will transform the farm into 'a wide area bio-factory that can be monitored and managed from a laptop' (ETC Group 2004a:8). For example, precision-farming technologies—such as seeds with inbuilt pesticides—could be released via remote control when remote nano-sensors detect pest infestation. This is likely to transform the nature of farm work and, with it, the identity of Australian farmers and farm workers.

The application of nanotechnologies to the Australian agri-food sector is also likely to pose challenges for farmers wishing to access the international market. The lack of nano-specific regulations across the world at this stage means that there are no additional constraints on domestic and international trade of agricultural goods produced using nanotechnologies. This situation could change, however, if and when national governments amend their current regulatory frameworks to specifically address nanotechnologies. As the first wave of nano-specific amendments to regulatory frameworks are likely to occur at the national level, rather than at the regional or international levels—despite harmonisation efforts by a number of multilateral bodies—Australian producers wishing to export their agricultural products could be required to conform to a number of different regulatory standards in order to access different markets. This could bring additional costs and bureaucratic procedures for Australian farmers wishing to export.

Consumer concerns regarding the potential risks could be of equal concern to Australian producers of nano-based agricultural goods. Fears in relation to GM foods within, for example, the European Union had a devastating effect on the sector (Bauer and Gaskell 2002). While public awareness of nanotechnology remains limited in Australia, the European Union and the United States (see, for example, Market Attitudes Research Services 2004; Mee et al. 2004; Gaskell et al. 2006; Cobb and Macoubrie 2004; Woodrow Wilson 2006), the prospects of a backlash against nano-foods would appear to be minimal at the present time. As consumers become increasingly knowledgeable about the technology, however, or if a nano-food scare makes its way to the front pages of the daily newspapers, the prospect of a consumer backlash is likely to increase. These market and consumer issues exacerbate economic vulnerability in rural communities.

## Human health risks from nanotechnologies

Nanotechnology applications in the agri-food sector could also give rise to a number of potential health problems for rural communities in their roles as agricultural producers, as rural residents and as food consumers. To begin, people living and working in rural communities will be exposed to engineered nanoparticles—including in the form of nano-pesticides and nano-sensors. These could pose a number of health risks for rural communities. The combination of nano-pesticides and nano-seeds in rural landscapes further extends the unpredictability of adverse health impacts. The Royal Society and Royal Academy of Engineering (2004) has warned of the potential human health risks of nano-toxicity. Reflecting these concerns, the International Union of Food, Farm and Hotel Workers has called for a moratorium on nanotechnology until the effects of human exposure to nano-materials are more thoroughly understood (Friends of the Earth 2007).

Nanotechnology applications in the agri-food sector could also pose social and health problems for rural communities in their role as food consumers. As previously stated, the current lack of nano-specific regulations or labelling requirements for food containing nano-ingredients enables producers of foods to replace conventional ingredients in commercial food products with nano-scale ingredients without triggering regulatory oversight. This poses a plethora of questions relating to the potential health risks of ingesting nano-materials (see, for instance, Swiss Re 2004). We know an Australian bakery currently selling a loaf of bread that contains nano-capsules of Omega 3 that are derived from tuna-fish oil, which is marketed as 'Tip Top Up'. The fish oil is encapsulated in a tasteless calcium and soybean lipid matrix that is made available only when the nano-capsules reach the stomach (Tip Top n.d.). Food industries argue that nano-capsules will improve the delivery of nutrients in processed foods (Kuzma and VerHage 2006). Similarly, the application of nano-cochleates could enable the release of encapsulated nutrients in targeted and specific ways, in response to individual consumers' needs (Gardener 2002). Proponents of these technologies argue that nano-capsules and nano-cochleates will increase the nutrient density of foods and the match between people's nutrient requirements (for example, for calcium or iron) and food consumption. Despite the claims, such novel foods could present a range of health risks to food consumers, the majority of which researchers are only beginning to examine (Rooker 2006). While it is widely accepted that materials behave differently and express different character traits at the nano-scale, experts disagree about what this means for exposure or ingestion of nano-materials.

As previously stated, the current lack of nano-specific labelling requirements for food that contains nano-scale ingredients has ensured that the number, or indeed identity, of commercially available nano-foods in Australia and elsewhere remains unknown. For consumers, the lack of mandatory labelling has ensured that consumers are unable to identify food derived from nanotechnologies and prevents the exercise of informed choice about the food that they consume. Despite the obvious difficulties therefore in predicting this figure, the Helmut Kaiser Consultancy Group reported that, by 2005, there were already more than 300 nano-food products in the international food market, and that sales of nano-food and packaging were valued at US$5.3 billion. The consultants anticipate that this figure will rise to US$20.4 billion by 2010, alongside the expansion of the nano-food industry.

## The environmental impacts of nanotechnological innovation for rural Australia

Alongside the social and potential health issues detailed above, there is a range of environmental issues and concerns associated with expanding nanotech innovation across the agri-food sector.

With the escalating and imminent problems associated with climate change, drought and declining water availability, as well as soil erosion and salinity problems, the need to transform the ecological relations of agricultural production has never been more pressing. In this context, nanotech applications and products are being strongly promoted on the basis of their environmental benefits and as enabling the shift to environmentally sustainable forms of production and consumption. In the agricultural sector, the general promise is for the development of more efficient, precise, flexible and adaptable systems of food production that will enable a more efficient and reduced use of chemicals, water and energy inputs.

Proponents of nano-agricultural innovations state the application of nanotechnologies will enable agricultural production to adapt to changing environmental and resource conditions. Proponents promise more efficient and safer chemical pesticides and fertilisers, and overall a more efficient and productive system that will minimise the use of pesticides, fertiliser and water inputs, including the more targeted use of chemical inputs, thereby reducing chemical pollution of the environment. These outcomes could be achieved by the introduction of 'smart' nano-pesticides able to be released in more controlled and precise ways; nano-sensors able to detect and inform a precise response to changing soil, water and pest conditions; and crops better adapted to particular environments. Among these high-tech visions of a smart, lean, green and efficient nano-industrial agricultural system, there has been little acknowledgment of or debate about the prospect of any specifically new environmental hazards that nano-agricultural innovations pose.

In considering the environmental implications of nanotech innovations in agricultural production, a distinction can be drawn between the impact on existing environmental problems on the one hand, and the possible introduction of a new range of environmental problems on the other. In terms of existing environmental issues, problems and dynamics—such as pollution from chemical pesticides and fertilisers, high water usage, soil degradation and diminishing biodiversity—the question is whether nanotechnology will exacerbate or alleviate some of these agro-ecological problems. Here we need to consider the case-by-case impacts of each innovation. There is, however, also the broader question of the type of agricultural production that nanotech innovation is likely to be used to support, and what are the environmental consequences of maintaining and entrenching this type of production. At the same time, nanotechnology potentially introduces an entirely new set of environmental hazards and risks, including the prospect of an entirely new form of environmental pollution: nano-pollution. In particular, there are immediate concerns relating to the release of nano-scale particles into the environment, such as nano-pesticides and nano-sensors, as well as concerns about the release of nano-engineered living organisms into the environment.

In the case of nano-pesticides, it is the very small scale of these nano-pesticidal compounds, in conjunction with a number of other physiochemical parameters including shape, particle size, crystalline structure and surface chemistry, that poses potentially greater toxicity and eco-toxicity risks in comparison with conventional chemical pesticides. The increased toxicity of some nano-scale toxins could mean greater harm not only to pests, but to all other living organisms—animals and humans. The ability for these nano-scale particles to penetrate the surface of plants could mean that pesticides also penetrate edible parts of the crop. Their size and dissolvability could mean that they contaminate soils and waterways across a wide area or travel into and affect other food chains.

Encapsulated pesticides could similarly be washed away and release their toxins in other environments, or even in the stomachs of other living organisms.

Despite concerns about the potential risks of nano-pesticides, the reformulation of a previously approved pesticide through the nano-sizing of active ingredients is likely to be considered by the regulator as an 'existing' product for the purposes of the regulatory framework. As such, despite the new properties exhibited by the nano-pesticide when compared with its conventional counterpart, the nano-pesticide will not have to be evaluated by a regulatory body on the basis of potential risks before it may be imported or manufactured in Australia.

Nano-pesticides are one of a number of new strategies being used to address the problems of the declining efficacy of older-style chemical pesticides, combined with the inevitable rising price of petrochemical-based inputs. Genetically engineered, insecticide-producing crops (that is, *Bt* crops) and genetically engineered herbicide-tolerant crops are other responses that have been implemented to create more precise and efficient forms of pesticide delivery. All these strategies maintain and entrench the toxic chemical approach to the control of insects, pathogens and weeds. Any efficiency gains and reductions in overall chemical usage will be portrayed as bringing environmental benefits, but they can equally be understood as providing ideological legitimation for the continuation of chemically dependent farming systems.

The large-scale release of nanoparticle-sized nano-sensors also raises a number of environmental concerns. Will they be biodegradable? What are the consequences of having these nano-sensors washed into soils, waterways and throughout the food chain? Their small scale means they could penetrate deeply into materials or living organisms.. There are also unlikely to be any regulations covering the release of these nano-sensors on the farm, since they would not fall under the banner, for example, of chemical inputs or novel living organisms.

Given that nano-sensors are likely to primarily support the growth of very large-scale, capital-intensive and chemical-intensive farming operations—usually at the expense of smaller-scale operations—we also need to ask what the long-term environmental implications of these technology-facilitated structural changes might be.

## Conclusion: developing a nano-regulatory agenda that engages with social, health and environmental issues

Nanotechnologies are being applied across the entire agri-food system. From remote nano-sensors and nano-seeds at the farm gate, to nano-packaging and nano-'super' foods on supermarket shelves and kitchen tables, nanotechnologies have captured the imagination of the agricultural and food industries. Many of these applications have already found their way onto the market. The scale of investment from the agri-food industries suggests the variety and quantity of nano-food products is set to expand rapidly in the next few years.

The overview of current approaches to the regulation of nanotechnology-based products and applications within the agri-food sector highlights how many commercial nanotech applications are falling beneath Australia's regulatory radar, and as such, are not adequately covered by the current regulatory frameworks. The patchwork of non-nano-specific regulations covers some products and processes to varying degrees, but clear gaps within these regimes have already emerged. As such, it is reasonable to conclude that there is a lack of rigorous review before the commercialisation of some nano-products within the agri-food sector, enabling agri-food nanotechnologies to enter the market untested and unlabelled.

The limits of current approaches to nano-regulation prohibit effective monitoring and mitigation of the potential health and environmental impacts of nanotechnologies. Our chapter demonstrates a diversity of social, health and environmental risks associated with agri-food nanotechnologies. The health and safety risks are particularly acute for rural Australians, due to their multiple roles as food producers, rural residents and food consumers. People living and working in rural communities will be, for example, directly exposed to engineered nanoparticles of which little is known about their potential toxicological effects. At the same time, nanotechnologies could give rise to new eco-toxicological effects within rural environments, posing new threats to the health of soils and water, as well as biodiversity. Rural Australians also face health risks in their role as food consumers—through the ingestion of nano-foods and food stored in new nanotechnologies (for example, nano-packaging, nano-fridges, and so on).

Looking more broadly at the social issues, nanotechnology is likely to impact on many rural producers due to the likely increased costs of purchasing such inputs. Farmers who adopt nano-seeds, nano-pesticides and other technologies also face the likelihood that their produce will be rejected in some markets, similar to the bans imposed on genetically engineered foodstuffs.

Governments and industry are currently portraying agricultural nanotechnologies as environmentally and socially responsible farming technologies, suggesting that they will bring financial benefits to the farming community. It is likely some farmers will choose to adopt nanotechnologies as part of their farming practices on these grounds, despite the potential health and environmental risks and the broader societal issues associated with nanotechnology. The current patchwork of non-nano-specific regulations, however, appears to be ill equipped to grapple with the complex and challenging array of health and environmental risks presented by nanotechnologies, along with the broader societal considerations raised by the technology.

Australian and other federal governments must begin the process of playing regulatory catch-up in order to protect the health and safety of their citizens, including those within the agri-food sectors. This might involve the revision of current regulatory frameworks, with consideration given to the new complexities and challenges posed by the nanotechnologies, or the formation of a new nano-specific regulatory framework. Revision of nanotechnology regulation will be required to ensure rural communities do not carry a disproportionate level of risk associated with the emerging agri-food nano-industries.

## Acknowledgment

The authors would like to thank Ms Diana Bowman for her insightful comments.

## Bibliography

Aitken, R., Creely, K. and Tran, C. 2004, *Nanoparticles: An occupational hygiene review*, Institute of Occupational Medicine for the Health and Safety Executive, Edinburgh.

Almas, R. and Lawrence, G. 2003, *Globalisation, Localisation and Sustainable Livelihoods*, Ashgate, Aldershot.

Associated Press 2006a, 'City of Berkeley wants to monitor nanotechnology', *Los Angeles Times*, 12 December, p. B1.

Associated Press 2006b, 'Berkeley first city in nation to regulate nanotechnology', *Mercury News*, 13 December.

Balbus, J. M., Florini, K., Denison, R. and Walsh, S. 2006, 'Getting it right the first time—developing nanotechnology while protecting workers, public health and the environment', *Annals of the New York Academy of Science*, vol. 1076, pp. 331–42.

Bauer, M. W. and Gaskell, G. (eds) 2002, *Biotechnology: The making of a global controversy*, Cambridge University Press, London.

Berkeley City Council 2006, Agenda—Berkeley City Council Meeting, 5 December, Berkeley City Council, Berkeley.

Bonanno, A., Busch, L., Friedland, W., Gouveia, L. and Mingione, E. 1994, 'Introduction', in A. Bonanno, L. Busch. W. Friedland, L. Gouveia and E. Mingione (eds), *From Columbus to ConAgra. The globalisation of agriculture and food*, University Press of Kansas, United States, pp. 1–26.

Bowman, D. and Fitzharris, M. 2007, 'Too small for concern? Public health and nanotechnology', *Australian and New Zealand Journal of Public Health*, vol. 31, no. 4, pp. 382–4.

Bowman, D. and Hodge, G. 2006, 'Nanotechnology: mapping the wild regulatory frontier', *Futures*, vol. 38, pp. 1060–73.

Bowman, D. and Hodge, G. 2007a, 'A small matter of regulation: an international review of nanotechnology regulation', *Columbia Science and Technology Law Review*, vol. 8, pp. 1–32.

Bowman, D. and Hodge, G. 2007b, Governing nanotechnology without government?, Paper presented at the Law and Society in the 21st Century Conference, Berlin, 25–28 July.

Bowman, D. and Hodge, G. 2007c, 'Nanotechnology "down under": getting on top of regulatory matters', *Nanotechnology Law & Business*, vol. 4, no. 2, pp. 223–33.

Busch, L., Lacy, W., Burkhardt, J. and Lacy, L. 1991, *Plants, Power, and Profit: Social, economic, and ethical consequences of the new biotechnologies*, Basil Blackwell, Cambridge.

Chaudhry, Q., Blackburn, J., Floyd, P., George, C., Nwaogu, T., Boxall, A. and Aitken, R. 2006, *Final Report: A scoping study to identify gaps in environmental regulation for the products and applications of nanotechnologies*, Defra, London.

Chaudhry, Q., George, C. and Watkins, R. 2007, 'Nanotechnology regulation: developments in the United Kingdom', in G. Hodge, D. Bowman and K. Ludlow (eds), *New Global Regulatory Frontiers in Regulation: The age of nanotechnology*, Edward Elgar, Cheltenham, pp. 212–38.

Cobb, M. D. and Macoubrie, J. 2004, 'Public perceptions about nanotechnology: risks, benefits and trust', *Journal of Nanoparticle Research*, vol. 6, no. 4, pp. 395–405.

Crow, M. and Sarewitz, D. 2001, 'Nanotechnology and societal transformation', in M. C. Roco and W. S. Bainbridge (eds), *Societal Implications of Nanoscience and Nanotechnology*, Kluwer, Dordrecht, pp. 45–54.

Davies, J. C. 2006, *Managing the Effects of Nanotechnology*, Woodrow Wilson International Centre for Scholars, Washington, DC.

Del Vecchio, R. 2006, 'Berkeley considering need for nano safety', *San Francisco Chronicle*, 24 November, p. A1.

Department of Industry, Tourism and Resources (DITR) 2006, Request for Tender: Requirements—review of possible impacts of nanotechnology on Australia's regulatory frameworks, Australian Government, Canberra.

Dunkley, R. 2004, 'Nanotechnology: social consequences and future implications', *Futures*, vol. 36, pp. 1129–32.

ETC Group 2002, *No small matter! Nanotech particles penetrate living cells and accumulate in animal organs*, Communiqué Issue no. 76, ETC Group, Ottawa.

ETC Group 2003, *No Small Matter II: The case for a global moratorium size matters!*, ETC Group, Ottawa.

ETC Group 2004a, *Down on the Farm*, ETC Group, Ottawa.

ETC Group 2004b, *Nanotech news in living colour: an update on white papers, red flags, green goo, grey goo (and red herrings)*, Communiqué Issue No. 85, ETC Group, Ottawa.

Friends of the Earth 2006a, *Nanotoxicity and health: the big risks posed by small particles*, Issue Summary, Friends of the Earth, Fitzroy, <http://nano.foe.org.au/filestore2/download/123/Nanotoxicity%20and%20health%20-%20Issue%20Summary%20May%202006.pdf>

Friends of the Earth 2006b, *An Analysis by Friends of the Earth of the National Nanotechnology Strategy Taskforce Report: Options for a national nanotechnology strategy*, Friends of the Earth, Melbourne.

Friends of the Earth 2007, International Union of Food Workers calls for moratorium on nanotechnology in food and agriculture, Press release, Friends of the Earth, Fitzroy, <http://www.foe.org.au/media-releases/2007/international-union-of-food-workers-calls-for-moratorium-on-nanotechnology-in-food-and-agriculture/>

Gardener, E. 2002, 'Brainy food: academia, industry sinks their teeth into edible nano', *Small Times*, 21 June.

Gaskell, G., Allansdottir, A., Allum, N. et al. 2006, *Europeans and Biotechnology in 2005: Patterns and trends*, European Commission's Directorate-General for Research, London.

Goodman, D., Sorj, B. and Wilkinson, J. 1987, *From Farming to Biotechnology. A theory of agro-industrial development*, Basil Blackwell, Oxford.

Helmut Kaiser 2004, *Study: Nanotechnology in food and food processing industry wide 2003–2006–2010–2015*, Helmut Kaiser Consultancy, Tübingen, Germany.

Huang, J., Hu, R., Pray, C. et al. 2003, 'Biotechnology as an alternative to chemical pesticides: a case study of Bt cotton in China', *Agricultural Economics*, vol. 29, no. 1, pp. 55–67.

International Centre for Technology Assessment 2006, Legal petition on the FDA's failure to regulate health threats from nanomaterials, CTA, Washington, DC, <http://www.icta.org/doc/Nano%20petition%20ex%20summary.pdf>

Jones, S. 2004, 'Progress without patents: public maintenance of agricultural knowledge', *Journal of Environmental Law and Litigation*, vol. 19, no. 2, pp. 469–71.

Kimbrell, G. A. 2006, 'Nanomaterial consumer products and FDA regulation: regulatory challenges and necessary amendments', *Nanotechnology Law & Business*, vol. 3, no. 3, pp. 329–38.

Kuzma, J. and VerHage, P. 2006, *Nanotechnology in Agriculture and Food Production: Anticipated applications*, Project on Emerging Nanotechnologies, Woodrow Wilson Centre for Scholars, Washington, DC.

Lawrence, G. 1987, *Capitalism and the Countryside: The rural crisis in Australia*, Pluto Press, Sydney.

Ludlow, K. 2004, 'Cultivating chaos: state responses to releases of genetically modified organisms', *Deakin Law Review*, vol. 9, no. 1, pp. 1–39.

Ludlow, K. 2005, 'Regulation on agricultural genetically modified organisms in Australia', *International Journal of Biotechnology Law*, vol. 2, no. 2, pp. 123–9.

Lux Research Incorporated 2005, Nanotechnology: where does the US stand?, Testimony before the Research Subcommittee of the House Committee on Science, Lux Research Inc., New York.

Macfarlane, I. 2006, Report into the technology of the small—nanotech, Media release, 06/362, Minister for Industry, Tourism and Resources, Canberra.

McMichael, P. 1999, 'Virtual capitalism and agri-food restructuring', in D. Burch, J. Goss and G. Lawrence (eds), *Restructuring Global and Regional Agricultures. Transformations in Australasian agri-food economies and spaces*, Ashgate, Aldershot, pp. 3–22.

Marchant, G. E. and Sylvester, D. J. 2006, 'Transnational models for regulation of nanotechnology', *The Journal of Law, Medicine & Ethics*, vol. 34, no. 4, pp. 714–25.

Market Attitudes Research Services 2004, *Short Report: Australian community opinion towards nanotechnology and the commercialisation of scientific research*, Department of Industry, Tourism and Resources, Canberra.

Maynard, A. 2006, *Nanotechnology: A research strategy for addressing risks*, Woodrow Wilson International Centre for Scholars, Washington, DC.

Mee, W., Lovel, R., Solomon, F. et al. 2004, *Nanotechnology: The Bendigo workshop*, CSIRO Minerals, Melbourne.

Miller, G. and Kinnear, S. 2007, 'Nanotechnology—the new threat to food', *Clean Food Organic*, vol. 4, May.

Monica, J. C., Heintz, M. E. and Lewis, P. T. 2007, 'The perils of pre-emptive regulation', *Nature Nanotechnology*, vol. 2, pp. 68–70.

National Nanotechnology Strategy Taskforce (NNST) 2006, *Options for a national nanotechnology strategy*, Report to Minister for Industry, Tourism and Resources, National Nanotechnology Strategy Taskforce, Canberra.

Nel, A., Xia, T., Madler, L. and Li, N. 2006, 'Toxic potential of materials at the nanolevel', *Science*, vol. 311, pp. 622–7.

Oberdörster, G. et al. 2005, 'Review: principles for characterizing the potential human health effects from exposure to nanomaterials: elements of a screening strategy', *Particle and Fibre Toxicology*, vol. 2, no. 8, pp. 1–35.

Phillips, P. 2002, 'International trade in genetically-modified agri-food products', in C. Moss, G. Rausser, A. Schmitz, T. Taylor and D. Zilberman (eds), *Agricultural Globalization, Trade and the Environment*, Kluwer Academic Publishers, Boston, pp. 503–20.

Roco, M. C. and Bainbridge, W. S. 2005, 'Societal implications of nanoscience and nanotechnology: maximising human benefit', *Journal of Nanoparticle Research*, vol. 7, pp. 1–13.

Rooker, J. 2006, 'Keeping a hand in nanotechnology', *Chemistry and Industry*, September, pp. 19–21.

Rowan, D. 2004, 'Are scientists putting you off your dinner?', *The Guardian*, 16 May.

Royal Society and Royal Academy of Engineering 2004, *Nanoscience and Nanotechnologies: Opportunities and uncertainties*, Royal Society and Royal Academy of Engineering, London.

Sandler, R. and Kay, W. D. 2006, 'The national nanotechnology initiative and the social good', *The Journal of Law, Medicine & Ethics*, vol. 34, no. 4, pp. 675–81.

Scrinis, G. and Lyons, K. 2007, 'The emerging nano-corporate paradigm and the transformation of agri-food systems', *International Journal of Sociology of Agriculture and Food*.

Swiss Re 2004, *Nanotechnology: Small matter, many unknowns*, Swiss Re, Geneva.

Taylor, M. R. 2006, *Regulating the Products of Nanotechnology: Does FDA have the tools it needs?*, Woodrow Wilson International Centre for Scholars, Washington, DC.

Tip Top n.d., Tip Top Up Omega 3 DHA, Marketing case study, Tip Top.

van Calster, G. 2006, 'Regulating nanotechnology in the European Union', *Nanotechnology Law & Business*, vol. 3, no. 3, pp. 359–72.

Wardark, A. 2003, *Nanotechnology & Regulation: A case study using the Toxic Substance Control Act (TSCA)*, Foresight Institute and Woodrow Wilson International Centre for Scholars, Washington, DC.

Weiss, J., Takhistov, P. and McClements, J. 2006, 'Functional materials in food nanotechnology', *Institute of Food Technologists*, vol. 71, no. 9.

Williams, C. 2007, 'Big talks over small tech.', *Mass High Tech: The Journal of New England Technology*, 15 June, <http://masshightech.bizjournals.com/masshightech/stories/2007/06/18/story1.html>

Woodrow Wilson 2006, *Report Findings Based on a National Survey of Adults*, Woodrow Wilson International Centre for Scholars, Washington, DC.

Woodrow Wilson 2007, *A Nanotechnology Consumer Product Inventory*, Woodrow Wilson International Centre for Scholars, Washington, DC, <http://www.nanotechproject.org/index.php?id=44&action=view>

## Endnotes

[1] Nano-cochleates or nano-encapsulation techniques are 'envelopes' that act as vehicles for the targeted delivery of micro-nutrients (including omega-3, antioxidants and polyunsaturated fatty acids). Nano-capsules 'protect' the active ingredient(s) inside and enable the controlled delivery of active ingredients under certain conditions (ETC Group 2004a; Weiss et al. 2006).

[2] Nanotechnology is an enabling technology for genetic engineering and other plant and animal breeding techniques. Nano-biotechnology refers to the intersection of nano-techniques and genetic and cellular-level techniques for the purposes of modifying living organisms. The use of nanotechnology to facilitate the breeding of new varieties of crops and animals is still in its infancy, and there is little information readily available about the kinds of research and development being undertaken.

# Conclusion

Francesca Merlan and David Raftery

The National Party, a political party that explicitly represents rural interests, experienced vastly different results on different sides of Australia in a single weekend of September 2008. In a by-election for the northern NSW federal electorate of Lyne, a seat formerly held by the National Party leader and Deputy Prime Minister, Mark Vaile, an independent candidate, himself a former National Party member, won the seat. In attempting to explain the reasons for this result, Senator Barnaby Joyce, a federal National Party MP, refused to entertain the possibility that a 'rural vote', one that explicitly recognised agrarian values, had diminished. Joyce maintained that the National Party vote was extremely strong, there were still lots of National Party voters, but the 'wrong net' (*Radio National Breakfast*, Australian Broadcasting Corporation, 8 September 2008.) was being cast to try to catch them.

In Western Australia, on the same day, a quite different result emerged. There, the National Party had five of its candidates elected to each house of parliament, thereby holding the balance of power between the two major parties. Each of the major parties had no choice but to negotiate with the Nationals so as to be able to form minority government. In these negotiations, the National Party eventually sided with the Liberal Party, on the condition that the National Party's promise to deliver 'royalties to the regions' was honoured. This policy proposal sought to reallocate funds accruing to the state government from mining royalties to regional health, infrastructure and community needs.

What can such different results tell us, with the same political party experiencing such different outcomes? Obviously, they tell us that the agendas of mainstream political parties have a weak hold in regional Australia. What they also tell us is that expressions of 'countrymindedness' (Aitkin 1985) are a political, counter-state reflex and one to which the National Party does not have exclusive rights. It is clearly much easier for the National Party to occupy this counter-state ground when it is not in coalition with the Liberal Party, a party that either forms government or is the major opposition.

The contributors to this volume have asked: what are the relationships between rural communities and policy? Where and what are these rural communities, these 'regions', which there is a moral struggle to legitimately represent? How would a rural political will be realised? What are the 'policy effects', intended and unintended, of state efforts to define roles for rural areas and people and to pursue economic and environmental goals in rural locales?

In terms of efforts to realise a rural political will, let us first take the example of Stefano Di Pieri, from Mildura on the Murray River. Di Pieri achieved some profile through his role in an ABC television program that promoted the Mildura region's cuisine and the relationship between its agriculture, tourism and social life. Di Pieri runs a successful restaurant and food business in a revamped Mildura hotel. Having formerly been an advisor to the Victorian Labor Government, Di Pieri, in 2006, ran for the Victorian upper house as an independent. Unlike other politicians, Di Pieri claimed that rural towns and farms in the Sunraysia region—his region—did face inevitable decline and he opposed sustaining them indefinitely. He did, however, propose concrete policy solutions: farmers in the marginal mallee regions would inevitably leave their farms and this departure would bring new 'settlers' into small, ailing rural centres. This increase in population would help revive these towns and a great deal of local human and other resources would be dedicated to 'managing' these ex-farming lands, which would be given over to environmental purposes. In effect, Di Pieri sketched out a concrete rural scenario, in which the productivist values of agriculture were not paramount. This sketch of a rural future came from the region.

Aitkin (1972) has explored the question of what the National Party stands for in great depth. Aitkin (1985) identified country-mindedness as the central political value of the National Party, the very thing that the party was organised around. Aitkin (1985:35) clearly identified country-mindedness as an ideology, as a

> system of values and ideas that among other things presents a more or less extensive picture of the good society, and of the policies and programmes necessary to achieve it; distinguishes goodies from baddies; accounts for the historical experience of a group; and appears as 'truth' to that group while being at least plausible to outsiders. Ideologies, unlike philosophies, obtain their force very much from social experience; they cannot be proved wrong, partly because they are sufficiently elastic to accommodate awkward facts.

The empirical basis of such an ideology, argues Aitkin, can be found in the nineteenth and early twentieth centuries. A growing primary sector, the basis of Australian economic booms, underpinned the development of a country-minded ethos. The crucial aspects of country-mindedness were, in equal parts, a distrust of urban and foreign outsiders and a mutual respect between graziers and farmers across different regions. Monopolistic commodity buyers allowed farmers and graziers to easily identify 'baddies' and to feel affinity with fellow growers. Railways and communications, in which Australian governments invested heavily, enhanced the possibility for political communities whose shared interests were based in the social experience of farming and grazing.

These conditions that have been the basis of country-mindedness have, Aitkin contends, been in retreat since the 1870s. The proportion of the population that is non-urban has steadily declined, farming numbers have fallen and technology has collapsed the spatial and cultural distances that formerly separated country and city. Aitkin (1985:40) thinks that country-mindedness is finished as an ideology, 'even though its institutional and administrative arrangements will continue indefinitely'. These institutional and administrative arrangements mean, presumably, political parties, community organisations and lobby groups. The foundation of organised rural politics—larger rural populations, farmers and graziers beholden to single buyers and country people prohibitively distanced from cities—has collapsed, as has the ideology that framed these empirical events in cultural terms.

If country-mindedness exists in remnant form only at administrative and institutional levels, what has taken its place? Is there a rural ideology that is dominant, a set of ideas and values that appears as 'truth' to that group while being at least plausible to outsiders (Aitkin 1985:35)? If country-mindedness has been uncoupled from the empirical conditions that gave rise to it initially, then what relationships between rural communities, rural land use and political organisation are being reconfigured?

The 'uncoupling' thesis, in its simplest form, posits that rural towns are disconnecting from the trajectories of major agricultural industries (Stayner and Reeve 1990; Rural Profile 1990; Campbell and Phillips 1993). Instead, the prosperity of rural towns is enmeshed with other economic activities (Campbell and Phillips 1993:47). Political parties rarely speak about this uncoupling of the rural from the agricultural. Moreover, 're-coupling', or the processes by which rural communities become wedded to the activities of non-agricultural industries, is seldom a topic of political debate. What also need clear specification are the different 'ruralisms' that are undergoing such transitions. In the introduction to this volume, we referred to the recognised ambiguity and variability of this term. In attempting to understand change, it is of little value to collapse all non-metropolitan regions into a category of ruralism that posits an equal distribution of resources, development opportunities and social capital.

The space opened up by this uncoupling of the agricultural from the rural is the ground that contributors to this volume are exploring. Clearly, there has been no complete de-coupling of agriculture from ruralism. Rather, agriculture's position in relation to the rural space and communities is more contested, qualified and partial.

## Modalities of change

This volume has documented different modalities of change in rural Australia, New Zealand and Europe. We have been concerned with rural transitions at the community level, whether these be within rural communities (Peace, Stehlik) themselves, or in the political contest for values over the 'rural' (Botterill, Morris, J. Gray). Let us briefly review tensions and dimensions that authors have identified in the processes of rural transformation in the settings they have considered.

John Gray identified the constant pressure on policymakers in the European Union to ensure the viability of rural areas through changing policy schemes, demonstrating the gradual broadening of what he called a 'policy effect'. Gray's chapter charts a shift from agriculture as the 'primary vehicle' for the construction of European communal space and presents a view of the Common Agricultural Policy (CAP) as a 'history' of the concept of rurality as it moves through various forms. The CAP was concerned to underscore the importance of rural areas not only as primarily agricultural regions, but as bearers of national identity. It also sought to ensure that goals of national food self-sufficiency were achieved. Another distinct phase of 'policy effect' becomes visible in the struggles to balance social equity and economic efficiency concerns: the focus of value in the operation of the CAP shifts from material production per se to the question of the economic viability of farming ventures that often tend towards overproduction. Lastly, there emerges an emphasis on forms of rurality no longer grounded in agrarian production but in a diversity of activities and spaces that have value as alternatives to urban forms of life. These transitions that Gray describes are accompanied and partly prompted by new forms of representation at the bureaucratic level. These new definitions of rural land use emphasise regional diversification and can involve the break up of larger landholdings into areas that are evaluated in terms of their potential for agriculture and for other activities. This uncoupling of agriculture and rurality creates a space in which diversification of activities can figure more prominently. In Europe, such diversification can take place because bureaucratic categories for such changes exist and many European regions have strong and effective traditions of local and regional government.

Gray indicates that the relationship between social and economic activities on farms on the one hand, and government actions to define, direct and support particular modes of economic production on the other, is a dialectical one, and thus is a relationship that requires constant 'adjustment'. What Gray also underlines is that the economic goals that initially drove the CAP—ensuring a food supply, guaranteeing affordable prices for European consumers and maintaining a social equity among farmers so as to achieve these two goals—have been superseded by more diverse and less measurable goals. Not only does ruralism, in the eyes of the European Union, comprise 'heterogeneous activities and types of spaces' (Gray this volume), its importance now involves environmental preservation and recreational amenity for urban populations, with each of these goals being defined as critical to the benefit of society as a whole.

Importantly, the history of the efforts to sponsor or legislate for the survival of rural communities within nations, and national rural sectors within the European Union, has its background in the evolution of distinct regions into nation-states and in the integration of the nation-states into the European Union. While local and regional political legacies are very strong in some parts of Europe, they are much less so in Australia and New Zealand. The rural economies of Australia and New Zealand that came to dominate indigenous societies were never closely wedded to the political power that was located in colonial capitals, and later, national, state and provincial governments. There is little tradition of effective regional governance in Australia (Gray and Lawrence 2001); unlike Europe, governance has been fomented from the outside in or from the top down.

Ian Gray's paper is an assessment of the legacy of this situation in Australia: he sees the nation as characterised by its administrative centrism and, correspondingly, rural administrative dependency. His examination of this dependency through several key forms of rural infrastructure reveals a disparity between the enthusiasm of farmers to acquire Graincorp, which they can envision as the capture of a government function, with the low levels of their real ownership of it; the difficulty farmers have in reimagining water management in localist and regionalist terms; and the lack of preparedness to engage in local ownership and management of railway systems. This leads him to the crux of the political potential generated in such a situation: there is no local government to which governmental functions might suitably devolve. At the same time, there is popular sentiment for rural regionalism. This can be the overt message of such vehicles of ruralism as the National Party, but with no realistic possibility of regional control and institutionalisation of government functions.

A memorable feature of Botterill's chapter is her argument that agrarianism, or country-mindedness (Aitkin 1985), is a value that has so thoroughly permeated Australian thinking that its existence and effects often go unrecognised. Now, in the often-painful struggles over rural viability and various forms of the uncoupling of agrarian activity from rural spaces—especially at a small, familial scale—agrarian sentiment and representation resurface. This is often epitomised by prime ministerial appearances in those troubled rural areas in an Akubra hat and R. M. Williams bush clothing. While this is taken as a 'natural' expression of government inclination, Botterill brings us to see this deep-seated country-mindedness as something that contributes to a lack of critical scrutiny of rural problems and prospects. It could contribute to supporting a continuously agonised process of uncoupling, which, on the other hand, has been driven for nearly three decades now by the ideological vehicle of neo-liberalisation.

Adrian Peace's chapter has given us the means to critically understand an often staged scenario. The non-viability of rural spaces deemed 'marginal' from an agrarian perspective makes them the object of projects of biodiversification and conservation, with their familiar modalities of national parks and wilderness areas. In Peace's case, biodiversification explicitly involves the issue of 'return' of a natural species and the practice of reversing the extinction and disappearance of species. In the Yorke Peninsula of South Australia, however, which is Peace's ethnographic focus, agrarian activity continues and his chapter shows the tensions that arise in the effort to merge the goals of different land uses. The superior institutional power of government proponents of biodiversity, compared with local farmers, results in what he calls 'rituals' of consultation. These consultations are rituals that are performed, but without genuine hearing or acceptance of the forms of local knowledge earned through lives of farming activity.

We can, however, neither merely point to the need for ethnographic research to better understand the nature of rural transitions nor uncritically champion the perspectives of long-term locals. While the immediate experience of rural populations and communities is crucial in understanding the nature of transitions and competing perspectives and interests, there must be a critical understanding of the framework of competing interests that converge in contests for legitimate identification with ruralism.

Carolyn Morris's chapter foregrounds a theme that also is relevant to the situation that Peace describes, but which is not his focus. Her chapter pivots on the anthropological theme of the mutual constitution of people and place. She discusses legal forms of land tenure in New Zealand grazing regions that, aside from defining and allowing particular land uses, are integral to the production of personal subjectivities. The topography and the pioneer history of the New Zealand high country have produced a form of agrarian activity in which farmers have been able to see themselves, and to be seen by others, as pioneers occupying a cultural position that dominates the lower valleys. The high country is home to a distinctive form of activity and those who live in and work this country are thus seen as stewards of lands that have been crucial to New Zealand imaginings of self, place and nation. In recent times, the high country has been admitted to prevailing processes of rural market liberalisation. This has meant the valuation of lands to determine their potential conversion to freehold or to conservation estate. Through this process, some high country graziers have come to regard themselves as business operators. Many others have had their morally sanctioned position as stewards of the high country challenged by conservationists, tourism operators and other non-agricultural actors. Morris reports a sense among high country graziers and others that liberalisation undercuts the kinds of personal and national imaginings fundamental to New Zealand.

Lesley Hunt's chapter also focuses on mutual constitution of people and place in New Zealand, but in other circumstances. She writes of ageing baby boomers, many of them former farmers, opting in their later years to become orchardists of kiwifruit. She examines differing kinds of relationships that these farmers establish between themselves and their orchards. She shows that the choices they make are based not only on economic calculations, but are, very importantly, oriented to creating continuity in their lives between their earlier, and usually more intensive, careers and those they adopt towards retirement. Hunt argues that the resulting diversity of farming modes is an important source of rural sustainability. This chapter might lead us to ask how consistent is later 'lifestyle' occupational choice among ageing baby boomers with other economic and aesthetic choices that have accompanied the trajectory of this large demographic cohort. It might also lead us to ask, more broadly, how this sort of development compares and contrasts in its implications for rural areas with early retirement schemes that have been used in some places (for Europe, see Shucksmith et. al. 2005) to achieve social and structural objectives.

Related to this, Daniela Stehlik's chapter takes up what has been a longstanding issue in rural sociology: the challenge posed by an ageing rural population. Her research on the rural farming populations of the Great Southern region of Western Australia takes as its original focus the problem of the transfer of social capital and knowledge at an intergenerational level. Now, as ever, this raises questions about the future demographic trajectory of rural areas. The pivotal sociological feature of her chapter is the proposal that we model various kinds of resources and relationships—including non-land goods, dimensions of information, social membership and position—within a more diversified framework that can better explore the challenges of intergenerational transfer as they will relate to rural areas.

Lyons and Scrinis, finally, emphasise how much technological change of relevance to rural production goes under the regulatory radar. Practically, their argument concerns the need for a present and forward-looking regulatory framework capable of dealing with the challenges of nanotechnology. Their chapter also, however, raises the wider anthropological question of the relationship of the public to scientific innovation—and here there is a growing literature on the range of orientations to biotechnology. In a New Zealand-based study, Fairweather et al. (2007) consider a range of ethical public positions and also the importance of 'post-materialist' values, as they relate to the practice of biotechnology and the prospect of nanotechnology. Fairweather et al. (2007) conclude that biotechnological applications in agriculture and food technology are perceived to be risky and the benefits of such applications are seen as flowing to commercial interests, not to individuals or communities. Importantly, though, Fairweather et al. (2007:17) stress that evaluations of the benefits and risks of scientific applications to agriculture and food are made in a context in which 'technological optimism' has diminished and the dominance of productivist agricultural values is in retreat. The social evaluation of risk, costs and benefits takes place alongside the evaluation of claims of productivist agriculture. What, then, could be an effective modality in the management and oversight of rural technological activities? Given the ubiquitous character of nanotechnological applications—in spheres of production and consumption—how can the regulation of its operation be fixed in place? Given the high level of technical expertise and political cooperation already demanded by the advent of genetically modified crops in Australia, we would foresee that one or more regulatory bodies would be created to manage nanotechnological developments. This would be another step along the path of administrative centrism to which Gray sees rural communities as subject. Lyons and Scrinis invite research on what policy structures can best fill the roles created by such novel developments.

These contributions illustrate that rural space and people who reside in rural areas are being progressively integrated with economic, cultural and social influences that are larger, more diverse and often contradictory. Or, to put it another way, at a societal level, more is being asked of rural spaces and people than ever before. The role of primary production that has been assigned to country areas has declined in terms of political priority, yet the food, fibre and fuel needs around which rural economies are organised are arguably greater now than in the period that Aitkin (1985) identifies as the high point of country-mindedness in Australia: 1925–60.

## Technology and rural transitions

In Australian and New Zealand contexts, the colonisation and development of rural regions have been achieved through the interplay of international commodity trade, emerging provincial and national governments and evolving agricultural technologies. It is these factors that, with varying degrees of success and failure, have dominated the indigenous societies and ecological conditions found in Australia and New Zealand.

It would be easy to focus on the role of the technological hardware and the introduced 'livestock' of agricultural practices: the ploughing, reaping and clearing technologies, the successes of farm animal breeding and the transplantation of foreign crop varieties. A host of other technologies, however, has been crucial in determining the course of rural development in Australia. The specific planning practices of governments, such as land selection legislation, government credit schemes, sponsored rural migration programs such as soldier settlement programs and other specific features of land tenure (Meinig 1962) all underwrote particular patterns of rural life. More recently, efforts to engage indigenous people and interests in conservation and management constitute new and complex areas of activity linked to specific histories of policy and practice in Australia and New Zealand (see, for example, for Australia: Yibarbuk et al.

2001; Bowman et al. 2004; Reid et al. 2004; for New Zealand: Todd et al. 1997; Gibbs 2005).

Historical and political research has helped to contextualise the role of infrastructure in promoting and shaping the character of the colonisation of rural lands in Australia and New Zealand. Railways, roads, ports, distribution networks, bulk handling and storage facilities and telecommunications have all been contextualised in wider patterns of urban and rural development (Wade-Marshall 1988; Eversole and Martin 2005; Denoon 1983; Williams 1974). This need for economic infrastructure is a constant refrain in the lobbying efforts of agricultural and resource industries and in the promises or complaints of governments. Removal of so-called 'capacity constraints' is put forward as crucial to the enhancement of export prospects in a competitive trading environment.

At a less visible level, though, are technologies that cut deep into agricultural practices. The application of fertilisers and pesticides in cropping and horticulture and the development and use of selected or cloned seed and plant varieties all potentially bring a new level of biotechnological dependence to agriculture. The patenting of biotechnologies and the willingness of patent-holders to enforce the rights associated with patenting ensure that agriculture's dependence on biotechnologies is grounded in a strong commercial imperative. Regulating the rights and interests in the agricultural sector has proved a significant challenge for governments and has sparked much controversy among rural communities. Regulation of the nano-level, where the objects of regulation are so deeply enmeshed in so many facets of production, distribution and consumption, is a challenge for which there is simply no precedent.

It would be too easy to focus on the specifically economic aspects of technology at the expense of an examination of the social and cultural possibilities and constraints that are afforded to rural communities through infrastructure such as telecommunications. Currently, there is a big emphasis on telecommunications (Commonwealth of Australia 2008); broadband and telephony services to regional and rural areas are seen as key factors not just in the productivity of rural-based industries, but in their potential social and cultural composition. Aitkin (2007) argues that broadband services would enable more people to operate businesses that have a wide geographical reach while residing in rural areas. With such business practices enabled by broadband technology, the very composition of a rural community would be less dependent on the industries traditionally associated with rural areas: agriculture, mining and associated service industries. Equally, in parts of Europe, for instance, this technological decoupling allows people to live outside urban areas and still perform jobs typically associated with urban living. In this way, the knowledge economy facilitated by telecommunications makes redundant not only the rural–agricultural nexus, but the knowledge economy–urban nexus also. This 'double de-coupling', with the cultural impacts it brings to rural communities, is an unprecedented phenomenon.

There is now a technological ability to financialise almost all rural/agricultural phenomena, to make land and its produce assets that can be the object of speculation and other forms of financial investment. Importantly, this is relevant not merely for agricultural products, such as the futures trading of agricultural commodities, but is something that is happening in the emerging post-carbon economy, in which ruralism has been assigned a big role. For instance, forestry plantations run by managed investment schemes, aided by generous tax concessions, have become sponges for large amounts of financial capital. There are many examples of this being a big, direct challenge to the operation of other rural enterprises (Hobson 2004; Herbohn and Harrison 2004).

## Policy and rural transitions

Schusky (1989) noted the phenomenon that he dubbed the 'neo-caloric revolution': the massive increase in the economic productivity of farms and the massive increase in agricultural energy expenditure that these productive regimes demanded. In Australia, the unsustainability of such a system is heralded by the Garnaut report (2008). This report seeks to cost the externalities of an economy, in particular carbon, and reduce these carbon emissions by various schemes. This signals a determined effort to mitigate the damage of climate change and shift to a 'low-carbon economy'—one in which the production and trade of goods and services are not as heavily dependent on fossil fuels. Such a transition poses a huge set of social, technical and policy challenges, which will undoubtedly be particularly felt in rural areas, since they are host to energy-dependent primary industries and are dependent on fuel-intensive transport infrastructure. Equally important is the prospect of rural spaces being increasingly dedicated to host projects and activities that 'offset' or reverse the adverse ecological impacts wrought by carbon emissions. We have already seen much evidence of the difficulties of accommodating these competing economic agendas within rural spaces (Schirmer and Tonts 2002; Ajani 2007). Bio-sequestration of carbon is a role that Garnaut suggests Australia is well equipped to play, and he designates rural Australia as the physical space where this could happen. At the very least, this would require significant new physical infrastructure in rural Australia, acquisition of land and the importation of a high degree of technical skill to rural areas. How might these developments be hosted in a way that allows rural communities to have a stake in the new economy (see, for example, Grubb and Neuhoff 2006)?

The Salzburg Conference (2003) organised by the European Union identified three broad policy objectives in relation to the rural sector. There was consensus on the need to work towards:

- a competitive farming sector
- managing the land for future generations
- a living countryside (including promotion of its sustainability and its diversification).

The proposal is to continue to improve the competitiveness of farming and forestry; to place emphasis on land management and environmental concerns; and to support improvements in quality of life in ways that recognise the need for and the reality of livelihood diversification. Other European perspectives propose variant phrasings of fundamental priorities linking agriculture with a shift to a wider framework of sustainable development, including food security, employment and income generation, environmental and natural resource conservation and popular participation (for example, van Mansvelt and Mulder 1993). Shucksmith et al. (2005:200) propose that even more encouragement should be given to diversification and that there is a great need to integrate policies at local, regional and national levels (p. 202). It must be noted that local structures are much stronger and more functional in some parts of Europe than others, but also that there is an evident polarisation between core areas and peripheries. The European Union is committed to a policy of balanced territorial development, which also spells commitment to considerable planning and management, and certainly something other than neo-liberal self-adjustment in rural areas.

While Australia and New Zealand remain overtly committed to neo-liberal policy (Peck and Tickell 2002; Larner 2003; Harvey 2005), recent events have showed some departures from this, in the sense that government interventions have been significant. In the introduction to this volume, one signal example was mentioned: the announcement in 2007 of $10 billion, subsequently increased to $12.9 billion, for a national water plan, the aims of which included reform of irrigation and water allocation in the troubled Murray-Darling river system of south-eastern Australia (<http://www.environment.gov.au/water/mdb/index.html>). A sum of $3.9 billion has been earmarked to purchase water entitlements from willing sellers in order to try to restore some of the rivers' flow. As a second example, numerous local and federal government initiatives have been announced to reward farmers and others for biodiversity and native vegetation conservation. Third, food and other exporters are able to apply to an Australian Government scheme called Export Market Development Grants (EMDG), which provides financial and other assistance supporting development for export of a wide range of industry sectors and products. These and other 'departures' suggest that measures not consistent with neo-liberal ideals of minimal state intervention in markets are adopted where it is felt to be politically strategic and necessary. They also raise fundamental questions concerning a neo-liberal agenda as an adequate overarching framework in the face of the large issues Australia will necessarily face in the immediate and longer term, including national resource management, population distribution, sustainability, climate change and the fostering of social and technological responses to these issues.

Le Heron and Roche (1997) apply an institutional building thesis (derived from Buttel 1997 and Redclift 1997) to the transformation of New Zealand agriculture since the 1950s. They outline the major transitions of New Zealand agriculture: first, the withdrawal of interventionist state structures from the agriculture sector; second, the 're-regulation' of agricultural sectors; and third, the paradoxical result—a proliferation of industry and region-specific governance arrangements. They chart the shift in responsibility for sustainable land use to individual landholders. The very commitment to individual responsibility, though, is unachievable without state regulation of particular regimes, including property rights, export controls and safety standards. Successful re-regulation of the agricultural industries, then, is dependent on a high degree of knowledge and empowerment among decision makers (Perry et al. 1997). Le Heron and Roche (1997) point to the need for social institutions that can meet community and commercial imperatives and the need to re-examine any singular adherence to market mechanisms in the social management of rural spaces.

It seems, in short, that although Australia and New Zealand took a bold pioneering position in initiating national neo-liberalisation projects with respect to the governance of rural areas in the 1980s, European states, in contrast, remained much more interventionist at various levels in practice and in overtly retaining a wide spectrum of policy concerns. At the same time, they have also had to participate in the reanimation of state-building projects in neo-liberal terms in the past two decades (Peck and Tickell 2002). Now that sustainability and climate change have become dominant agenda items of governance everywhere, it remains to be seen how neo-liberal regulatory methods focusing on marketisation and commoditisation can be implemented in relation to them. It seems ever more doubtful that the usual tools of the neo-liberal tool kit can be an adequate basis of coordinated approaches to the range of issues involved. The examples given above from Australia have shown the regularity and the extent of departures in practice from that position.

## References

Aitkin, D. 1972, *The Country Party in New South Wales: A study of organisation and survival*, The Australian National University Press, Canberra.

Aitkin, D. 1985, '"Countrymindedness": the spread of an idea', *Australian Cultural History*, no. 4, pp. 34–41.

Aitkin, D. 2007, *'Building Australia', Under Construction: Nation-building in Australia, past, present and future*, Canberra.

Ajani, J. 2007, *The Forest Wars*, Melbourne University Press, Melbourne.

Bowman, J. S., Walsh, A. and Prior, L. D. 2004, 'Landscape analysis of Aboriginal fire management in Central Arnhem Land, north Australia', *Journal of Biogeography*, vol. 31, no. 2, pp. 207–23.

Buttel, F. 1997, 'Some observations on agro-food change and the future of agricultural sustainability movements', in D. Goodman and M. Watts, *Globalising Food: Agrarian questions and global restructuring*, Routledge, London.

Campbell, Hugh and Phillips, Emily 1993, 'The uncoupling thesis: a critical appraisal', *Regional Journal of Social Issues*, vol. 27, pp. 47–50.

Commonwealth of Australia 2008, *Regional Telecommunications Review Report: Framework for the future*.

Denoon, D. 1983, *Settler Capitalism: The dynamics of dependent development in the southern hemisphere*, Oxford University Press, New York.

Eversole, R. and Martin, John 2005, *Participation and Governance in Regional Development: Global trends in an Australian context*, Ashgate, Aldershot, England.

Fairweather, John, Campbell, Hugh, Hunt, Lesley and Cook, Andrew 2007, *Why do some of the public reject novel scientific technologies? A synthesis of results from the Fate of Biotechnology Research Programme*, Research Report No. 295, Agribusiness and Economics Research Unit, Lincoln University, Lincoln.

Garnaut, R. 2008, *The Garnaut Climate Change Review: Final report*, Port Melbourne.

Gibbs, M. 2005, 'The rights to development and indigenous peoples: lessons from New Zealand', *World Development*, vol. 33, no. 8, pp. 1365–78.

Gray, I. and Lawrence, G. 2001, *The Future of Regional Australia: Escaping global misfortune*, Cambridge University Press, Cambridge.

Grubb, M. and Neuhoff, K. 2006, *Allocation and Competitiveness in the European Union Emissions Trading Scheme: Policy overview. (Options for Phase II and beyond)*, Emissionsportal.de.

Harvey, D. 2005, *A Brief History of Neoliberalism*, Oxford University Press.

Herbohn, J. L. and Harrison, S. R. 2004, 'The evolving nature of small-scale forestry in Australia', *Journal of Forestry*, vol. 102, no. 1, pp. 42–7.

Hobson, K. 2004, '"Say no to the ATO": the cultural politics of protest against the Australian Tax Office', *Social Movement Studies*, vol. 3, no. 1, pp. 51–71.

Larner, W. 2003, 'Neoliberalism?', *Environment and Planning D: Society and Space*, vol. 21, pp. 509–12.

Le Heron, R. and Roche, Michael 1997, 'Commentary on part VI: sustainability and institution building: issues and prospects as seen from New Zealand', in D. Goodman and M. Watts, *Globalising Food: Agrarian questions and global restructuring*, Routledge, London, pp. 366–74.

Meinig, D. W. 1962, *On the Margins of the Good Earth: The South Australian wheat frontier, 1869–1884*, Rigby Limited, Adelaide.

Peck, J. and Tickel, A. 2002, 'Neoliberalizing space', *Antipode*, vol. 34, pp. 380–404.

Perry, M., Le Heron, R., Hayward, D. J. and Cooper, I. 1997, 'Growing discipline through total quality management in a New Zealand horticulture region', *Journal of Rural Studies*, vol. 13, no. 3, pp. 289–304.

Redclift, M. 1997, 'Sustainability and theory: an agenda for action', in D. Goodman and M. Watts, *Globalising Food: Agrarian questions and global restructuring*, Routledge, London.

Reid, H., Fig, D., Magome, H. and Leader-Williams, N. 2004, 'Co-management of contractual national parks in South Africa: lessons from Australia', *Conservation and Society*, vol. 2, no. 2, pp. 377–409.

Rural Profile 1990, *Agriculture and Rural Towns: A relationship re-examined,* Rural Development Centre, University of New England, Armidale.

Schirmer, J. and Tonts, M. 2002, *Plantations and Sustainable Rural Communities. Prospects for Australian forest plantations, conference proceedings,* Department of Agriculture, Forestry and Fisheries, Canberra.

Schusky, E. L. 1989, *Culture and Agriculture: An ecological introduction to traditional and modern farming systems*, Bergin and Garvey Publishers, New York.

Shucksmith, M., Thomson, K. J. and Roberts, D. 2005, *The CAP and the Regions: The territorial impact of the Common Agricultural Policy*, CABI Publishing.

Stayner, R and Reeve, I. 1990, *'Uncoupling': Relationships between agriculture and the local economies of rural areas in NSW*, Rural Development Centre, Armidale.

Todd, T., Lyver, P., Horsley, P., Davis, J., Brag, M. and Moller, H. 1997, 'Co-management of New Zealand's conservation estate by Maori and pakeha: a review', *Environmental Conservation*, vol. 24, pp. 236–50.

van Mansveldt, J. and Mulder, J. 1993, 'European features for sustainable development: a contribution to the dialogue', *Landscape and Urban Planning*, vol. 24, pp. 67–90.

Wade-Marshall, D. 1988, *The Northern Territory: Settlement history, administration and infrastructure*, Strategic and Defence Studies Centre, The Australian National University, Canberra.

Williams, M. 1974, *The Making of the South Australian Landscape: A study in the historical geography of Australia*, Academic Press, New York.

Yibarbuk, D., Whitehead, P. J., Russell-Smith, J., Jackson, D., Godjuwa, C., Fisher, A., Cooke, P., Choquenot, D. and Bowman, D. M. J. S. 2001, 'Fire ecology and Aboriginal land management in Central Arnhem Land, northern Australia: a tradition of ecosystem management', *Journal of Biogeography*, vol. 28, no. 3, pp. 325–43.

www.ingramcontent.com/pod-product-compliance
Lightning Source LLC
Chambersburg PA
CBHW061246270326
41928CB00041B/3438
* 9 7 8 1 9 2 1 5 3 6 5 2 6 *